Judaism Since Gender

edited by
Miriam Peskowitz
and
Laura Levitt

ROUTLEDGE
New York and London

Published in 1997 by

Routledge
29 West 35th Street
New York, NY 10001

Published in Great Britain by

Routledge
11 New Fetter Lane
London EC4P 4EE

Printed in the United States of America on acid-free paper.

Library of Congress Cataloging-in-Publication Data

Judaism since gender / [edited] by Miriam Peskowitz and Laura Levitt.
p. cm.
Includes bibliographical references and index.
ISBN 0-415-91460-4 (cloth). —ISBN 0-415-91461-2 (pbk.)
1. Feminism—Religious aspects—Judaism. 2. Women in Judaism.
I. Peskowitz, Miriam, 1964– . II. Levitt, Laura, 1960– .
BM729.W6J83 1996
296'.082—dc20 96-42109
CIP

To our students,

past,

future,

present.

Judaism Since Gender

Contents

Foreword

Virginia R. Dominguez

I come to this book via Jerusalem more than via Berkeley, Philadelphia, New York, Chicago, or the myriad smaller locations throughout the United States in which feminist Jewish scholarship is being produced by women and men, Jews and non-Jews, who take both feminist and Jewish scholarship seriously.

Jerusalem was home for me when Israel invaded Lebanon in the summer of 1982. Sitting in Jerusalem glued to *Mabat leHadashot* (the evening news broadcast on Israeli television) day after day, I felt part of a historical community to which I had no formal attachment. I experienced the obsession, the agony of fear, violence, disgust, and instability that I could feel more than articulate. I kept a diary. By early July, wanting friends elsewhere to understand what I was seeing and feeling, and wondering if my raw experiences sitting in the middle of it all might serve some useful purpose for possible readers far away from Israel and Lebanon, I took its entries, made a few copies, added a title and mailed it off for feedback. I called it "Falling in Love with a Criminal?"

I never did publish that piece but I still have it—nearly 14 years later. Something had gotten into me that both energized me and constantly challenged me. Like Daniel Boyarin, whose essay "Justify My Love" appears in this book, I had fallen in love with something that frequently caused me deep consternation. What the Talmud is for Boyarin, life in contemporary Israel was for me: each a nearly mysterious, only partly explicable draw, appealing beyond belief because of its constantly unfolding intellectual difficulty and the personal, interpersonal, emotional attachment it inspired in us, an "obsession" we love, but not easily.

"From within a cauldron of utopia and dystopia," Miriam Peskowitz and Laura Levitt write in the introduction to this volume, "this book embraces arguments, disagreement, and 'passionate and acrimonious intellectual debate.'" These concern Judaism, jewishness, and Jewish Studies just as much as gender, feminism, and Women's Studies. But there is a passion in their engagement that such description defies. Here are 25 feminists, men along with women, with a passion both for justice and for Jewish life. Here are 25 scholars, primarily but not exclusively Jewish, with a passion for knowledge both of and through Jews. And here are 25 teachers teaching in and out of classrooms, with a passion for passing on their questions and not just answers, their critiques and not just applause, their training along with a thoughtful and at times painful assessment of aspects of that training they now seek not to reproduce.

Each contributor has her or his way of framing it. The architectural design of past and present synagogues is Karla Goldman's "way in." The special needs of two sons frames Jonathan Boyarin's reflections and commitments. The continued Orientalist representation of Middle Eastern Jews provokes Joëlle Bahloul's gendered take on colonialism. Canons of discipline and practice in Jewish philosophy paradoxically enable Susan Shapiro to read "for gender." Everyday women's responses to Jewish laws and interpretations, typically considered the province of male scholars and rabbis, becomes Tamar El-Or's handle on the internalization of authorized knowledge and the quotidian expressions of its variations. For others, the link may be the challenges of being a feminist and not over-privileging gender in every analysis; or the ethical challenges of making Holocaust women's gynecological experiences visible and useful knowledge without enabling a disrespectful voyeurism.

At its simplest level, this book asks what it means, in practice, to internalize feminist scholarship and to participate in the production and reproduction of Jewish scholarly traditions at the same time. Or, as Laura Levitt puts it at the end of the book, what does it mean "to do Jewish feminist scholarship at the end of the twentieth century in America?" The question is neither just rhetorical nor necessarily negative. What do we know, after all, about what the range of things (questions, perspectives, bodies of knowledge, questioning theories) that feminist scholars bring to Jewish scholarship? Or, about the range of things (questions, perspectives, bodies of knowledge, questioning theories) that Jewish scholars bring to feminist scholarship? Or, what a scholar deeply rooted in historical traditions of Jewish learning, debate, and interpretation brings to contemporary disciplines, practices, questions, and agendas that are not recognizably Jewish? The answers that may readily come to our lips are the overly easy—and dangerously simplifying—answers the contributors to this book seek to transcend.

What is sought and evident throughout this book is something less additive than transformative. Feminist scholars clearly do not just add women to the mix any more than Jewish scholars just add Jews to the mix. By the same token, feminist scholarship is no more a simple addendum to scholarship unmotivated by feminism than Judaic scholarship (by which I mean scholarship deliberately and deeply conversant with historical traditions of Jewish learning, debate, interpretation, and canonized textual knowledge) is a simple addendum to scholarship unmotivated by Judaism and at least 2000 years of Jewish learning. Both have scholarly agendas, institutional practices, evaluative debates and discussions, and theoretical/philosophical discourses that are far richer and significantly more autonomous than a simple additive or derivative or oppositional argument would imply. The question, clearly, is not about adding Jewish women (or even studies of Jewish men in relation to Jewish women) to the general body of feminist literature, nor about adding women (or even gender) to the topics covered within Jewish Studies. More extensive and transformative effects are sought.

We all discard certain things in our lives, but not others. Sometimes we choose to keep certain things even when they seem antagonistic to values we hold dear. Often they are at odds with other values and principles in our lives, but something else binds us, ties us, commits us, and convinces us to maintain a connection to these things, rather than to discard them altogether; to salvage what we do value in them and fight for a greater transformation based on those qualities, those knowledges, those skills, or those commitments.

Take Daniel Boyarin's dilemma. He admittedly and evidently loves the Talmud. Yet, since at least the late 1980s, after a sustained engagement with feminist scholars, he has come to think of himself as a deeply committed male feminist and of his project as a "feminist one, to the extent that it owes its life to feminism and the work of feminist critics." Much in the rabbinic texts and culture disturbs him, but something else keeps him mining it and drawing on it.

Or take Miriam Peskowitz. The frequent ghettoization of "women" and "gender" within Jewish Studies circles is something she faces when putting together syllabi for teaching, when writing, when presenting papers at conferences. But her commitment to producing knowledge of—and knowledge *through*—Jewish learning and history keeps her from throwing in the towel. Does the U.S. feminist scholarly community not also ghettoize Jewish Studies, after all? Jewish Studies and Judaica, not Jews themselves?

Laura Levitt calls what they're doing, and problematizing, in this book "embracing." The metaphor is compelling: a strong hold, a connection to be dealt with, an interactive felt experience, a nonverbal assertion, a social act, the appearance of equality, a way to ease tension, a way to apply pressure, an expression of love. Not all are good, not all are desired, not all are peaceful. But all are felt, all are grounding, all—at the very minimum—demand a response.

It is this palpable intangible that cuts across all contributions to this book, all styles of intervention, all arguments, and all invocations of theory—an embodied, engaged, critical practice that seeks responsible social transformation, drawing on Jewish history and Jewish learning alongside women's history and feminist theory.

Editors' Introduction: "A Way In"

Miriam Peskowitz and Laura Levitt

Conversations about Jews, Judaism, and jewishness happen all over, in both expected and surprising places, as do conversations about women, men, feminism, and gender. This book collects essays that, themselves, offer openings into new thinking about women, men, Jewish culture, history and religion, feminism and gender—and a number of other things besides. Many of these essays make their own case for the importance of the more systematic reflections of university intellectuals on figuring out the complexities of everyday life. Most of the essayists here resist platitudes and certainties. They offer, instead, provocations—Jewish men as sissies, Jesus as transvestite, the problematic eroticizing of Holocaust survivor narratives. Many of the nearly thirty essays take on familiar topics. They stop to peer closely at current debates and, in doing so, provide more nuanced and philosophical underpinnings for these. They consider ramifications; they talk about ethics and politics in ways that open up topics from different angles. Others make new topics familiar. They introduce readers to a wide range of intellectuals and scholars. We aim to accommodate readers without the time or leisure to work through longer pieces whose dense and difficult arguments may be rewarding but are also intensely demanding. This short-essay format should appeal, then, to those of us who read and think in many ways: in libraries, offices, or studies; upright at a desk or reclining on a couch; on the subway or bus to work, or while waiting for a doctor's appointment; during lunch breaks; for a quiet Sunday-afternoon hour, or for ten minutes before bed.

From within a cauldron of utopia and dystopia, this book embraces arguments, disagreements, and "passionate and acrimonious intellectual debate."[1] The essays are intellectual adventures—"thought-experiments"—that risk the comforts of certainty for a different way of understanding. Their authors stake out some temporary position—or take even a few minutes to write—as "thoughtful lovers and compassionate scholars" commuting "on the shuttle connecting freedom to constraint . . . political loyalties to scientific disinterest." We must admit that none of this is easy. There are simultaneous and conflicting desires, allegiances, and critiques. Desires for nostalgia and cultural myths of wholeness—"traditions" of various sorts—collide with the joys of transgression and the fascination with fragmentation. The authors in this volume hold various commitments and multiple desires: stances they will defend, conclusions they are willing to change, positions they will hold no matter what. Arguments arise among them, and with others who are not represented here. And often their arguments take place internally, as ambivalences, as different forms of disputes among "the multiple, diverse voices within our selves." As Chava Weissler writes, "What does loyalty to Judaism demand? What does loyalty to women demand? What does loyalty to scholarship demand? I too may reach a point at which the conflicting loyalties block any response but silence."[2] To the possibility of silence we propose a cacophony of unsettling and sometimes uncertain voices. Upsetting the myth of detached scholars, we offer instead embodied intellectuals who draft articles about patriarchy and Jewish studies with live guitar music in the background, who think about Walter Benjamin's "Theses on History" while fetching a child from its great-grandmother, and who write about colonialism while caring for infants.

Once we re-admit "desire," knowledges about Judaism, jewishness, and Jews—the word *Judaism* in our title is meant only in the broadest sense—become less predictable, more uncertain, less stable, and more fun. This speaks to what we hope to add to the current intellectual and cultural climate. If, as intellectuals, thinkers, writers, teachers, speakers, and more, we are concerned primarily with the production and distribution of knowledge, these concerns cannot be narrowly defined by either topic or place. In many of the essays, knowledge about Jewish Studies is not separate from "everything else," nor is it confined to classrooms, lecture halls, offices, or academic hallways. Rather, teaching and learning happen also in airport lounges, on museum tours, at home, at writers' desks, on e-mail and cyberspace discussion groups, in conversations over bottles of wine or cups of afternoon tea. The conversation that began this book, in fact, happened over a casual dinner in Philadelphia's Chinatown; its details were initially imagined on the sidewalk outside. We began by asking contributors to envision their roles in reconfiguring Jewish Studies; we commence now with a collection of essays that demonstrates how a (reconstituted) Jewish Studies might become a feminist practice. We make a utopian move, but where else might utopian gestures emerge if not from impassioned *and* intelligent conversations with the present and its pasts?

Studying Jews

We begin with the complicated—and complicating—recognition that all knowledge about women, gender, and Judaism is mediated through a series of interpretive frames and explanatory frameworks. From this starting point, this book attempts to shift a discourse that encompasses both a field of study and a set of common and uncommon knowledges. In reconstituting the production of Jewish knowledges as a feminist project, we identify two frames that have prevented it from being such. The first is masculinism. As an ethos for organizing knowledge about Jews, jewishness, and Judaism, this frame privileges men and maintains commitments to the values and categories of specific kinds of masculine intellectuality. This masculinist framing of Jewish Studies is also part of and has been intertwined with another significant frame: the legacy of the European Enlightenment of the seventeenth and eighteenth centuries. From the Enlightenment, with its critiques of "religious" authority and its commitments to restructuring society and reorganizing knowledge within the terms of "rationality," emerged (in the nineteenth century) the *Wissenschaft des Judentums*, the so-called scientific, or nonreligious, study of Judaism. The terms of the Western and central European academy became those in which the *Wissenschaft des Judentums* produced knowledge about Jewish history and Hebrew language. A central factor in this nineteenth-century production of knowledge was the acceptance of notions of scientism and objectivity, fictions that hide the explicitly political origins of the *Wissenschaft* and that continue to hide scholars' investments in their work and arguments. As Jews producing knowledge about Jews, *Wissenschaft* scholars were making an overt (and conscious) bid for Jewish membership in the community of "Europeans." These political origins are often rendered invisible, through an ideology that these Enlightenment methods (even in their modified forms) produce "objective" scholarship. This desire for the authority of objectivity can be measured by the hostility and passion with which scholars in Jewish Studies have accused one another of "polemics" or, borrowing the terms of Christian culture, of "apologetics." This same desire for objectivity is revealed in their denunciations of feminist scholarship as "political," an ironic accusation that merely tries to hide the political stakes in all scholarship. By bringing this genealogy of commitments to the fore, we wish to challenge the claim that any study is disinterested or detached, just as we suggest that such stances of authority are problematic rather than desirable.[3] This infrastructure of objectivity is one of the starting points for our feminist reconstitution of knowledges, as we attempt to explain the various ways that European inheritances prefigure, organize, and mediate the knowledges that scholars and other intellectuals produce about Jews, jewishness, and Judaism.

Both Jews and women, and the disciplines of Jewish Studies and Feminist Studies have ambivalent relations to these traditions. On the one hand, their promises of civil rights and entry into universal conversations have been empowering, and at the same time the terms of these promises constrain as they empower. As intellectuals attempting to problematize our commitments to certain ways of knowing the world, we face a basic tension. The same Enlightenment ethos that promotes objective scholarship and "master" narratives also made possible the promotion of law and policy that gave European Jews their primary source of standing in modern society. Enlightenment sensibility ensured some Jews some access to certain forms of European culture and knowledges but still limited what they could accomplish through these knowledges. Still, consciously or less than consciously, many Jewish intellectuals and writers have maintained an ongoing faith in the promises of inclusion provided by the social contract of classical European liberalism. They have been reluctant to question critically the scholarly methods that are one of its legacies.

These loyalties bear critique. The disembodied Enlightenment mind has been shown to be, in fact, a most embodied—and masculine—subject. Universal "reason" has been situated as a form of thinking linked particularly—and politically—with elite and literate sectors of western Europe. The Enlightenment-spawned collection and division of knowledge have been shown to be tied closely to the history of Europe's colonial ventures. The systematic and repeated acts of genocide in the twentieth century expose the fallacy of Western assertions that science, technology, and human reason ensure freedom, pleasure, and even survival. A critique of these assumptions forces a reassessment of how we, as scholars, teachers, intellectuals, and students—and as "regular people"—will produce and distribute knowledge. Some of the essays in this volume defend these commitments and offer reasons. Other essays are particularly concerned with the limitations of these promises of progress and emancipation. They note the constraints encased within these terms, and they seek alternative possibilities. These possibilities start with, but are not limited to, the kinds of knowledge that can render more possibilities imaginable.

Jewish Studies as practiced has not by itself provided space for feminist thinking, so it has been necessary to interrupt it in fairly dramatic ways.[4] The newest round of interruptions, which we suggest, happen on the way to configuring a radically new Jewish Studies that is not a "feminist Jewish Studies," or a "Jewish Women's Studies," or even a "Jewish Cultural Studies." We are not content with any formulation in which "Jewish Studies" remains the norm and a feminist difference is noted as an additional, interruptive adjective (e.g., "Feminist" or "Women's" or "Cultural"). Rather, we imagine a reformulated Jewish Studies in which a different set of assumptions is practiced as "normal." Many of these essays offer maps of alternate possibilities, with suggestions for how to get from "here" (wherever "here" is) to a desired "there" (wherever that might be). They gesture in new directions, and they demonstrate some specific results. Feminist critiques and reformulations of classic studies and familiar explanatory categories are well under way, and in some cases, these reconfigurations have been going on for some time.[5] But the research, writing, and publication of new and carefully thought feminist knowledge take time. They present their own challenges and raise very practical questions. For instance, if feminist scholars are producing new information about women and gender and also altering the very terms and values of scholarship, how will these new knowledges be distributed, taught, and learned? What introductory and teaching books must be (re)written and made available, for all levels of education? With questions like these, we solicit visions: What might Jewish Studies and familiar knowledges about Jews look like in ten years? Or five?

Feminist Theory

These visions have many versions. There is no single feminist approach, no one theory of gender's construction, no single agreed-upon definition of *gender*. Broad generalizations about "Jewish feminists" entirely disregard the fact that "Jewish feminists" have never spoken with a unified voice and have taken many divergent positions. Feminist acts, feminist theory, and feminist study have developed in diverse and complicated ways.[6] There is no longer (and in fact there never was) a singular feminist position. In the essays, concepts such as "gender," "sexuality," "masculinity," and "femininity," as well as "Jew," "jewishness," and "Judaism," are used and deployed in multiple and sometimes conflicting ways. Readers should sense immediately the numerous fault lines of contention. Rather than cover over and harmonize differences among and between us, we wish to bring debate and difference to the fore, to offer glimpses into the fractiousness of these ongoing and impassioned discussions. This conflict and multiplicity, and not a move toward canonized definition, are precisely what we find intellectually exciting.

Scholarship on topics about Jews and Judaism produced from a feminist ethos is both new and not new. Today's discussions take place amid a number of histories, including a long registry of female Jewish scholars and Jewish women as the topics for study. Here we can point to the first wave of feminism in western Europe and the United States in the mid-to-late nineteenth century. From the ranks of Jewish feminists come intellectual women such as the German Bertha Pappenheim. Another, the London activist and writer Lady Katie Magnus, was among those whose work was published (along with the poetry of Grace Aguilar) in the founding issue of *Jewish Quarterly Review*. The first American edition of her book *The Outlines of Jewish History* (1890) was the initial publication of Philadelphia's Jewish Publication Society (founded 1888) and one of the few English-language Jewish history textbooks available to several generations of English and American Jews in the late nineteenth century and early twentieth.[7]

Feminist critique and revision of Judaism and Jewish life began, then, as a late-nineteenth- and early-twentieth-century phenomenon. But this first-wave feminism was largely unknown to the so-called second wave of feminists, and has had to be rediscovered through research. Consequently, we can identify another history here that is barely twenty-five years old. In this second wave, Women's Studies and academic feminism appeared as widespread political and cultural critiques fostered a search for new information about women. From this ethos of critique developed an active Jewish feminist critique of Judaism and Jewish life (and its accompanying backlash). Later, and coinciding with this activism, a feminist scholarship on these topics emerged. The result has been a history of twenty-five years of feminist scholarship, much of it generated by women who were our teachers, including such scholars as Paula Hyman, Marion Kaplan, Judith Baskin, Carol Meyers, Ross Kraemer, Bernadette Brooten, Judith Hauptman, Ellen Umansky, and numerous others. Many among them made the initial arguments for different kinds of feminist scholarship and produced the first demonstrations of the difference this makes.[8]

Ongoing feminist analysis must continuously consider what we know and how we study. This means critiquing the basic assumptions that are part and parcel—still—of the study of literature, history, anthropology, and so on. And we must continue to make visible the constructedness of knowledges and its ramifications. But even as we engage in these scholarly practices and the powerful critiques they offer, we find ourselves at a conflicted juncture. The conversational and intellectual mode that we call feminist theory has become increasingly sophisticated and difficult to enter, especially for feminists outside academia. Professionalized in the university, feminism's critical language has become very abstract and theoretical, and sometimes necessarily so. One result of this is a widening gap between how feminist theorists write (and the subjects we choose to write about) and other kinds of feminism and feminists. The practical issue of words and what they mean has created a division—some of us use words and phrases that others use in very different ways, and that still others of us find unfamiliar or even unfathomable. What indeed, the educated reader might ask, are the meanings of words like *postmodern*, *representation*, *trope*, or *mediation*? What is denoted by *subject*, or *subject position*? What are the positive meanings of the word *critical*, and why is *critical* bandied about so much? What is conveyed by *sign*? Words like these are bread and butter to some university thinkers who are already engaged in these critical moves. To other readers, they can be obtuse and unmeaningful jargon that hampers, rather than promotes, any kind of understanding. What are *rhetoricity* and *textuality*? How does *genealogy* differ from *history*, and if *genealogy* (in common parlance) is what you do to locate family ancestors, then what is a genealogy of culture, or of an idea?

All of these are useful questions, but we offer no simple glossary, no immediate explanation. Part of the intellectual fun of reading is figuring out what writers mean by the words they use. Searching out "dictionary" and other kinds of definitions, and recognizing the differences generated by the "real-life" uses of words are the tasks of readers who actively engage with what they read. These are tasks that help each of us to cultivate her or his own glossaries of theoretical terms and critical tools. Definitions are both helpful, and impossible. And in all honesty, many terms, *Judaism* or *woman*, for example, mean very different things to different people. Each essay favors different modes of explanation. Some will offer temporary definitions. Ann Pellegrini, for instance, offers her readers a clarifying definition of *interarticulation*. Others work through demonstration, as does Sara Horowitz in her account of ongoing engagements with Holocaust survivors. In other words, to speak back to critics, theoretical language does not have to be subterfuge and occlusion. This language of critical terms and concepts can matter when it enables us to do what we do, and to do it more powerfully.[9]

A second effect of this professional turn also concerns us. Feminist theory and gender studies have moved so far from their starting points that some basic insights and critiques have been forgotten, or brushed to the side, or considered too naive to mention. It has become unfashionable, for example, to repeat feminism's basic critique: that structural inequities of all sorts exist and are unjust. While drafting their essays, some contributors found themselves in this recurring conversation: How do we keep critiques of patriarchy and the structural inequities of women's lives in a male-dominated society as at least a partial rationale for our work when these very ideas have become passé or unpopular to discuss? One set of responses looks to the reasons for this shift in feminist terminology. Words such as *patriarchy* have been rightly critiqued for presuming a universal or unchanging social mode, one that does not allow for differences. Other words—*misogyny, masculinism, sexism*—have also been critiqued, from within, by feminists. Over time, our concern for careful use of language has led feminist scholars to reject (or at least find problematic), in turn, all the words that describe gender-based inequity. But, at the same time that feminist scholars are working to speak clearly and fairly about inequality, these critiques have not found their way into social and scholarly commonplaces. The conditions of inequity are, themselves, constantly reiterated in the worlds in which we live (and with significantly less concern for clear and accurate terms). Consequently, it has become necessary for many of us to come to terms with our terms because rejecting feminist language (even for thoughtful and valid reasons) has had quite conservative effects, and has prevented us from talking about what needs to be spoken. Thus, even if some things are not "new," even if other scholars, writers, and intellectuals have already "said it," several essays in this volume work to rethink and reclaim some of these feminist terms, finding in words like *patriarchy* (once again) necessary tools for feminist critique.[10]

As theory has become more sophisticated, the conditions of our families, workplaces, and societies have not changed so positively or dramatically. Structural inequities, masculinist and other oppressive discourses, and the naturalized suppositions that support these do not change just because we uncover their genealogies or trace their histories or call attention to their constructedness or imagined alternatives. But when we recall the origins of feminist scholars and scholarship in several centuries and different contexts, we are reminded of the practicalities we face. This brief account of the history and current conditions of Jewish feminist thought, we hope, can help us to resist the tendency to let the production of knowledge become detached from the many reasons why informed intellectual critique might matter.

Attempts at Conversations

We have asked a wide variety of writers to envision their role in reshaping our collective imaginings. The book's essays come in two sections. Part One, "Knowledges," is imagined as a conversation, one without the spontaneity of spoken exchange but with the artfulness and craft that writing proffers. We distributed one essay—Miriam Peskowitz's "Engendering Jewish Religious History"—and asked younger and older scholars, as well as intellectuals who have chosen to work outside the university, to read the essay and respond to the issues it raises. We posed some questions and asked them to think with us about feminism and gender, to consider where they had been and where they are going.[11] In conceptualizing this as a conversation with a starting point, we experiment with a format that, as one contributor notes, "allows us to stop talking past and around each other." Feminist scholars can and do speak extensively and critically, with one another. Part One, then, can be read as an intersection, a positive place to stop and reflect.

A second set of invitations and questions was posed to contributors to Part Two, "Studies." Here, six scholars present longer essays that offer more extensive analyses of practices and possibilities for conceptualizing readings of Jewish texts, and analyses of issues that Jews face. Most of these studies defy conventional disciplinary restrictions. Others could be named according to a "subfield," but at the cost of a false narrowing of their claims. For example, Susan Shapiro's essay, "A Matter of Discipline," speaks to the specific case of Jewish philosophy, but her discussion of reading for gender and of reading for literary tropes and figures has much wider implications. Points made with regard to a specific discipline of study can and should be applied to others. Whereas some of these essays attend centrally to questions of women and gender, others use feminist and other critical theory as a starting point for thinking—and thinking again—about all sorts of things.

The resulting essays are more delightful than we could have imagined, and readers should prepare themselves for both a sense of recognition and a certain epistemic messiness. To different readers, the resulting collection may seem alternately disorienting, congenial, boring, challenging, or familiar. What becomes evident is multiplicity, tension, and contention, as well as unexpected points of connection. Readers will see immediately that neither section of the book is concerned with (the fiction of) "covering" a certain number of academic disciplines and fields (after all, who could claim to cover "everything"). In fact, we call attention to the various constraints of these disciplines. Indeed, outside the university's boundaries, the practice of dividing the world into categories of "anthropology," "history," "literature," or "religion" already seems somewhat bizarre. Instead of adhering to these and other strictures, we aim to demonstrate a new ethos for studying, one that is multilayered and attends continuously to the terms of its conversations, to the ways that it makes "truths" true. Many of the essayists resist the pressure to posit "universal" truths, to push complicated information into more confining "explanations." Most eschew broad generalizations in favor of exploring the very local and specific contexts in which knowledge, gender, and power are constructed and perpetuated. Letting go of what used to seem normal and natural, they point to complicated and competing ways of making sense of the world. These essays offer information, insights, and imagination. They take risks to change the terms of intellectual conversations, and show how different and more interesting these subjects begin to look once we let go of some of the certainties around which they have been organized.

As part of the exciting and often utopian process of envisioning new knowledges and new ways to write, think, and teach, several of the essays call attention to the economies of intellectual life. For feminist intellectuals, the traditions of academe provide both a starting point and a set of restraints. Beth Wenger, for instance, writes of the material conditions of the conferences and classrooms that make up professional intellectual life. We could add to her list of concerns its hiring practices, its tenuous record of recognizing and promoting women and feminists, and the increasingly difficult economic conditions of the university as a workplace. Feminist knowledges do not—and usually do not pretend to—come from nowhere. Conditions such as these have direct effects on scholarship and writing, the products of intellectual workers who write from within the pressures and constraints of the current economy. As well as specifically material constraints, the current conditions include working against the university's entrenched intellectual conservatism. As Ammiel Alcalay writes, this is the place from where we begin "our explorations out of the echo chamber." On the other hand, freedom from "academic" constraints also means the denial of its relative privileges and the status it confers. Irena Klepfisz—poet, activist, teacher, and intellectual—writes of another site of conversation, the noisy camaraderie of the kitchen table as a place of discussion, friendship, and argument.

Intellectual life is a communal venture. A book seems perhaps the most static translation of the ways in which we think and write. Pages might quell the burble, the banter, the excitement of working with texts and experiences and desires and ideas, the anxiety and happiness of developing knowledges on new terms, of calling into question previously held positions. We hope that the vibrancy of conversation will not be lost in the move to the book, in the experience of these debates as something read. Most readers will never know precisely the interchange of conversations, telephone calls, decisions, principled arguments. But we hope these crafted essays convey the discussions, compliments, disagreements, and respect between authors and editors, among authors in conversation with one another and—as we know most closely—between us, as editors and friends.

There are many people without whom this book would not be possible: David Watt, Rob Baird, Marlie Wasserman, Eric Zinner, our editor Bill Germano, and especially, Maxine Grossman. We thank Phyllis and Irv Levitt for the generous use of their Fenwick Isle beach house for editorial meetings, and we thank Myra and Danny Peskowitz for other kinds of enthusiasm and support. We thank all contributors for their generosity and for the pleasure of our interchanges, no matter how fractious. We especially wish to recognize Susan Shapiro, Naomi Seidman, Beth Wenger, Judy Baskin, and Karla Goldman, and to recognize as well the members of our editorial committee. We thank Joseph Haberer and Nancy Lein, editor and managing editor of *Shofar: An Interdisciplinary Journal of Jewish Studies*, for sponsoring the special issue "Engendering Jewish Knowledges" (*Shofar* 14.1 [1995]), which contains slightly different versions of some of these essays, along with additional articles and a long series of reviews of recently published books. We extend our appreciation to those whose work appears there: Gail Labovitz, Richard Freund, Hollis Glaser, Jennifer Gubkin, Moshe Re'em, Cynthia Baker, Michelle Friedman, Deborah Eisenbach-Budner, Kim Haines-Eitzen, Mary Potter-Engel, Sylvia Barack Fishman, Marina Rustow, Oren Stier, Lauren Granite, Ruti Kadish, and Tania Oldenhage. We thank as well Irene Fine, Clare Kinberg, Judith Plaskow, Harry Brod, Evelyn Beck, Madelaine Adelman, Melanie Kaye/Kantrowitz, James Young, Susan Handelman, Howard Eilberg-Schwartz, and Elliot Wolfson. We thank Barbara DeConcini and the American Academy of Religion for their Collaborative Research Award, which greatly facilitated our work. At the University of Florida, we thank several people for crucial material support: Azim Nanji, Chair of the Department of Religion; Catherine Holbrook, Vice-President for Research; and Warren Bargad, Director of Jewish Studies. Our thanks go also to Julia Smith and to Annie Newman. At Temple University, we thank the Research and Study Leave Committee of the Faculty Senate for a Summer Research Grant.

Notes

1. We quote from Rebecca Alpert's essay. Note Seyla Benhabib's comment in *Feminist Contentions: A Philosophical Exchange* (New York: Routledge, 1995): "This exchange brought four of us who share profound ties of personal friendship into open political disagreement about our theoretical and political commitments. This process has not always been easy: public disagreements have strained personal loyalties and friendships. Nonetheless, serious intellectual exchanges are processes through which the life of the mind and the community of scholarship is enhanced. And as is to be expected from a deep controversy, no one has remained untouched by its consequences" (31).

2. Chava Weissler, "Women's Studies and Women's Prayers: Reconstructing the Religious History of Ashkenazic Women," *Jewish Social Studies* 1.2 (1995): 28–47.

3. It is not uncommon to find in scholarship published in the past few years the language of Enlightenment critique. See, for example, David Biale, "Confessions of an Historian of Jewish Culture," *Jewish Social Studies* 1 (1994): 40–51, and Howard Eilberg-Schwartz, *The Savage in Judaism: An Anthropology of Israelite Religion and Ancient Judaism* (Bloomington: Indiana University Press, 1990).

4. Nor has Jewish Studies provided much space for women, until very recently, and then, as several essays indicate, not unambivalently. In Paul Ritterband and Harold Wechsler's recent *Jewish Learning in American Universities: The First Century* (Bloomington: Indiana University Press, 1994), female scholars are almost entirely absent. See the similar situation in Shaye J. D. Cohen and Edward Greenstein, eds., *The State of Jewish Studies* (Detroit: Wayne State University Press, 1990). Surveys by feminist scholars of various fields in Jewish Studies are available in Lynn Davidman and Shelly Tenenbaum, eds., *Feminist Perspectives on Jewish Studies* (New Haven: Yale University Press, 1994). The chapters show the specific ways and the different degrees to which these fields have incorporated and/or been reshaped by feminist scholarship and critique. To be consulted as well is Susan Shapiro's "Voice from the Margin: Women and Jewish Studies," *Association for Jewish Studies Newsletter*, 2d ser., 4 (1990): 1–4. At the same time, it has been difficult to integrate Jewish Studies into the concerns of Women's Studies/Feminist Theory; see Evelyn Torton Beck, "The Politics of Jewish Invisibility," *NWSA Journal* 1.1 (1988): 93–102.

5. For example, note the relationship between the classic of S. D. Goitein, *A Mediterranean Society: The Jewish Communities of the Arab World as Portrayed in the Documents of the Cairo Geniza* (Berkeley: University of California Press, 1978), and a feminist reading of some of this material by Judith Baskin, "Jewish Women in the Middle Ages," in *Jewish Women in Historical Perspective*, ed. Judith Baskin (Detroit: Wayne State University Press, 1991), 96–102. The classic text by Jacob Katz, *Out of the Ghetto: The Social Background of Jewish Emancipation, 1770–1870* (Cambridge: Harvard University Press, 1973), has been subject to critical re-evaluation by these two collections: Jonathan Frankel and Steven J. Zipperstein, eds., *Assimilation and Community: The Jews in Nineteenth Century Europe* (Cambridge: Cambridge University Press, 1992); and Pierre Birnbaum and Ira Katznelson, eds., *Paths of Emancipation: Jews, States, and Citizenship* (Princeton: Princeton University Press, 1995). Yet, although these volumes offer rereadings of the question of emancipation, they offer little by way of a feminist critique. For a third example, note the second edition of Paul R. Mendes-Flohr and Jehuda Reinharz, eds., *The Jew in the Modern World: A Documentary History*, 2d ed. (New York: Oxford University Press, 1995). The second edition begins to redress some of the gaps in the first edition by adding texts by women. There is, however, still much work to be done. Although Ellen Umansky and Dianne Ashton, eds., *Four Centuries of Jewish Women's Spirituality: A Sourcebook* (Boston: Beacon Press, 1992), offers readers a broad range of religious sources by Jewish women that fill in some of the remaining gaps in the Mendes-Flohr and Reinharz collection, it is a very different kind of volume. What is still needed is a focused reader that looks at both secular and religious sources by Jewish women, and that organizes "primary" sources in ways that conceptualize both male and female Jews as central within various practices and experiences of Judaism and jewishness. Also of interest are works by scholars such as Daniel Schroeter and Joëlle Bahloul, whose critiques show the European orientation of the terms of Jewish studies, especially when examined from the perspectives of the histories and anthropologies of North African Jewish and immigrant communities and experiences.

6. We are especially concerned with situations in which one feminist (or one Jew) is picked as a token to "speak for" the whole. This has been particularly the case with feminists who are other than the white and invisibly Christian norm. Hence, instead of allowing for multiple

black/African-American, or Latina, or Jewish voices, one feminist becomes a de facto spokesperson for all. See Michelle Wallace, "For Whom the Bell Tolls: Why America Can't Deal with Black Feminist Intellectuals," *Voice Literary Supplement* (November 1995): 19–24. For those who wish additional introductions into feminist theory, we suggest the following: Teresa de Lauretis, ed., *Feminist Studies/Critical Studies* (Bloomington: Indiana University Press, 1986); Dianna Fuss, *Essentially Speaking: Feminism, Nature and Difference* (New York: Routledge, 1989); Patricia Hill Collins, *Black Feminist Thought: Knowledge, Consciousness and the Politics of Empowerment* (New York: Routledge, 1990); Judith Butler, *Gender Trouble: Feminism and the Subversion of Identity* (New York: Routledge, 1990); Chandra Talpade Mohanty, Ann Russo, and Lourdes Torres, eds., *Third World Women and the Politics of Feminism* (Bloomington: Indiana University Press, 1991); Judith Butler and Joan Scott, eds., *Feminists Theorize the Political* (New York: Routledge, 1992); Susan Bordo, *Unbearable Weight: Feminism, Western Culture, and the Body* (Berkeley: University of California Press, 1993); Linda Kauffman, ed., *American Feminist Thought at Century's End: A Reader* (Cambridge, MA: Basil Blackwell, 1993); Kathy Ferguson, *The Man Question: Visions of Subjectivity in Feminist Theory* (Berkeley: University of California Press, 1993); and Seyla Benhabib, Judith Butler, Drucilla Cornell, and Nancy Fraser, *Feminist Contentions: A Philosophical Exchange* (New York: Routledge, 1995). As feminist theory has developed to see the interarticulation and imbrication of gender and masculinism with other constructions and practices of power, texts based in feminist theoretical assumptions tend less and less to display the key words *feminist, gender*, or *women* in their titles. This reflects both a critique of Western feminisms for the erasure of or complicity with practices and epistemologies of racism and colonial relations (see Chandra Talpade Mohanty, "Under Western Eyes: Feminist Scholarship and Colonial Discourses," 51–80, in *Third World Women*). At the same time and in other circumstances it reflects discomfort with the political signal of "feminism" or in the supersession of feminism by queer theory; in this regard see Judith Butler, "Against Proper Objects," *Differences: A Journal of Feminist Cultural Studies* 6 (1994): 1–26. See Russell Ferguson, Martha Gever, Trinh T. Minh-ha, and Cornel West, eds., *Out There: Marginalization and Contemporary Cultures* (Cambridge: MIT Press, 1990); Trinh T. Minh-ha, *When the Moon Rises: Representation, Gender and Cultural Politics* (Bloomington: Indiana University Press, 1991); Toni Morrison, ed., *Race-ing Justice, En-Gendering Power: Essays on Anita Hill, Clarence Thomas and the Construction of Social Reality* (New York: Pantheon, 1992); Rey Chow, *Writing Diaspora: Tactics of Intervention in Contemporary Cultural Studies* (Bloomington: Indiana University Press, 1993); Rajeswari Sunder Rajan, *Real and Imagined Women: Gender, Culture and Postcolonialism* (New York: Routledge, 1993); and some of the essays in Angelika Bammer, ed., *Displacements: Cultural Identities in Crisis* (Bloomington: Indiana University Press, 1994).

7. On Pappenheim, see Marion A. Kaplan, *The Jewish Feminist Movement in Germany: The Campaigns of the Jüdischer Frauenbund, 1904–1938* (Westport, CT: Greenwood Press, 1979). Pappenheim was the "Anna O" of Sigmund Freud's writing; see Lucy Freeman, *The Story of Anna O* (New York: Paragon, 1990), and Max Rosenbaum and Melvin Muroff, eds., *Anna O: Fourteen Contemporary Re-interpretations* (New York: Free Press, 1984). Magnus's life and writing has not as yet been studied, despite a plethora of available materials, including her own books and articles and letters, and articles written about her, in London's "Jewish Chronicle" and elsewhere. On the U.S. re-publication of *Outlines*, see Shuly Rubin Schwartz, *The Emergence of Jewish Scholarship in America: The Publication of the Jewish Encyclopedia* (Cincin-

nati: Hebrew Union College, 1991), 12. If both Pappenheim and Magnus were concerned to write about Jewish women, there is an additional and different history of Jewish women as religious scholars, most often by virtue of being the daughters of important figures of Talmudic and other religious study. See Gerda Lerner, *The Creation of Feminist Consciousness: From the Middle Ages to Eighteen-seventy* (New York: Oxford University Press, 1993), 28. Regarding another example of Jewish and female intellectuality, note the salon "Jewesses" of eighteenth-century Berlin. See Deborah Hertz, *Jewish High Society in Old Regime Berlin* (New Haven: Yale University Press, 1988), and Jay Geller's essay in this volume.

8. We apologize in advance if we have inadvertently left anyone off of our list. Some of this early work (with more recent expansions) includes Charlotte Baum, Paula Hyman, and Sonya Michel, *The Jewish Woman in America* (New York: Dial Press, 1976); Paula Hyman, "Gender and Jewish History," *Tikkun* 3 (1988): 35–38, and *Gender and Assimilation in Modern Jewish History: The Roles and Representation of Women* (Seattle: University of Washington Press, 1995); Marion Kaplan, *The Jewish Feminist Movement in Germany: The Campaigns of the Jüdischer Frauenbund, 1904–38* (Westport, CT: Greenwood Press, 1979); Judith Baskin's article "The Separation of Women in Rabbinic Judaism," in *Women, Religion, and Social Change*, ed. Y. Y. Haddad and E. B. Findly (Albany: SUNY Press, 1985), and note the two important collections she edited: *Jewish Women in Historical Perspective* (Detroit: Wayne State University Press, 1991) and *Women of the Word: Jewish Women and Jewish Writing* (Detroit: Wayne State University Press, 1994); Carol Meyers, *Discovering Eve: Ancient Israelite Women in Context* (New York: Oxford University Press, 1988); Ross Kraemer, "Women in the Religions of the Greco-Roman World," *Religious Studies Review* 9 (1983): 127–139, and the more recent *Her Share of the Blessings* (New York: Oxford University Press, 1992); Judith Hauptman, "Women's Liberation in the Talmudic Period: An Assessment," *Conservative Judaism* 26 (1972): 22–28, and "Image of Women in Talmud," in *Religion and Sexism: Images of Woman in the Jewish and Christian Traditions*, ed. Rosemary Radford Reuther (New York: Simon & Schuster, 1974); Ellen Umansky, *Lily Montagu and the Advancement of Liberal Judaism: From Vision to Vocation* (Lewiston, NY: Edwin Mellen Press, 1983); Ellen Umansky, ed., *Lily Montagu: Sermons, Addresses, Letters and Prayers* (Lewiston, NY: Edwin Mellen, 1985), and co-edited with Dianne Ashton, *Four Centuries of Jewish Women's Spirituality: A Sourcebook* (Boston: Beacon Press, 1992); Bernadette Brooten, *Women Leaders in the Ancient Synagogue: Inscriptional Evidence and Background Issues* (Chico, CA: Scholars Press, 1982). See also Aviva Cantor, *A Bibliography on the Jewish Woman: A Comprehensive and Annotated Listing of Works Published, 1900–1978)* (Fresh Meadows, NY: Biblio Press, 1979); Rachel Biale, *Women and Jewish Law* (New York: Schocken Books, 1984); and Sydney Stahl Weinberg *The World of Our Mothers: The Lives of Immigrant Women* (New York: Schocken Books, 1988).

In emphasizing a certain kind of feminist scholarship, we find ourselves in a bit of a bind. We wish to recognize specifically the intellectual production of feminist research scholars, and to recognize their achievements within the university, both as graduate students at times when there were very few women in these fields and when research on women was almost entirely devalued, if even imaginable, and as scholars whose groundbreaking work on women's lives, and later, on gender slowly has changed what we know. Simultaneously, we wish to recognize that study, research, and writing are not limited to academically trained women. Despite its difficulties, the academy has been a more fruitful terrain for Jewish and feminist writing. Nevertheless, much writing has also been produced on these topics by women who are not connected by profession to the university.

Other additional important feminist writings on Judaism include Elizabeth Koltun, ed., *The Jewish Woman: New Perspectives* (New York: Schocken Books, 1976); Blu Greenberg, *On Women and Judaism: A View from Tradition* (Philadelphia: Jewish Publication Society, 1981); Evelyn Torton Beck, ed., *Nice Jewish Girls: A Lesbian Anthology* (Watertown, MA: Persephone Press, 1982, and Boston: Beacon Press, 1989); Melanie Kaye/Kantrowitz and Irena Klepfisz, "Tribe of Dina: A Jewish Women's Anthology," a special issue of *Sinister Wisdom* 29/30 (1986), republished with the same title (Boston: Beacon Press, 1989); Susannah Heschel, ed., *On Being a Jewish Feminist: A Reader* (New York: Schocken Books, 1983; 2d ed., 1995); Susan Weidman Schneider, ed., *Jewish and Female: A Guide and Sourcebook for Today's Jewish Woman* (New York: Simon & Schuster, 1984); Judith Plaskow, *Standing Again at Sinai: Judaism from a Feminist Perspective* (San Francisco: Harper Collins, 1990); Melanie Kaye/Kantrowitz, *The Issue Is Power: Essays on Women, Jews, Violence and Resistance* (San Francisco: Aunt Lute Books, 1992). Work by Jewish feminists can be found in some of the "women and religion/feminism and religion" collections; see, for example, Carol Christ and Judith Plaskow, *Womanspirit Rising: A Feminist Reader in Religion* (San Francisco: Harper & Row, 1979); and Judith Plaskow and Carol Christ, *Weaving the Visions: New Patterns in Feminist Spirituality* (San Francisco: Harper & Row, 1989). Journals such as *Bridges: A Journal for Jewish Feminists and Our Friends, Lillith, Neshama,* and *Journal of Feminist Studies in Religion,* as well as the few feminist articles published in *Tikkun,* are additional places to find Jewish feminist writing, produced both in and out of the academy.

For notices of recent and forthcoming articles and books, please refer to the notes of individual articles, and to Notes on Contributors.

9. Much of the language of "theory" comes from western philosophy and/or literary theory, and in this regard we send readers to helpful volumes, such as Frank Lentricchia and Thomas McLaughlin, *Critical Terms for Literary Study,* 2d ed. (Chicago: University of Chicago Press, 1995).

10. See also Susan Bordo, "Material Girl," in *Unbearable Weight,* 245–276; and Teresa Ebert, "Ludic Feminism: Bringing Materialism Back In," *Cultural Critique* 23 (Winter 1992–1993): 5–50.

11. These questions included (1) What are the different and often conflicting definitions of "feminism" and "gender" out of which we work? (2) Since the vast majority of work in Jewish feminist studies has been tied either implicitly or explicitly to the Enlightenment's project of emancipation, what are some of the consequences of this strategy? What are some alternatives to this way of constructing knowledge? (3) How are the terms "gender," "sex," and "sexuality" deployed in current Jewish scholarship? (4) What are the different and often conflicting definitions of "jewishness," "Judaism," and "Jews" at work in Jewish Studies and Feminist Studies?

Part One:

Knowledges

Engendering Jewish Religious History

Miriam Peskowitz

Scouting for Discourse

The experience of undoing long-accepted histories, logics, and truths provides feminist intellectuals with a "heady sense of encountering the future," as we work to complete these tasks.[1] Although I speak here of feminist pursuits, in my study of Judaism I imagine kindred spirits and ancestors among the early *maskilim.*[2] This fantasy of connection evokes an ethos of Jewish intellectuals meeting in living rooms in Berlin, drinking wine in Parisian cafes, reveling in ragingly new Enlightenment challenges to long-standing truth claims, roaming among a terrain of fractured traditional authorities, and in the midst of all this "headiness," returning "home" on the Sabbath to a coeval world that still presumed itself whole and intact. With the new tools of the European Enlightenment, my imagined *maskilim* came to recognize the outlines of the world that had been familiar to them. Their commitments to "modernity" painfully highlighted the newly perceived differences.

Of course, there is some irony in my use of the *maskil* as hero and predecessor, especially since I challenge the permanence of much of what the *maskilim* and the consequent academic movement, the *Wissenschaft des Judentums,* or Science of Judaism, achieved.[3] The irony extends through to my objections to the Enlightenment fantasy of a universal human subject who is unified, seamless, and coherent, a fantasy that is as false as it is culturally persuasive. Even more ironic, this universal, unified, seamless, and coherent subject is masculine, hardly an obvious starting point for feminist work. Despite these ironies, the fantasy of the *maskilim* provides a nostalgic comfort. If only momentarily and provisionally, I have retrieved some prepackaged and easily available Jewish ancestry for my feminist project.[4] At the same time, I recognize the seduction of this nostalgia, the seductive offer of even the transient comfort of a perceived intellectual ancestor. Such nostalgia for an intellectual heritage is simultaneously comforting, contradictory, and complicated. It romanticizes those thinkers who propounded the very same Enlightenment and/or *Wissenschaft* paradigms that currently keep us from seeing and writing Jewish religious history with both male and female agents. It ignores the fact that these same thinkers posited "gender" as a series of "natural" sex differences, which has of course made more work for those of us who insist that neither sex nor gender is a naturally occurring difference but, rather, is a cultural product constantly in (re)production. And such nostalgia hides the fact that these same thinkers were almost exclusively men.

Feminist accounts of women and gender intend to challenge masculinist traditions (long perceived as "neutral") for presenting the past. Important new insights and information have emerged from feminist studies of Judaism. Yet, even as we change histories and challenge history, many feminist studies of Judaism still work within the categories (and utilize the methods) of Enlightenment-based scholarship. These categories and methods are highly restrictive, but for the most part they have not yet become a topic of sustained, public discussion among those of us who are feminist scholars. At their best, though, our intellectual engagements will challenge not only "traditional" masculinist conversations but the very terms of our own conversations as well.[5]

My starting point lies in the recognition that some aspects of feminist analysis have been strategic and necessary. They have served us well, for a time. Given our location in European and American intellectual life, these choices made sense, they were readily available, familiar, and helpful. But they need not always organize and limit our inquiries. In what follows, I work to undo very real conceptual constraints. I scout out some emerging and already-present discourses, and I consider the possibilities for thinking about women, gender, and feminism.[6]

In the beginning years of feminist scholarship, institutional discouragement and impediments provided external challenges to feminist research. Currently, additional challenges for feminist scholarship come "from within." Feminists take many positions, and this sometimes puts us at odds with one another. Some college and university environments have changed, making it easier for some of us to do our work. Institutional barriers have not ceased (far from it), but differences among and between feminist thinkers today can be as great as between thinkers along the whole continuum from feminist to masculinist. Writing feminism has not become easier; only the specific challenges have changed. Scholars in the late twentieth century are surrounded by a proliferation of theoretical possibilities and scholarly performances, many of which are intellectually enticing, and none of which are essentially or necessarily liberatory. As I write, I realize (and attempt to make real) the necessary critique of the contents of Jewish religious history. I see, and attempt to make visible, the categories of traditional scholarship.[7] "Traditional scholarship" refers to the overlapping discourses of domination that organize knowledge in ways that hide the basic categories by which that knowledge is produced: to name just a few, these discourses include masculinism, colonialism, the European Enlightenment inheritance that veils a specific Christian-ness behind its claims to the universal. In naming problems, I purposely shift attention away from the sexism of individual authors, since such a focus repeats and reinscribes the Enlightenment fallacy of human subjects that can be independent of culture. The analysis of these constraints makes it possible to detect the categories that have structured knowledges, and that have come to seem familiar, normal, objective, and true. These are also the most easily, and the most problematically, replicated.

This essay, then, is about complexities and comforts such as these, about how they provide the terms of conversations within which we feminist thinkers may conceptualize, research, teach, and write a gendered Jewish religious history. I offer this as work-in-process. In places I remain speculative, even idealistic and optimistic in a quest for more powerful questions and more convincing explanations of how gender works and is worked in Jewish religious culture. The essay contains at least some of the traces of its own production, traces left visible as a gesture to a critical practice that does not smooth over the seams nor attempt to erase the construction of knowlege within culture. And I have attempted to identify and expose those constructs that constrict each of us, individually and collectively, from thinking best about things that demand our best thinking.

Constrictions (Spring 1993)

One place that I perform as a feminist thinker of Judaism is in a classroom of undergraduate students.[8] This spring I have been teaching a course with a familiar title: "Introduction to Judaism." The course is taught within Duke University's Department of Religion, and is cross-listed in History. No matter who teaches it, it aims to give students basic knowledge of Judaism "as a religion" and basic knowledge of the historical development of Jewish communities.[9] In addition, each semester around registration time, the Women's Studies Program at Duke compiles and distributes a list of courses under two rubrics: first, courses that place women's lives and experiences explicitly at the center of study; and second, "other" courses in which women's lives and/or the construction of gender are not at the center of curricular attention but are attended to in intellectually defensible ways. My course, "Introduction to Judaism," ended up in the second category. I had been away from campus that fall and couldn't be reached to confirm that my course was appropriate for this second category. But the Women's Studies office had assumed such, given my training in feminist theory, my work as a research assistant for the introductory course in Women's Studies, and all my other involvements in producing new scholarship on women and gender,

I had assumed this also. In a workshop on pedagogy the previous summer,[10] I had spent time conceptualizing the integration of "women" into a course on "Judaism." I was concerned to do this in a way that did not continue to marginalize—

and would in fact reverse the marginalization of—women's experiences. I wanted to avoid the model that teaches "Judaism" and then, as an additional gesture, speaks to "women in" Judaism. I found that the current state of conceptualizing the problem does not yet facilitate this project in ways that are elegant and/or consistent. "Women" remain marginal, extra. The religious tradition's use of gendered relations to organize itself remains invisible and critically untouched. This was the problem with my conception that summer of the need to "integrate" the two: the liberal model of "integration" is impossible because it ignores the categorical structures that marginalize "women" in the first place.

It is already a truism that one cannot "add women and stir."[11] The earliest second-wave feminist historians had worked hard to achieve the addition of women to history. And their earliest feminist critics soon realized that women cannot truly be added unless—and until—the historical frameworks have been changed and the masculinist ideologies of those frameworks exposed. Most recently, scholars writing on women, Judaism, feminism, and gender have further articulated the point that the many varieties of "adding women and stirring" are insufficient.

There is a second truism, that gender must be a category of analysis. Yet, even as we repeat it to one another, this truism remains mostly untheorized within most studies of women, gender, and Judaism. Beyond the repetition of the axiom "gender is a category of feminist analysis," some of our research continues pre-"gender-as-a-category" methods, assumptions, and results. Currently, and for a variety of reasons, large gaps exist between these recognized truisms, the production of critical feminist scholarship, and a satisfactorily gendered religious history of Judaism.[12] So, I pose and pursue the following question: Why has it been so difficult for women and gender to be part of the narrative of Jewish religious history?

"Women in X"/"Women and X"

The other place that I perform as a feminist thinker of Judaism is in the production of scholarship. My project for the past several years has used cultural texts about spinners and weavers to investigate the construction of gender in Roman-period Judaism.[13] Roman-period Judaism includes the earliest centuries of rabbinic Judaism. And feminist studies of rabbinic Judaism had already established a topic called, variously, "women in rabbinic Judaism," or "women in early Judaism," or "gender and Talmud." These include surveys of "images of women," explanations for patterns of rabbinic law for women, and others. Adding to these concerns, I wanted to know *how* specific and partial accounts of the activities and personae of men and women were naturalized into truths about gender. I was interested in Roman-period images of Jewish women as initial data for an inquiry into how images of femininity, masculinity, female work, and female sexualities "got to be the way they were." In other words, I decided to eschew "what" for "how," as in *how* did the kinds of genders and sexualities articulated in Jewish texts of the Roman period become possible?

We cannot fully explain and account for the development of Judaism during its classical period without taking into account the presence and the constructedness of gender in all aspects of Jewish religion and history. Current scholarly practices in the field have continued to divide "Jewish religion" and "women." For instance, the very terminology of the subject—"women and rabbinic Judaism"—implies that "rabbinic Judaism" and "women" are separate entities. Consequently, the study of "women" is inadvertantly kept marginal to the enterprise of studying rabbinic Judaism.[14] Conceptualizing these things as separate has another ramification: it allows some scholars to continue to study "rabbinic Judaism" without considering women and gender. The "and"—the space between "rabbinic Judaism" and "women/gender"—is never bridged. The "and" both connects these things and simultaneously keeps them separate. In practice, the model of "women in rabbinic Judaism" or "gender in rabbinic Judaism" (although much better than ignoring women/gender in the first place) contributes to the traditional and ongoing strength of the dichotomy that places men and masculinity at the center of study, and positions women and femininity at the periphery. It allows us to continue investigating "rabbinic Judaism" without asking how that entity is itself gendered, and how the history of its study has been gendered.

The polarized division between "women" and "rabbinic Judaism" in the phrase "women in rabbinic Judaism" is neither essential nor natural. We don't have to think about these things in these ways, through constructs whose strategic usefulness has for the most part come to an end. These ways include a set of inherited intellectual modes for examining men and women as participants—of whatever kind—in Jewish life and religion in Roman Palestine. These modes—the mostly unspoken, unwritten, unarticulated notions that underwrite and provide the logic for our reconstructions of Jewish religion in that period—should be understood as a master code of rabbinic studies. This particular, and peculiar, master code shapes the field of study.

When we locate master codes and make them explicit, we begin to see why it is still so difficult to write a (gendered) Judaism. For example, the phrases "Women in X/Women and X" and "Gender in X/Gender and X" are tools—or codes—used by various scholars and writers, including feminists. But at the same time, these phrases ("Women and Judaism," and especially the closely related "Gender and Judaism") "make sense" only within a misogynist and masculinist framework. To speak of "women" or "gender" as separate from (or even as an aspect of) Judaism can take meaning only within a collective intellectual imagination that cannot yet conceptualize Judaism as always already gendered. The twin formulations "Women in X/Women and X" and "Gender in X/Gender and X" take meaning within a collective imagination that may just be beginning to consider the constructed character of terms and entities such as women, gender, and Judaism.

Working out of the current state and categories of knowledge about Judaism and Jewish religious history, and working from a new kind of critical feminist ethos, how can we imagine, conceptualize, and study a historical moment and a set of texts and cultural constructs called "rabbinic Judaism"? The goal of resisting the formulation of "Women in X/Women and X" is to make the marginalization of women intellectually impossible. It is to refuse to pretend that gender is absent, in cases when it is merely invisible.

Teacher-Student-Text (Spring 1993)

On the first day of class I had a problem: introducing the two main textbooks we would use in the course "Introduction to Judaism." The textbook quandary had been resolved. I chose two: Robert Seltzer's *Jewish People, Jewish Thought* and Judith Baskin's edited volume *Jewish Women in Historical Perspective.*[15] With these books in hand I had solved the immediate problem of teaching a class "in Judaism" that included information about "women." It is a problem faced by many who teach broad-ranging surveys, titled implausibly and impossibly as "introductions." The solution was not satisfactory, but it was probably close to the best possible in the early nineties. The main text (Seltzer), a bible-to-modernity, start-to-present narrative of Jewish religious history, would be supplemented—and interrupted—by Baskin's chapters about Jewish women.

In formulating an introductory course on Jewish religious history, I faced this problem: the current narrative of Jewish religious history—and of most histories of most religions—represents as whole what is in fact a partial story of male Jews, and educated male Jews at that. I am certainly not the first to recognize this. A sweeping view of multiple centuries of Jewish religious history in one semester shows that Judaism in most places and times has made sexual difference and gender a central feature. Within its gender systems, those in control of material conditions have been men, not women. Further, the recording of Jewish pasts has transmitted the texts and experiences of male authors and actors. The result is that the story of a religion in which (in most premodern historical contexts) women and men engaged in very distinct practices, and a religion that maintained changing notions of the need for separateness between men and women, has been told as the story, simply, of men.

Any discussion of women must begin here. Because the standard schema fails to see how gender was made and how gender mattered, this narrative has no room for the new information about Jewish women, men, gender, and sexuality that the current generation of feminist scholars is producing. Their new information and insights do not fit the old picture. The lack of fit presents a radical challenge. Also, I realized with trepidation, the lack of fit was going to complicate terribly the introductory course I was about to teach.

Three days before class was to start I had afternoon tea with Jean O'Barr, who directs Duke's Women's Studies Program. I described my quandaries. Despite my training in feminist theory, the history of Judaism, and gender studies, I was stuck on the problem of how to make the introductory course in Judaism a course about the religious lives of both men and women. I was stuck on how to organize a course that would simultaneously present knowledge and problematize knowledge. Jean thought for a moment and sipped her tea. "Now I know you've probably already thought about this," she said. "But just the other day, I heard this formulation of feminist teaching. Feminist teaching problematizes a three-part relationship between teacher, student, and text." She paused and smiled and said, "But I think you already know that."

In some ways, I did already know that a good part of feminist teaching is about exposing the threads that hold together traditional masculinist stories and histories.[16] But as basic as the point is, some of us need to be reminded again and again. We need to figure out how to do this in new places and situations. To create intellectual room for thinking gender and women into our stories of Jewish religious history, it is necessary to locate, and then to dismantle, the currently available masculinist narratives that constitute that curriculum. On the first day of class I discussed the syllabus—the reading expectations, the theoretical framework of the class, the tests, the papers, and so forth. And then I held up the two textbooks: Seltzer's maroon-covered 874 pages and Baskin's mustard-yellow-and-black-covered 300-page volume. I announced to the students the problem: at this moment in time, scholars in Jewish studies have not yet figured out how to tell the combined story of religious Jewish men and women in history. Nor have we figured out how to make gender explicit. We might see the critical problem as a confrontation between, on the one hand, historical narratives that invoke the quality of seamlessness and, on the other hand, historical narratives that would "expose the threads" of their own production. The term *seamless* refers to historical narratives that claim a cohesiveness and completeness, doing so despite the significant gaps and lacunae in the evidence available to reconstruct almost any period, place, and aspect of Jewish religious history. "Seamlessness" refers also to texts that tie together what they perceive negatively as "loose ends." "Seamlessness" stands in opposition to "exposing the threads." The latter is a critical practice that marks the places where ideas, documents, texts, artifacts, and other pieces of evidence are joined together in a "reconstruction" or historical narrative. "Seamlessness" makes the traces of production disappear. It smooths over the specific intellectual practices that make disparate and discontinuous data into something coherent, connected, and even calming in its familiarity.

In Seltzer's *Jewish People, Jewish Thought*, the writing of the historical narrative as seamless and self-contained corresponds to Seltzer's vision of Judaism's own seamlessness and cohesiveness. In his words, and with reference specifically to the medieval period, Judaism is "a seamless garment—an identity cut from a whole cloth woven of tradition, intellection, and social ties" (515). The problem resides both in the content of the narrative and in the mode of narration, and also in the interrelation of the two. Seltzer's construction of Judaism as "a seamless garment" is a metaphor that prefigures his organization of the disparities and divergent evidence of Jewish religious history into the smoothness of a seamless narrative.[17]

I decided to offer the students some tools to undertake an intellectual quest, not to discover old knowledges but to produce their own knowledges about how old knowledges became knowledges in the first place. To do this, to call these books a problem, was extraordinarily difficult. I was asking the students to memorize and know "facts" about Jewish religion and its history at the same time that they analyzed the process by which this organization of facts was put together and authorized. I was asking them continually to ask who is telling the story and what particular and peculiar story is being told. I was asking the students explicitly to admit complexity into their classroom.[18]

Dismantling authorized narratives of religious histories requires explicit critical tools: tools that can expose the peculiar masculinist logics upon which these narratives rest, tools that can show how these masculinist and other discourses and conditions have come to seem natural and normal. This dismantling requires combining these critical tools with feats of imagination, permissions of some sort, and intellectual courage. Finding ways into and out of these conceptual problems demands that we pay explicit attention—in the formality of our writings and in the informalities of our classrooms—to the construction of knowledge. Explicit attention to the metanarratives through which we produce knowledge is a necessary precondition for producing better scholarship on gendered histories of Judaism. It is a necessary precondition for educating an extended community that can think about issues of gender and women's lives within Judaism with nuance, sophistication, and justice.

Construction Sites

Most of the time, gender is knowledge about sexual difference, which means at least two things: knowledge of the notions of difference that circulate among those we study;[19] and knowledge of the notions of difference within which our production of "history" takes place, and to which our production of histories about other times contributes. Far from being transcendent, "knowledge" is a construction site. The past and its histories are places where gender is produced and reproduced. These places and times, and our recountings of them, are sites where concepts of sexual difference are figured out, clarified, distributed, enforced, challenged.

Picture an actual construction site, in which you can see day by day the process and materials that construction workers use to create a building. Eventually the frame and inner steel bars and concrete pillars are hidden. The supporting structures are invisible to view and the building stands as if naturally and by itself. Eventually, most viewers forget the alternatives: the prior site, the dug-out basement, the exposed wiring, what else might exist. Similarly, for the construction of gender, what exists comes to be the apparent and only reality. Architectural historians figure out how buildings were built, down to the most intricate details. Historians of gender and culture do the same. Both gender and Judaism are constructed. Both are authorized, legitimized, made natural through various means. Both are mediated to us viewers through vast mechanisms of representation. Both can be examined with critical tools to find how the pieces are put together, how the pieces are made into a whole, how that whole is made to appear coherent, sensical. In architectural terms related to images of the artifacts with which I work: How are stones shaped and smoothed? How are the roughly hewn stones hidden from view? How are the textures and colors of stone paved with plaster and painted with frescos?

Tools from the Toolbox

With these issues in mind, I moved the problem of the constructed nature of gender to the forefront of the "Introduction to Judaism." The syllabus read in part as follows:

> This course provides an historical introduction to Jewish religion and culture. We will begin with a survey of contemporary Judaism and then pivot around chronologically to consider earlier forms of Jewish religious culture. The ensuing journey through Judaism's various stages of development is intended to highlight the continuities and ruptures in Judaic religious history and ideas. Since religions do not develop naturally, or of their own essential accord, we will need to consider how Judaism "got to be the way it is." Furthermore, we will investigate the new understandings made possible by applying the very basic insight that there is in fact no "Judaism" but rather many "Judaisms," no "homo Judaicus" but Jewish men and women. Finally, as students of religion, we will have to engage methodological questions of "how we know what we know" about Jewish history, religion and culture, and consider the religious and cultural ramifications of the present state of knowledge about Jewish religious history.

Critical tools, like the practical tools they are, come in the form of new questions and new starting points. Such tools can come in the form of permission and encouragement to critique the familiar and the canonical. A critical tool can also take the form of an explicit acknowledgment that academic claims to produce complete explanations are an anomaly within a late twentieth-century culture of complexity.[20]

Dismantling/Building

In the second chapter of *Standing Again at Sinai* (1990), a work of Jewish feminist theology, Judith Plaskow presents suggestions for making the Jewish past useful to Jewish feminists and to Jewish women. "Torah: Reshaping Jewish Memory" considers the use of Jewish women's history as part of a constructive theological project. "History" is many things. In reading and analyzing this chapter, I am especially interested in Plaskow's theological discussion of the cultural and personal uses of history, and the authority relations at work among different ways of "knowing" the Jewish past(s).[21]

Plaskow's starting point is that nearly all historical accounts of Jewish women's religious activities are based on traditional Jewish texts. These texts—Bible, Talmud, Midrash, Responsa literature, and so forth—were written by men and cannot represent the "totality of women's experiences." In approaching these texts, the feminist critic's first action must be to critique the masculine origins of received texts and traditions. A feminist critic's next response entails the project of "reclaiming" and recovering Jewish women's history, that is, reconstructing women's history with new sources or through new readings of old sources. Plaskow discusses some of this new research on women's history, with particular attention to Carol Meyers's 1988 book on Israelite women and Bernadette Brooten's 1982 study of female leaders in synagogues during the Roman and Byzantine periods. The work of both Meyers and Brooten, and Ross Kraemer as well, is significant in that each scholar finds nontextual evidence—material culture, archaeology, and inscriptions—and introduces it into the set of data used to produce "history."[22]

Plaskow points out that these dual readings of religious texts and material culture have produced new and more specific histories, in which Israelite and Jewish women (in the Roman and Byzantine periods) have more variegated and status-giving roles than previous histories, based solely upon male-written textual sources, have led us to perceive. These new alternate histories of women's experiences are significant. Instead of representing women as victims controlled by masculinist religion and culture, historical Jewish women may be comprehended as agents "struggling within and against patriarchal culture." Implicitly and explicitly both, these new histories point out the specific and partial truths of the available histories about Jewish religious life. New knowledges of women's experiences in history confer the "power to shift our view of the present and the future" (40–46). In these new histories feminist critics read between the lines, and against the grain, of texts invested with religious and ritual importance. The new historical knowledges about women can be used to challenge the theological claims of "so-called normative texts" (50). This challenge to authoritative religious texts provides an opening into, and a foundation for, new feminist theologizing. Hence, the practical importance of the new feminist historiography for the creation of a Jewish/female past for Jewish feminist theology.

Then, at a key point in her argument, Plaskow asserts that these historical projects have limited effectiveness for feminist theology. At best, these histories provide only glimpses into Jewish women's lives. Their effect is limited by several things: the shortage of available and extant evidence for women's lives; the recent growth of this new research; and the relatively small number of projects and studies that currently address aspects of Jewish women's history. Not enough is being produced quickly enough. Few of these sources, especially from the ancient periods, come "directly from women's hands" (47), and here, Plaskow shows both her frustration with the mediated quality of historical data and her desire for some unmediated connection.

To navigate out of these confines, and to produce the "past" needed for a feminist Jewish religion, Plaskow proposes "more traditional strategies for Jewish remembrance . . . [specifically] the open-ended process of writing midrash—simultaneously serious and playful, imaginative, metaphoric" (53).[23] She invokes midrash as a process of knowing that can be both "authentically Jewish" and "feminist." Establishing a Jewish process for "remembering" the past, she links this process for Jewish feminists with Monique Wittig's instruction: "There was a time when you were not a slave, remember that. You walked alone, full of laughter, you bathed bare-bellied. You say you have lost all recollection of it, remember. . . . Make an effort to remember. Or, failing that, invent."[24]

In the paragraphs that follow, Plaskow elucidates the quotation from Wittig:

> This passage, evocative and haunting, names a distinction [i.e., remembering or inventing] to be both honored and ignored. Certainly there is a difference between an inscription about Yahweh and his Asherah or an ancient Aramaic divorce document written by a woman, and a modern midrash about Miriam or Sarah. The first provides us with information that can be ignored or variously interpreted, but that also confronts and challenges, inviting us to find a framework for understanding the past broad enough to include data at odds with selective memory. The second is more fully an expression of our own convictions, a creative imagining based on our own experience, albeit developed in dialogue with traditional texts. To be sure, all historical reconstruction also involves conviction and imagination, but still it tries to accommodate itself to data that midrash feels free to skip over or reshape. (56)

Plaskow's use of midrash aims to give Jewish feminist imaginations access to a past. Access to that past is located within the authority and "authenticity" of the Jewish exegetical tradition of midrash.[25] This use of "midrash" may be helpful for certain projects, but any helpfulness it achieves comes at the cost of several sidesteps. First, confirming the "distinction" between history and midrash presents these as the only possible options for feminist thinkers. Instead of privileging this disinction, we need to historicize and analyze its construction. Plaskow's feminism is radical in intent but constrained by her unarticulated loyalties to Enlightenment categories through which "modern Judaism" has been imagined and practiced. First, the category "history" is neither an essential human or Jewish need; the first question might be, why does a feminist Jewish theology need to claim this kind of past? Second, the positing of these either/or choices is consistent with an Enlightenment framework that would organize things into simple oppositions: objective "evidence" and subjective "selective memory." Committed to this Enlightenment legacy, much of contemporary Jewish thought retains these limits. Yet, having to make the "choice" of either "honoring *or* ignoring," history *or* midrash, severely limits Jewish feminist thought.

Highlighting the distinction between "history" and "memory," as a means of describing how Jews and Judaism might imagine the past, is a practice popularized by the writings of Yosef Yerushalmi, especially *Zakhor: Jewish History and Jewish Memory* (1989). Plaskow cites Yerushalmi's distinction and uses it as the foundation for her own. This gives to Yerushalmi's distinction of history and memory (which has since become a more widespread truism) a feminist approval, when it really warrants a critical analysis. Other questions could have been asked; for instance, what are the historical specificities of Yerushalmi's work? Are these distinctions as categorical and/or as operative for Jewish women as they are for the Jewish men who are the universalized subject of Yerushalmi's text? Yerushalmi's dichotomy ascribes to "memory" an authenticity that needs to be questioned. Memories are social and cultural products. Both Plaskow and Yerushalmi rely upon a notion of "collective memory" that could be understood more creatively, critically, and helpfully in James Young's terms of "collected memory."[26] Young's formulation pushes to the forefront the dynamics of power and discourse that inhere in the construction of "memory."

Conceptualizing an ideal relation for feminist Jews to the past as a turn from "history" to "midrash" (or "memory") gives away "history" and its ongoing intellectual authority and socioreligious uses. This turn to midrash ignores the powerful role of books of Jewish religious history in formulating a "remembered," or even an "invented" landscape. "History" matters because it is distributed orally, at various types of schools and universities, through popular magazines and journals, and through film, video, museums, and other media. This turn to midrash (and of course, Plaskow sees this as augmenting, and not absolute substituting for, history writing) forecloses too quickly the analysis of how history writing is related to memory making. Plaskow writes that "history provides a more and more complex and nuanced picture of the past; memory is more selective" (52). This perpetuates a notion that "history" is not "selective" and that it does not "reshape." But, "history" is not a natural occurrence. It is a culturally specific conceptual category that organizes evidence from the past into a more-or-less coherent chronological narrative. It is a practice built on specific claims to specific kinds of authority. In her division of history and memory, remembering and inventing, Plaskow claims to sidestep and ignore history; instead, she ends up reasserting history's authority.

My deconstruction of the binary terms of "history" and "midrash/memory" has several ramifications for our feminist projects. Plaskow's contradistinction posits history as an enterprise that creates broad frameworks; "history" deals with the complexities of data "at odds with" memory. In contrast, memory is understood to comprise "our own convictions" and "our own experience." My quarrel with Plaskow's notion of "history" is that it ignores complexities. These new histories are necessary precisely because they are complicated. In that they start to demonstrate how gender was organized and women and men were made, these histories are "messy." They critique the terms of the conversation and the authority of inherited frameworks, and they show historical Jewish subjects as temporal "others" who do not always look like "us." Within the conceptual economy that Plaskow describes, complexity resides only in feminist history; its "opposite" (midrash/memory) is construed as nonconfrontative and nonchallenging. Alternatively, I suggest that if we desire a past or a history—no matter what terms of authority these are constructed through—we must allow our notions of identity to contain more complexity and ambiguity. Subjectivity need not be based on a model wherein identity and desire and the past are understood as necessarily unified, congruous, harmonious, and coherent. Like Plaskow's notion of "history," memory, too, could contain within itself things "at odds."

Plaskow's turn from history to midrash ends with the following words: "remembering and inventing together help recover the hidden half of Torah, reshaping Jewish memory to *let women speak*" [my emphasis] (56). The project of "letting women speak" is a particular strategy adopted by some feminist theorists and theologians. "Letting women speak" was an initial response to a situation, such as the historiography of Judaism, that had not included women's lives. "Letting women speak" was (and still can be) strategically useful in its appeal to a woman's voice that has been denied a hearing in the ears of men and other women. It can demonstrate female agency where this has been denied.[27]

Yet, the feminist project that centers primarily on a female voice—on "letting women speak"—brings with it certains risks. It risks essentializing women (where does this female voice come from?) and erasing significant differences between women. We know that women's speech, thoughts, feelings, stances, and positions are multiple, complicated, and often contradictory and at odds with one another. But theorizing feminism primarily as a project that "lets women speak" risks conflating women's voices with feminism. Not all speaking women speak feminism. "Letting women speak" brings with it the risks of underestimating the problems of feminisms and feminists that conflict with one another. It overlooks a critical problem for feminism at the century's turn: determining which of the women among us can speak "for women."[28]

The ideal of "letting women speak" can empower certain women (and men) in certain places, but, as feminist theory, it ignores the problem of the social construction of voice. Afer all, the same masculinist societies and discourses that foster and construct men's voices construct our female voices as well.[29] Women perform femininity in all sorts of different ways. Women speak through the mediations of masculinist culture, and through negotiations with what we determine to be "horizons of possibility."[30] "Letting women speak" means accepting as feminist those women whose speech reinforces and legitimates masculinist discourse and society. Plaskow does recognize and write about differences among women, but I am concerned that her formulation does not challenge, in the most powerful ways possible, the masculinism of the culture that constructs the ongoing possibilities under which we women speak. Focusing on women's voices can sometimes mean than we forget about the power of culture. Recognizing complexities in the power relations of language and culture means that our forms of resistance to them must become more nuanced in order for resistance to be as powerful as the real conditions of our lives, so that our theories reflect the way we live now.

The Misnomer of Engendering

Often I see the word *gender* used as a practical synonym for *women* or for *feminism.* When this substitution happens, there is a problem. The critical force of *gender* is lost. Masculinity is still assumed as the universal, and femininity continues to function as the mark of difference. *Gender* becomes a replacement for more specific and critically acute words. Sometimes, too, *gender* becomes a euphemism or replacement for the term *feminist.* This usage is as problematic—in that it neutralizes feminist critique—as it is inaccurate. Gender is only sometimes an element of feminist discourse, and gender is not exclusively found in feminist discourse. This point bears development. Such semantic slippages are evident, for example, in the title of this essay, "Engendering Jewish Religious History." To speak of "engendering" as the essay's positive contribution might suggest that "Jewish religious history" is not already gendered, or that this topos is not already engendered. Further, it might even smooth over the various and conflicting modes of engendering that are precisely at issue here. A reader might interpret this title to mean that "engendering" adds something to "Jewish religious history." But "Jewish religious history" is always already gendered. Titling the essay "engendering Jewish religious history" risks using a more sophisticated terminology to replicate the logic that merely adds women. It risks substituting an additive project for an analytic one.

Hence, the misnomer of engendering, a misnomer that points to the always-present minefield of addition. "Engendering" is a contested discourse and topos of study. The field of rabbinic studies and Roman-period Judaism already is situated within a gender discourse. This discourse contains multiple strategies for organizing women into its historical narratives. These gender tactics include, at minimum and in various combinations: a tendency to avoid overt and careful analysis; a reliance on stereotype; apologetic valorization; a subtle masculinizing of rabbinic subjectivity; as well as, in other places, a downplaying of rabbinic "masculinity" and an erasure of "women" through the claims that all Jews and Judaism are "feminine." This gendering occurs most often within a masculinist discourse, but its result is one type of an engendered Jewish religious history.

Telling Stories

A brief example might illustrate the differences made by entertaining—and practicing—a more sustained critique of gender's construction. My research investigates the production of gender in Roman-period Judaism in Palestine, with a specific emphasis on the period after the destruction of Jerusalem and its Temple, 70–250 CE. My work details in historically specific ways how Jews negotiated the meanings of male and female. My particular concerns are with the development of notions of gender in the tannaitic religio-legal documents of Mishnah and Tosefta, commonly dated from the late second to the late third centuries. My current conceptualization of this period of Jewish religious culture expands the traditional field of Rabbinic Studies into a broader and more complicated matrix of Roman-period Judaism. In this expansion, material culture from archaeological excavation comprises a significant set of newly available texts with which to investigate both women's lives and the everyday lives of women and men. Material culture provides artifactual texts that can be read with (or against) contemporary early rabbinic texts. In putting these varied texts into conversation with one another, mediated through my scholarly imagination, there rests the potential for reassessing nearly all the traditionally held viewpoints on the early Rabbis that have structured this field of knowledge.

According to rabbinic genealogies, in the late second century Judah ha-Nasi moved with his circle of sages to the city of Zippori, or Diocaesarea. Zippori was a small Roman city in the lower Galilee. There, and through a process still largely unknown to us, the Rabbis edited and promulgated the Mishnah, the earliest of what would become the classic Rabbinic law codes. Roman-period Zippori, called Sepphoris in English, was excavated initially in the early 1930s by Leroy Waterman. In the mid-1980s new excavations were begun.

Excavations of the significant Roman and Byzantine levels of this archaeological site are showing the birth city of the Mishnah to be wonderfully decorated and very Roman/pagan. The excavations also provide new information about domestic architecture and daily life in the Roman and Byzantine periods, as well as new evidence for art and aesthetics in Roman Palestine and for the cultural environment of at least some generations of tannaitic Rabbis. The most spectacular and widely reported finds are the mosaics excavated in various precincts of Zippori. Floor mosaics include scenes of Alexandria and the Nile, Dionysiac processions, a portrait of a woman, zodiac circles, depictions of gods and goddesses, and more.[31] The published and public commentary on these mosaics, and on Zippori/Sepphoris more generally, reveal the generalizing tropes through which the cultural history of the site is understood. These "public" tropes and figures also shape the "scholarly" commentary. The site joins scholarly and popular discourse on Judaism in Roman antiquity. In the case of Zippori and the study of Roman-period Judaism in Palestine, the presentation of the excavation site makes these tropes and figures easier to see.

One of the earliest of the floor mosaics excavated at Zippori is the so-called Mona Lisa of the Galilee mosaic excavated by the Joint Sepphoris Project. This mosaic, or stone carpet, features, in a medallion on its north side, a very well-executed mosaic representation of a woman. The mosaic itself was the centerpiece of the *tri-*

clinia (dining area) of a villa located on the eastern side of the city's acropolis (or high point), nearly adjacent to the theater. After the first several excavation seasons, and in the midst of ongoing excavation, the site was turned into an archaeological park by Israel's National Parks Authority. A small museum was built to cover and display the mosaic and to explain the mosaic to the public.[32]

I had excavated at Sepphoris several seasons before, and I revisited the site in December 1992. While the entire organization of the site is significant in terms of an Israeli presentation of Judaism and paganism, here I will focus on only one aspect. Upon walking into the museum, visitors first see an illuminated drawing, placed directly on the wall opposite the entrance. In it, banqueters lounge in various positions. They are draped over one another, receiving abundant portions of foods. The drawing intends to illustrate the ancient function and use of the room, to prepare the visitor to understand the mosaic down the hall and below, to move from a "now" to a Roman/Byzantine "then." Closer inspection shows that all the banqueters are female. Presumably, the display is intended to illustrate for the museum-going public a normative use of the ancient dining room in the villa. Yet, a normative use of a main *triclinia* in a late Roman villa would not be an all-female event.[33] The drawing of a women's banquet to depict the use of the room is curiously inaccurate, contextually odd. It doesn't represent "history" as we historians might know it. Furthermore, the bodies are bulbous and large, drawn in the style of a late-nineteenth-century European type: the "Oriental" or Eastern woman.[34] What is interesting is the drawing's role in constructing an ancient culture in gendered and neocolonial terms.

In the kind of feminist analysis that celebrates the presence of women but does not necessarily consider the terms of women's inclusion, the drawing could be applauded. In contrast to the usual absence of women from archaeology and history, here women are not absent but present and prominently displayed. Their lives are part of the museum's popular production of the history of Roman Palestine. However, such an analysis engages in a misconception that sees the inclusion of most pictures of women (or the inclusion of "women's voices") as a "positive" interruption of traditional historical practices. This analysis is based in a logic of addition. Yet, instead of responding to the usual absence of women by celebrating the inclusion of women's bodies in a museum presentation, a range of other responses and questions are possible: How are women's bodies being portrayed? What cultural work is being accomplished by a particular portrayal? On what terms are women included?

The evidence of Roman-period Sepphoris suggests that its population included "pagans," Jews, and at a certain point, Christians. What the illuminated drawing accomplishes is related to the discourse that assigns gender to each of these religio-cultural groups, but in varying ways. The illuminated drawing participates in the masculinization of rabbinic Judaism, a masculinization as apparent in popular culture as it is in scholarly books and articles, and in textbooks for students. In the case of the illuminated drawing that introduces the mosaic at Sepphoris, the drawing first constructs "pagans" (to use a term that problematically groups together a series of religions, *ethnoi*, and practices) as Judaism's Roman-period "other." In the banquet scene, "paganism" is being feminized. As encapsulated in this introductory drawing, the "pagan" is illustrated as a culture inhabited by women. The feminization of the "pagan" serves to protect its "opposite" gender—the masculine—for the imagining of the Jewish. This gendering of two religio-cultural groups overtly feminizes "paganism" and hence contributes to the masculinization of Judaism. This gendering of an aspect of Jewish history may not have been conscious on the part of the artist who produced this drawing, but it need not have been a conscious act for my analysis to hold. In fact, this kind of gendering is so in line with current practices for envisioning sexual difference in the Jewish past that it most likely went unnoticed, and seemed "natural."[35]

It is this process of naturalizing gender that must become a more articulated focus of feminist analysis and conversation about Jews, jewishness, and Judaism. The plights and plots of women were part of the past but are absent—for the most part—from history writing. Gender is different. Gender both was present in past time and is present in modern history writing. The problem is not that *gender* is absent from either the past or from our renderings of history; even a womanless history is simultaneously and necessarily gendered. The claim of such an absence is possible only when *gender* is mistakenly used as a simple synonym for *women*. The problem is not gender's absence, but the absence of a critical analysis of gender. A more powerful project investigates something that is present but hidden, largely through our familiarity with masculinist histories and culture. When we ignore things that are already there, when we let masculinist constructions of categories stand, feminist work can actually bolster and protect these historical and cultural narratives of Rabbinic and other forms of Judaism. Any intellectual venture—feminist and nonfeminist—can reify sexual difference, in startlingly similar ways. Historically varied Jewish cultures have articulated and reified sexual differences. Cultural productions—scholarly and popular writing and other media—that formulate knowledge of Judaism and Jews in past time can participate, or not participate, in the construction and reification of sexual difference.

A study of Judaism that is feminist and critical demands our increasingly nuanced analysis of how these notions of difference are articulated, argued, made persuasive, given authority, and made to seem normal. Attending to women's experiences and to the construction of the possibilities for women's experiences really does alter the conditions and terms of our projects. Feminist research of the past two decades has made clear the nuance, intransigence, and sophistication by which gender was produced and reproduced and retained within Jewish traditions. As intellectuals who are engaged in the production of knowledge that is always already politicized, we need critical tools sufficiently powerful to demonstrate and explain how gender is engendered.

Notes

I thank Laura Levitt for her repeated readings of and critical suggestions for this essay, as well as for the pleasure of our ongoing conversations. Appreciative admiration goes to Susan Shapiro, for reading this text more delicately and subtly than I could ever have done. I thank Judith Plaskow for her responses to an earlier, oral version, and thank various other readers for their suggestions. Much of this essay could not have been written but for Jean O'Barr, Professor of the Practice of Women's Studies at Duke University, and it is in recognizing her efforts at our common endeavor that I dedicate this essay to her. This essay is a revised version of that which appeared in *Shofar* 14.1.

1. The phrase is Carolyn Heilbrun's.

2. The term *maskil* refers to a participant in the Haskalah in central and western Europe, that is, to the specifically Jewish intellectual activity informed by the then-new Enlightenment formulations. This blatantly ahistorical fantasy is informed by my curiosities regarding the apparent blindness in the common ascription of the term *secular* to putatively (post)-Christian *philosophes* educated in Christian schools, with priestly brothers and reverend fathers and pious mothers.

3. For readers unfamiliar with the history of Jewish Studies, the *Wissenschaft des Judentums* adopted and adapted Enlightenment categories of philology, history, and other European academic categories to study Judaism; see Gershom Scholem, "The Science of Judaism—Then and Now," in *The Messianic Idea in Judaism and Other Essays on Jewish Spirituality* (New York: Schocken Books, 1971), 304–313; Salo Baron, "Jewish Studies in Universities: An Early Project," *Hebrew Union College Annual* 46 (1975): 357–376; and Ismar Schorsch, "Breakthrough into the Past: the Verein für Kultur und Wissenschaft des Juden," *Leo Baeck Institute Yearbook* 33 (1988): 3–28.

4. I am reminded here of a repeated motif in Gayatri Chakravorty Spivak, *Outside in the Teaching Machine* (New York and London: Routledge, 1993), that of "critical intimacy," and her suggestions, for example, of "the legacy of patriarchy which, like the culture of imperialism, is a dubious gift that we can only transform if we acknowledge it" (123), and later, significantly: "Favorite sons and daughters who refuse to sanctify their father's house have their uses. Persistently to critique a structure that one cannot not (wish to) inhabit is the deconstructive stance" (284).

5. These problems are not new among some feminist thinkers (although a good deal of writing by and about female religionists continues to ignore, argue against, or dismiss the complexities of the constructedness of gender and sexual difference). We thinkers and theorists of Judaism are beginning—individually and collectively—to tackle them in ways that reflect the specific relations, complexities, and interpretive histories of working with Jewish texts.

6. One point of this paper is that each of these terms—*women, gender, feminism*—is understood and deployed in many and contradictory ways. Nonetheless, by *gender* I mean attention to several overlapping things: the constructed nature of differences ascribed to women and to men; the constructedness of the cultural significance given to distinctions between male and female humans; and the politics of empowering these notions of differences into authorized, or canonical, knowledge.

7. By "categories" I have in mind the divisions and distinctions around which knowledges and the interpretation of evidence (as well as the partitioning of evidence) is organized.

8. The classroom is not, of course, the only site for the distribution and reproduction of knowledges to people other than peers and colleagues. Some Jewish feminist writers have quite frequently and successfully written for and spoken in many other venues; I have in mind Judith Plaskow's regular contributions to *Tikkun* magazine, the work of *Bridges* magazine, and feminist intellectuals active in community endeavors, occupations, and educational institutions other than the university.

9. I have actually smoothed over some very significant differences in the history and practice of this course. Continual discussions were had, specifically regarding how and whether to teach "Judaism" as a "religion" and/or as a "culture" and/or as a "civilization." Depending on who taught it, this course used these categories very differently.

10. The American Academy of Religion (AAR) had organized, together with the Lily Foundation, a yearlong Workshop on Teaching Religion, comprising staff, twelve faculty, and three advanced graduate students, and hosted by Raymond Williams at Wabash College, Crawfordsville, Indiana. This was the first workshop in an ongoing effort by the AAR to promote new conversations about the teaching and study of religion. Feminist theory, Women's Studies, and other issues regarding gender formed significant aspects of these conversations and proceedings.

11. The move beyond "add women and stir" has become a truism in some places and not others, and is language common in discussions among feminist historians and women's historians at a certain moment in the development of those practices. In general, it signals a cognition that knowledge categories are not innocent of their traditional and containing exclusion of women and gender construction. Recognition of the limits also recognizes the limits of the liberal dream of integration. See essays in Gerda Lerner, *The Majority Finds Its Past: Placing Women in History* (New York: Oxford University Press, 1979); Peggy McIntosh, "Curricular Re-Vision: The New Knowledge for a New Age," in *Educating the Majority: Women Challenge Tradition in Higher Education*, ed. Carol Pearson, Donna Shavlik, and Judith Touchton (New York: American Council on Education, 1989); Margaret Andersen, "Changing the Curriculum in Higher Education," in *Reconstructing the Academy: Women's Education and Women's Studies*, ed. Elizabeth Minnich et al. (Chicago: University of Chicago Press, 1988), 36–68; Linda Gordon, "What's New in Women's History," in *Feminist Studies/Critical Studies*, ed. Teresa de Lauretis (Bloomington: Indiana University Press, 1986). The end of reliance on liberal models is related in significant ways to a turn by (some) feminist scholars to other ways of theorizing "women," and to the attractions of some feminist scholars to Foucault and other continental theorists. On the "turn" to gender and newer modes of conceptualizing "women's agency and subjectivity in history," see Joan Scott, *Gender and the Politics of History* (New York: Columbia University Press, 1988). On applications of feminist theory to Jewish studies, or explications of feminist theory within Jewish studies, see Susannah Heschel, "Women's Studies," *Modern Judaism* 10 (1990): 243–258; Shulamit Magnus, "Out of the Ghetto: Integrating the Study of Jewish Women into the Study of 'the Jews,' " *Judaism* 39 (1990): 28–36; and Susan Shapiro, "Voice from the Margins: Women and Jewish Studies," *Association for Jewish Studies Newsletter*, 2d ser., 4 (1990): 1–2, 4.

12. It has been possible to adopt and adapt new aphorisms from feminist theory and then not figure out their ramifications.

13. See Miriam Peskowitz, "'The Work of Her Hands': Gendering Everyday Life in Roman-Period Judaism in Palestine (70–250 CE), Using Textile Production as a Case Study," Ph.D. diss., Duke University, 1993), and *Spinning Fantasies: Rabbis, Gender and History* (Berkeley: University of California Press, forthcoming).

14. Paradoxically, the moment of their association is also that of their separation from each other.

15. Robert Seltzer, *Jewish People, Jewish Thought: The Jewish Experience in History* (New York: Macmillan, 1980); and Judith Baskin, *Jewish Women in Historical Perspective* (Detroit: Wayne State University Press, 1991).

16. There is a large literature on the theory, vision, and practices of feminist teaching. More recently, several books explore feminist teaching practices in ways that are informed explicitly by feminist theorizing. See Gail Griffin, *Calling: Essays on Teaching in the Mother Tongue* (Pasadena, CA: Trilogy Books, 1992); Jean O'Barr, *Feminism in Action: Building Institutions and Community Through Women's Studies* (Chapel Hill: University of North Carolina Press, 1994). In the past decade, feminist thinking about pedagogy focused in part on unraveling the relations of power and authority between teacher and student. I think that this is now being taken in a related direction, that of unraveling and reconstructing the power relations between traditional producers of knowledges, presented by teachers and (text)books, and traditional receivers of knowledge (students). In reflecting on the power relations of student, teacher, and text, I think that it is ineffectual, and politically fruitless, to expose and undermine our authorities to speak as teachers, scholars, and trained intellectuals without simultaneously exposing the authorities and truth claims of the textbooks and other texts introduced into teaching situations.

17. A significant "bulge" in the seams occurs at the few points at which Seltzer's text on Jewish people mentions Jewish women. "Women" appear at most two or three times in *Jewish People, Jewish Thought.* At one point, p. 583, women enter the narrative of Jewish religious history in the figures of Henriette Herz and Rahel Varnhagen, that is, as German salon women who broached the boundaries of Jewishness and became Christian, i.e., "susceptible" women who left "Judaism" for "Romanticism." Despite the many places where research on women existed (at the time when Seltzer's text was written and published), it is suggestive that here, women signify a breach in the seamlessness and lead the way out of Judaism. Other introductory surveys of Judaism share similar problematics of ignoring women and hiding their own masculine engenderment. What is necessary are new classroom texts for Jewish religious history that speak to the critical problems of "doing history" while narrating the practices and lives of male and female Jews, and attending to Judaism's canonical use of gender in its own narratives, halakhic practices, ritual, and so forth.

18. Despite warnings by some colleagues that this type of teaching would be too difficult for undergraduates or applicable only to well-educated students at elite universities, I have found that students at both institutions at which I have taught, Duke and the University of Florida, become excited and empowered by, as well as show resistance to, teaching that includes complexities such as these, teaching that recognizes "messiness."

19. My work is in the cultural history of Jewish religion in antiquity, but my discussion at this general level can be applied to work within other disciplines and regimes of knowledges, such as anthropology, cultural studies, and literature.

20. I begin this course "in the present" in part to introduce and problematize the Enlightenment categories through which "the past" is understood and organized, while simultaneously presenting the intellectual, political, and cultural origins of contemporary Western Judaism.

21. Judith Plaskow, *Standing Again at Sinai: Judaism from a Feminist Perspective* (San Francisco: Harper, 1990). I thank Judith Plaskow for her comments when I first presented this analysis in April 1993 at the Gender and Judaism conference at the Ohio State University. During our conversation the next day, she remarked to me that she had herself been uncertain about and uncomfortable with the distinctions contained in this section. I see my expanded analysis here as an acknowledgment of our conversations, and as a provision of theoretical tools and explanatory language that help to untangle and explain that uncertainty and discomfort.

I choose Plaskow's text primarily because she is well known and her writings are widely read. I do not wish to reify her positions and stances, especially as her new writing and projects emerge. Recent Jewish feminist thought is moving and changing rapidly, and I am aware of the dynamic of critiquing a text published in 1990 as if it were my exact contemporary as I write in 1994 and publish even later. I do so because the theoretical assumptions in this section of Plaskow's work are still operative for much Jewish feminist thought and historiography.

22. Carol Meyers, *Discovering Eve: Ancient Israelite Women in Context* (New York: Oxford University Press, 1988); Bernadette Brooten, *Women Leaders in the Ancient Synagogue* (Chico, CA: Scholars Press, 1982); and Ross Shephard Kraemer, *Her Share of the Blessings: Women's Religions among Pagans, Jews, and Christians in the Greco-Roman World* (New York: Oxford University Press, 1992).

23. Plaskow refers not to the collections of midrash but to an understanding of a midrashic process of reading sacred text.

24. Plaskow, *Standing Again at Sinai*, 56. The quotation from Wittig comes from *Les Guérillères* (New York: Avon Books, 1973), 89. This particular Wittig citation recurs regularly in feminist theologies located in various religious traditions; of course, the move to "theology" is to locate Jewish feminist thought within explicit frameworks—"theology"—of the Christian West.

25. The reach for Jewish textual authority flattens the distinctions of various documents within that canon. Specifically, the authority of Midrash within the traditional economy of rabbinic texts was marginal because these texts were accorded lesser status than halakhic forms.

26. James Young, *The Texture of Memory: Holocaust Memorials and Meaning* (New Haven: Yale University Press. 1993), xi. Young uses the term to discuss the production of memory through Holocaust memorials.

27. I want to emphasize the ongoing necessity of some of these strategies. That sectors of Jewish knowledges and Jewish Studies scholarship remain so intransigently committed to the exclusion of both women and the explicit study of gender and sexuality means that these temporally "earlier" "stages" in feminist work need be constantly repeated, strategically, in order to interrupt both intransigence and active resistance to feminist scholarship.

28. For example, contention over women's voices in certain Orthodox communities, precisely with regard to which women get to represent "women's" desires is described and theorized by anthropologist Deborah Kaufman, in *Rachel's Daughters: Newly Orthodox Jewish Women* (New Brunswick, NJ: Rutgers University Press, 1991).

29. That women do not live free of masculinist culture and structures provided the initial and ongoing impulses that spawned feminist scholarship.

30. "Horizons of possibility" is an adaptation from Teresa de Lauretis, "Feminist Studies/Critical Studies: Issues, Terms, and Contexts," in de Lauretis, ed., *Feminist Studies/Critical Studies* (Bloomington: Indiana University Press, 1986), 8. "In other words, these different forms of consciousness are grounded, to be sure, in one's personal history; but that history—one's identity—is interpreted or reconstructed by each of us within the horizons of meanings and knowledges available in the culture at given historical moments, a horizon that also includes modes of political commitment and struggle." I thank Laura Levitt for this helpful reference.

31. There is a growing literature on these mosaics. For starters, see R. Talgam and Z. Weiss, " 'The Life of Dionysos' in the Mosaic Floor of Sepphoris," *Qadmoniot* 21 (1988): 93–99; Eric Meyers, Ehud Netzer, and Carol Meyers, "Artistry in Stone: The Mosaics of Ancient Sepphoris," *Biblical Archaeologist* 50 (1987): 223–231, and *Sepphoris* (Winona Lake, IN: Eisenbrauns, 1992). Yearly reports can be found in *Israel Exploration Journal*, and more popularized accounts in *Biblical Archaeology Review.*

32. The excavation and public presentation of Zippori/Sepphoris has been subjected to much attention, popular, scholarly, and pseudo-scholarly. For an excellent account, see Joel Baumann, "Between Tourism and Zionism: Israeli National Parks and the Politics of Historical Representation," *MERIP*, forthcoming.

33. Kathleen Corley argues that women were generally participating with men at public meals. See her "Were the Women around Jesus Really Prostitutes? Women in the Context of Greco-Roman Meals," *SBL Seminar Papers* 28 (1989): 487–521, and *Private Women, Public Meals: Social Conflict and Women in the Synoptic Tradition* (Peabody, MA: Hendrikson, 1993). On the evidence for separation of men and women in some contexts, see Ross Kraemer, "Monastic Jewish Women in Greco-Roman Egypt: Philo on the Therapeutrides," *Signs: Journal of Women in Culture and Society* 14 (1989): 342–370. For an interpretation of domestic space at Herod's fortress at Macheros into separate dining rooms for women and men, see B. Schwank, "Neue Funde in Nabatërstidten und Ihre Bedeutung für Neutestamentliche Exegese," *NTS* 29 (1983): 429–435. I thank Kathleen Corley for this last reference, and for her help on this topic. A main dining area would either seat men and women together in the same room, in various configurations, or serve men, with women eating separately elsewhere. There seems to be no evidence for a normative cultural pattern in which female diners would

occupy the main formal *triclinia.* See also William Slater, ed., *Dining in a Classical Context* (Ann Arbor: University of Michigan Press, 1991).

34. I thank Beatrice St. Laurent for this insight. For examples and analysis of this style, see James Thompson, *The East Imagined, Experienced, Remembered: Orientalist Nineteenth Century Painting* (Dublin: National Gallery of Ireland, 1988), esp. figures 13, 21, 22, and 28.

35. That is, the gendering of Judaism as masculine and paganism as feminine is sufficiently naturalized so as to seem natural. My hunch is that my insight could be extended to a re-evaluation of the feminizing of "paganism" in scholarship. Ross Kraemer has made remarks in this regard, and comments as well on Roman-period "feminizing" of certain specific formulations of what we could now call "religion." See her *Her Share of the Blessings,* and "The Other as Woman: An Aspect of Polemic among Pagans, Jews, and Christians in the Greco-Roman World," in *The Other in Jewish Thought and History: Constructions of Jewish Culture and Identity,* ed. Laurence Silberstein and Robert Cohn (New York: New York University Press, 1994), 121–144.

Theorizing Jewish Patriarchy *in extremis*

Naomi Seidman

The focus on Jewish men and masculinity has turned out to be a more productive critical approach, it seems to me, than one might have predicted a few years ago. Once attention had been drawn to the maleness cloaked by the general terms *Jew* or *Judaism*, an extraordinary number of historical and cultural phenomena took on a new and more curious cast. In Sander Gilman's pioneering reading, for example, Freudian psychoanalysis (and the cultural production of such other central European Jewish men as Heine, Marx, and Weininger) emerges as a response to stereotypes of "the [male] Jew as woman";[1] in Michael Berkowitz's work, Zionism is similarly viewed as a therapy program for wounded Jewish masculinity, an attempt on the part of European Jewish males to be "manly men."[2]

Although the work of Gilman and Berkowitz proceeds from Jewish men's internalization and rejection of antisemitic perspectives on Jewish masculinity, other critics have attempted to recover and transvalue traditional Jewish masculinity. Thus, what appeared as a pathetic lack of virility, an inability or unwillingness to work productively and provide for one's family, or (in Freud's Vienna) an incapacity for "scientific objectivity," is now marked as a coherent value system, in which nonviolence, early marriage, and Torah learning are prized over and against heroic, romantic (or celibate), and economic Christian/European ideals of masculine behavior.[3] To complicate matters, this traditional Jewish system produces its own "feminized" Jewish men, as in one of the conventional addresses to the reader that appeared in premodern Yiddish literature: "For women and men who are like women," a category that included under the rubric of the feminine those (far from anomalous) men who failed to live up to the masculine requirement of Hebrew literacy.[4] In Ashkenaz, in particular, the "feminization" of Jewish men appears to be a widespread, overdetermined phenomenon, one with its corollaries, presumably, in other colonized, marginal, or belated cultures.

Although the study of Jewish masculinity owes an undeniable debt to feminist criticism, the one area that remains least developed in this growing body of work is the analysis of patriarchy or gender inequality—important masculine issues, one would think. The fascination with an alternative or degraded Jewish masculinity, in study after study, fixes on the contrast between Jewish and non-Jewish men, or between more-learned and less-learned Jewish men. The notion that Jewish men are like women has been, if anything, profoundly unproductive of feminist analysis or anti-patriarchal critique. Thus, the suggestion is made in one essay that Christian culture "masculinizes Jewish women" as it has "emasculated Jewish men" and "robs Jewish women of their femininity";[5] this analysis leaves open the question of whether "emasculation" and "masculinization" are equally disempowering or reverse mechanisms, while laying the blame for the woes of Jewish "masculinity"or "femininity" solely at the feet of antisemitic culture. In other analyses, Jewish men's embrace of the "natural" feminine virtues of humility and accommodation (though not to their wives!) produces a supremely balanced religious culture, a perfect union of the masculine and feminine. Jacob Neusner, arguing that the "feminization of rabbinic Judaism accounts for its success," describes how this "androgynous Judaism," as he calls it, translated into a "remarkably successful" cosmic and domestic order:

> Men had to find virtue in the political status of inferiority that history accorded to them as their lot. . . . [T]he authentic Israelite man exhibits virtues that, for women, come quite naturally. What was asked of the women was no more than what the men accepted at the hands of the nations. What was demanded of men was no more than the relationship that their wives endured with them, which was identical to that relationship Israel affirmed with God. The circle then is closed: God is to Israel as the nations are to Israel as man is to woman.[6]

Neusner's reading of the equivalence between "what the men accepted at the hands of the nations" (as if Jewish women did not also suffer this oppression) and "the relationship their wives endured with them" is disturbing in its serenity, a signal of where the (il)logic of the analogy "Jewish men are like women" can ultimately lead. What is needed, it seems to me, is a willingness to think through the intersections between Jewish patriarchy and the various disempowerments of Jewish men—to negotiate, in other words, the multiple displacements and unstable categories of a marginal and partially colonized gender system without losing track of its hierarchies and inequities. What follows is no more than a sketch of how such a project might proceed.

S. Y. Abramovitsh's 1878 novella, *The Travels of Benjamin the Third*, could be called a central text of late nineteenth-century eastern European Jewish masculinity (as *Portnoy's Complaint* could be said to fulfill that function for postwar American Jewish masculinity).[7] Many of the themes current in contemporary studies of Jewish masculinity are remarkably close to the surface of Abramovitsh's novella; one of the two male protagonists, in fact, is nicknamed "*di yidene,*" a usually denigrating term for a Jewish woman. It should come as no surprise that Yiddish literature produced what is perhaps the most direct treatment of the feminized Jewish man. This literature arose, after all, in the gap between two mutually contradictory gender systems; Abramovitsh began writing firmly within the Haskalah (Jewish Enlightenment) program, with its critique of Jewish male unproductivity and what was seen as the Jewish distance from nature and sexual instinct. Moreover, there was the more widespread sense—among maskilim and the masses alike—that the eastern European Jews were a people of long-faded greatness. Thus, the Jewish man was feminized not only by contrast with European codes of masculinity but also within the Jewish order, where diasporic Yiddish culture was the feminine counterpart to Hebraic masculinity and the legendary glories of Israel's royal past.[8]

Travels recounts the adventures of two men, Benjamin and Senderl *di yidene,* who venture from their small town in the Pale of Settlement to search for the legendary and heroic Red Jews, using the often fantastic medieval literature of the "great Jewish explorers" as their eminently unreliable compass. The novella is a complex satire with multiple targets, and has been read, for instance, as both a critique of Jewish political passivity and a deflation of proto-Zionist fantasies.[9] For the purposes of this paper, I will focus only on the ways in which Abramovitsh, or his narrator Mendele, presents Benjamin and Senderl as inadequate, emasculated, or feminized men. The men are feminized in at least three separate ways. Benjamin and Senderl are described as inadequate in comparison with other men, both Jewish and non-Jewish; men they meet, or read about, or with whom they are implicitly compared through the novella's numerous intertexts. Senderl is also described as Benjamin's female counterpart in the quasi-marriage of the two men. Most explicitly (although this aspect of the novella is also consistently overlooked) Senderl and, to some degree, Benjamin are described as feminized in relation to their wives. These three modes of feminization, as it turns out, are interwoven in a number of ways.

The narrative works very much within the realm of what could be called "comparative masculinity." Benjamin and Senderl are explicitly or implicitly measured, to their detriment, against an array of Jewish and non-Jewish masculine models: their longing to reach the Ten Lost Tribes or Red Jews, who live in royal splendor and military invulnerability on the other side of the magical river Sambatyon, reminds us of their own sorry lives in the Pale of Settlement. Another military figure, Alexander the Great, is Benjamin's particular hero (the name Senderl, pointedly enough, is the Yiddish diminutive of Alexander). In Benjamin's first misconceived foray into the countryside surrounding his *shtetl,* he is rescued by a burly Ukrainian farmer who takes pity on the terrified Jew (Benjamin is sure he is a "brigand"). Finally, the officers of the czarist army, into which Benjamin and Senderl have been kidnapped, regard the two men as ludicrous buffoons and discharge them.

Although Benjamin and Senderl are generally the targets of Abramovitsh's satire, the army episode at the novella's end partially reverses the satirical charge. Benjamin and Senderl are, predictably, woefully inadequate at soldiering, but their very buffoonery exposes the ridiculousness of the soldiers they are trying to emulate: "Looking at them, you'd think the two men were dressing up just to make fun of the army, just to show how foolish the whole thing was."[10] In fact, Senderl and Benjamin do present an implicit challenge to the army, seeing it as a place where men are stripped of their proper masculinity—beard and sidelocks, for example. Senderl, immediately before their abduction into the army, has a prophetic nightmare about being transformed into a woman, losing his beard, wearing a housecoat, about to give birth to his first child. And, in fact, their uniforms hang on them "like women's housecoats;" and when they hold a gun, they look as silly as "a man ["a mansbil"] messing around by the kitchen stove."[11] The joke is partly on Benjamin and Senderl, but it also lets us see that, from *their* perspective, it is the rituals of military life that are inappropriate and even effeminate. It is significant that Senderl, the more passive partner in the duo, is less impossible a soldier than Benjamin, who at least has a wily and spirited opposition to the absurdities of goose-stepping upon command. Their discharge from the army is something of a qualified triumph—not at having achieved an ideal masculinity but at having recovered the dignity of the masculinity, degraded as it is, that was always theirs.

Travels presents both Benjamin and Senderl as ineffectual, but it is Senderl who is more consistently described as womanlike, even in relation to Benjamin, the "husband" for whom he plays wife. This farcical quasi-marriage, from one point of view, is an extension of the comparison between Jewish and non-Jewish masculinity, part of an extended parody of *Don Quixote*, itself a mock-heroic parody of the chivalric romance, as a *shtetl* narrative (the Yiddish novella was translated into Polish as "The Jewish Don Quixote"). In contrast with Quixote's emblematically European pursuit of love and honor, Benjamin and Senderl are married men in flight from their wives, and they are generally intimidated by women. When Senderl appears disguised in women's clothing on the morning of their escape, for example, Benjamin hides at the sight; it's only when he realizes that the figure is Senderl that he emerges from behind the windmill. Where Don Quixote turns peasant girls into noblewomen, Benjamin's sexual adventures include waking up in the embrace of a donkey and conducting a mock-sublime courtship, romance, and "elopement" with the cross-dressed Senderl.[12] The erotic life of the traditional Jewish man, Abramovitsh seems to suggest, is no more than a grotesque version of the valorized heterosexuality of both European literature and the Bible.[13]

Benjamin and Senderl's quasi-marriage also serves as a commentary on what constitutes masculinity and femininity in the traditional gender system. Benjamin is that masculine staple of Jewish comedy, the *luftmensch*, full of dreams and ideas but lacking in the means to implement them. Senderl, by contrast, has the stereotypical qualities of the Jewish wife: he is earthbound, enabling, practical. Benjamin has read the books that provide the men with their quest, but Senderl, "like a good housewife," remembers the provisions, and for that "Benjamin thought even more highly of him."[14] Benjamin and Senderl's partnership, then, reconstitutes the traditional division of labor (if you can call masculine reading and dreaming "labor"), but in the male sphere; "femininity" is reclaimed as the missing component of Jewish masculine empowerment. The Europeanized writer's satirical target here is not so much the "feminized" Jewish man but a gender system that marks productivity and practicality as female attributes, and views them as unusual if not unnatural when they appear in a man.

The feminization of Senderl arises not only from the confrontation between two gender systems but also from within Jewish patriarchy, a system divided against itself. Senderl acquires his nickname, "*di yidene*" because his shrewish wife "wore the pants [literally, caftan] in the family,"[15] beating Senderl and and making him clean the house with a kerchief over his beard—a humiliating concealment of the primary sign of traditional adult Jewish masculinity with an article of clothing ordinarily associated with both women and domesticity. Senderl's domestic situation, which is an extreme version of Benjamin's marriage and others, makes use of the stereotype of the dominant, shrewish Jewish woman as another aspect of the disempowerment of Jewish men. But Senderl's relationship with his wife also reveals patriarchy as the incompletely realized ideal of the community—if we define patriarchy, for the moment, in the simplest sense of institutional male superiority. To call Senderl a *yidene* is, after all, to state clearly that the submissive position in marriage properly belongs to women, just as cooking and cleaning are perverse activities for men (unless, as it turns out, the female function is performed in the context of a male homosocial relationship, as when Senderl acts as breadwinner and "wife" to his *luftmensch* companion). Patriarchy not only structurally underwrites Senderl's "femininity," it also explains Senderl's shame at allowing his wife to treat him so poorly and propels him to search for the power that is his birthright—as it turns out, this search is, in one sense, absolutely successful.

The disparity between ideal Jewish masculinity and Senderl's present degraded state is underlined by a series of textual allusions in the scene in which Benjamin approaches the bruised and battered Senderl to invite him to come along on his travels. Senderl, we are told, sits in the kitchen "like a woman whose husband had abandoned her and gone abroad," or, the narrator continues in a lower register, "like a woman whose husband had just slapped her." The passage elaborately reiterates what is already implicit in Senderl's nickname: the position of the abused is properly feminine. And this is true not only in the case of Senderl but also elsewhere in the Jewish library—after all, the first, grandiose simile refers to a midrashic parable comparing Israel in exile to a deserted woman, a famous parable that paves the way for an equation of Senderl with the humiliated Jewish man in the diaspora and grants the deserting man divine precedence, if not justification. But the comparison of Senderl and the abandoned woman functions only partly through the *similarity* between his situation and that of the punished woman. It derives most of its force from the difference between Senderl (or the male collective) and the individual deserted wife. The reference to an *agune* (deserted wife or "grass widow") occurs first in the novella, not in this passage but in the humorous chapter title "How Benjamin Became a Martyr—and Zelda an Agune."[16] As we are told, Benjamin's wife, Zelda, acquires that nickname during his first aborted foray, although the joke is soon to become a more serious problem when Benjamin leaves for good. And Senderl, of course, is about to desert his own wife to join Benjamin, so the description of him as an *agune* prefigures and justifies his own actions. Senderl and Benjamin's desertions of their wives dramatize the difference between being treated as if one were a woman and being subject to Jewish marital laws by virtue of actually being a woman. Senderl's wife's absence from the kitchen enables Benjamin to proposition Senderl. In other words, her absence frees him to pursue his own fortune. By contrast, the *agune* is most helpless precisely when her spouse is most absent. In a society where male domination is secured most strongly, and perhaps solely, by Jewish law, language, and texts, men can easily disappear, leaving patriarchal law to guarantee their power. The paradox implicit in the concept of the *agune*—literally a woman "anchored" by her husband's absence—is testimony to the power of a symbolic order that is independent of its apparently powerless agents.[17] And in contrast to their disruption of the military order, Benjamin and Senderl continue to assert and uphold the asymmetrical terms of Jewish marriage, even and especially in their apparent deviations from it.

Wife abandonment is always present in traditional Jewish patriarchy, not only as an option or threat but also as part of the homosocial structure of everyday life. As Bluma Goldstein perceptively points out, leaving one's family is no more than an extension of the "routine of daily life" in the shtetl: "After all," she writes, "the impoverished *shtetl,* as Mendele notes, consists of unemployed men who, congregating in study hall or bath, 'sit all day long until late at night, abandoning wife and children,' discussing politics and finance."[18] Desertion, then, is part of the fabric of Jewish life, from the traditional site of the study hall, where removing oneself from the company of women is a valorized part of Torah learning, to the more secular site of the bathhouse, where the "men's business" of politics and finance forms the basis for new homosocial discourses. By the same token, the homoerotic bond that Abramovitsh satirizes enables Benjamin and Senderl to triumph over and subjugate the women they have left.

The structural inequality that governs and limits Senderl's feminization in the domestic sphere, I argue, in fact underlies all the ways in which Senderl or both men are feminized, in contrast with each other or with other men. In each case the feminine is the denigrated term, and the masculine is an incompletely realized ideal that propels and motivates the gender system. Whatever the context, the "feminization" of Jewish men either already involves the (discursive or physical) disappearance of women or motivates masculine desertion of women. Benjamin and Senderl leave their wives in search of masculine mobility and ascendance; to the extent that they succeed, they do so by appropriating "feminine" virtues for their program. In a final ironic triumph Benjamin even pleads to leave the army (though not to return to his wife!) because he and Senderl are "praise God, married men."[19] Thus, the initial terms of their disempowerment are translated into a new kind of freedom.

I do not mean merely to reverse what I consider the elisions of contemporary scholarship on Jewish masculinity by asserting that Benjamin and Senderl are more misogynistic, more reliant on patriarchal codes, to the extent that they experience themselves as deficient men. It may well be that a sense of inadequacy is an integral part of the construction of the self as a gendered subject, or indeed as a subject at all. Nevertheless, my approach is meant to suggest that the disempowerment of Jewish men (voluntary or coerced, in relation to non-Jews or in relation to Jewish women, ideal or degraded) may as easily be an aspect of the patriarchal economy as it is its antithesis or its negation.

To draw the larger consequences of this analysis: the "feminization of Jewish men" is a perception and self-perception whose ubiquity cannot be denied. This perception, as I've tried to indicate, is thoroughly dependant on a patriarchal system whose hierarchies and misogyny it encodes or even reinforces. The Jewish man-woman, that is, is not *necessarily* a culture subversive, a sexual outlaw, or a woman's dream come true; to put it differently, the feminized Jewish man may as easily feed patriarchal power as qualify or negate it. And, that the recent studies of Jewish masculinity should so thoroughly have obscured the structural imbalances of Jewish patriarchies is only the latest expression of this dynamic.

Notes

1. Sander Gilman, *Jewish Self Hatred: Anti-Semitism and the Hidden Language of the Jews* (Baltimore: Johns Hopkins University Press, 1986), 200. Gilman's discussion of the feminization of European men begins with *Jewish Self-Hatred* and is further developed in *The Jew's Body* (New York: Routledge, 1991), and *Freud, Race, and Gender* (Princeton: Princeton University Press, 1993). See also Jay Geller, "(G)nos(e)ology: The Cultural Construction of the Other," in *People of the Body: Jews and Judaism from an Embodied Perspective* (Albany: SUNY Press, 1992), 243–282. My own thinking on this subject began with a review article I wrote entitled "Carnal Knowledge: The Body in Jewish Studies" for the first issue of the new series of *Jewish Social Studies*, edited by Aron Rodrigue and Steven Zipperstein. In that article, I voiced a vague disquiet with what I perceived as the occlusion of feminism and Jewish women in works that focused on Jewish masculinity. Here I attempt to outline one approach to negotiating a feminist reading of male disempowerment.

2. Michael Berkowitz, *Zionist Culture and West European Jewry Before the First World War* (Cambridge: Cambridge University Press, 1993), 19.

3. See Daniel Boyarin, *Carnal Israel: Reading Sex in Talmudic Culture* (Berkeley: University of California Press), 215, in which Jewish ideals of masculine beauty are compared with those of Hellenistic culture, and also, especially, the upcoming *Unheroic Conduct: The Rise of Het-*

erosexuality and the Invention of the Jewish Man (excerpted in this volume), in which the issue of Jewish masculinity takes center stage. This essay, however, was written before I read Boyarin's latest work.

4. For an analysis of the feminization of the male Yiddish reader, see Chava Weissler, "For Women and Men Who Are Like Women: The Construction of Gender in Yiddish Devotional Literature," *Journal of Feminist Studies in Religion* 5.2 (1989): 9.

5. Barbara Breitman, "Lifting up the Shadow of Anti-Semitism: Jewish Masculinity in a New Light," in *A Mensch Among Men: Explorations in Jewish Masculinity*, ed. Harry Brod (Freedom, CA: Crossing Press, 1988), 112.

6. Jacob Neusner, *Androgynous Judaism: Masculine and Feminine in the Dual Torah* (Macon, GA: Mercer University Press, 1993), 187.

7. All references are to the Yiddish version of Shalom Yakov Abramovitsh, *Kitzer Masoes Binyomin Hashlishi* (The abridged travels of Benjamin the third) (New York: Hebrew Publishing Company, 1920 [1878]) (cited hereafter as *Masoes*). The novel has been translated into English by Moshe Spiegel as *The Travels of Benjamin the Third* (New York: Schocken Books, 1968) and also appears in a collection entitled *The Shtetl: A Creative Anthology of Jewish Life in Eastern Europe*, trans. and ed. Joachim Neugroschel (New York: Richard Marek Publishers, 1979), 179–264. All translations here are my own.

8. The narrator/editor/publisher Mendele, in the introduction to *Travels,* takes his own measure as a Yiddish publisher/editor against what he describes, in explicitly sexual terms, as the greater masculinity of the Hebrew writers: "So I said to myself: until my brothers the Hebrew writers, whose little fingers are thicker than my loins, wake from their deep sleep to transcribe the story of the travels of Benjamin from the beginning to the end for the good of all Israel, I will try to print a short version of them as a temporary measure. So I girded my loins like a man and got to work." Not only does Mendele describe himself as sexually deficient in relation to another category of Jewish males, we should note, he also draws his comparison from a Jewish repertoire of images of strong biblical men. As Mendele's reversal of Rehavam's aggressive boast ("My little finger is thicker than my father's loins," 1 Kings 12:10) implies, the poles of masculine self-image, from the grandiose to the pathetic, are intertwined at the very center of Jewish patriarchy, in the great royal narratives of the House of David. Male aggressivity, then, may derive as powerfully from sexual anxiety as from sexual certitude.

9. David Aberbach calls *Travels* "a classic satire on the idea of *aliya*," adding that Abramovitsh was "at root an assimilationist who believed . . . that the future of the Jews lay in Russia." See his *Realism, Caricature. and Bias: The Fiction of Mendele Mocher Sefarim* (London: Littman Library of Jewish Civilization 1993), 2.

10. *Masoes,* 84.

11. Ibid. Spiegel's translation of the novella misses the transgendered point here: "They handled their weapons with all the dexterity of butter-fingered cook's helpers working with breadshovels." *Travels of Benjamin the Third,* 116.

12. For an excellent extended analysis of Benjamin and Senderl's mimicking of heterosexual literary conventions, see Dan Miron and Anita Norich, "The Politics of Benjamin the

Third," in *The Field of Yiddish: Studies in Language, Folklore, and Literature* (Fourth Collection), ed. Marvin I. Herzog, Barbara Kirshenblatt-Gimblett, Dan Miron, and Ruth Wisse (Philadelphia: Institute for the Study of Human Issues, 1980), 55–70.

13. The fairly explicit homosexuality of Benjamin and Senderl's quasi-marriage lends itself to a number of readings. See Miron and Norich, "Politics," 58ff., and Aberbach, *Realism*, 98–101. Aberbach views Benjamin and Senderl's relationship as evidence of Abramovitsh's confusion over gender roles, and traces this to the author's difficult adolescence. My own approach is sociological rather than psychological, viewing the male marriage, at least for the purposes of this paper, as satire on the supposed absence of heterosexual romance among traditional Ashkenazic Jews (and the presence, I would add, of strong homosocial bonds). The ubiquity of apparently homosexual themes and characters in nineteenth-century Yiddish literature (and expressions of romantic love among the authors of this literature) has been noted but not, to my mind, adequately theorized. Clearly, the discourse of repression and latency is somewhat misplaced in analyzing a literature that seems so unself-conscious about its presentations of male romance, "serious" or parodical. Nor do theories of sexual identity ("the homosexual") or sexual minority (the "10% hypothesis") account for a phenomenon simultaneously so widespread and intertwined with heterosexuality. For an exploration of the interconnections between hetero- and homoeroticism in a Yiddish modernist work, see Naomi Seidman, "Between Two Worlds: Tradition, Modernity, and Same-Sex Love in Ansky's *Dybbuk*" (unpublished paper). I am also at work on a book-length manuscript titled *From Senderl the Yidene to Yentl the Yeshiva Boy: A Queer History of Yiddish Literature.*

14. *Masoes*, 32.

15. Ibid., 20.

16. The Yiddish *kodesh* has been translated as both "holy man" and "martyr." Arguments could be made for either translation here.

17. For an analysis of the abandoned woman in Jewish literature, see papers presented by Bluma Goldstein at the Association for Jewish Studies in 1993, 1994, and 1995.

18. Bluma Goldstein, "The Spoils of Adventure: Deserted Women/*Agunes* in Abramovitsh's *The Travels of Benjamin the Third* and Rabinovitsh's *The Adventures of Menachem-Mendel*" (paper presented at the Association of Jewish Studies, Boston, December 1994), p. 5. This paper is part of a larger project of reading the narratives of abandoned wives in Jewish literature and culture; other papers in what will be a book-length study of the *agune* include "Doubly Exiled in Gerrnany: Deserted Wives/*Agunes* in Glikl Hameln's *Memoirs* and Solomon Maimon's *Autobiography*" (Association of Jewish Studies, 1992) and "*Agunes* Disappearing in a Gallery of Men: Recovering Women's Voices" (Association of Jewish Studies, 1993). My own thinking on the subject is greatly indebted to Goldstein's fascinating and important work.

19. *Masoes*, 97.

Interarticulations: Gender, Race, and the Jewish Woman Question

Ann Pellegrini

Attention to the ways in which axes of difference may mutually inform, cross, and contradict one another is among the energizing concerns of much recent feminist, queer, and postcolonial theories.[1] But what does it mean, in critical practice and not simply as a theoretical piety, to attend to and historicize the interarticulations (a concept I will return to presently) of sexual and racial difference? Among other things, it means *not* taking gender, race, and sexuality for granted as categories for analysis or even as categories of experience. Instead we attempt to see *whether* they mean, what and how they mean if they do, and what and how they mutually construct—interarticulate—in a specific place and at a specific time.[2] For example, I do not assume that race expresses the same set of relations from one cultural or national context to another, even within the same historical period. Nor do I assume that its meanings or effects within any one cultural or national context have been at all times the same. But I also do not take for granted that "race" means at all; this seems to me one of the things I am aiming to find out, not to assume in advance.

I borrow the term *interarticulation* from Judith Butler, who describes identity categories, such as gender and race, as "vectors of power" that "require and deploy one another for the purpose of their own articulation."[3] This formulation insists that gender, race, sexuality (to name the three axes that will interest me here) are not mutually exclusive but interimplicating and interstructured. To ask into these interarticulations is to look not to nature but to the discursive embeddedness of categories of identity and bodily experience in history and culture.

I am, to put it mildly, surprised and pleased that my own attempts to think gender, race, sexuality together should have brought me to a central concern with "the Jewish question" in Freud's Vienna and should have landed me in this forum, *Ju-*

daism Since Gender. Neither of these "destinations" seemed foreordained, even if, in hindsight, nothing could appear more obvious.[4] What began for me as a project to trace the discursive production of "the" lesbian body in the post-Enlightenment West gave way to considering the ways that body was raced, sexed, and (though this remains undertheorized in my work to date) classed; which gave way to thinking about one of the central narratives in the production of the lesbian body, psychoanalysis; which gave way to thinking about how the sexualized racial difference "Jew" haunts psychoanalytic theory, psychoanalytic theory's privileged difference (woman's from man), and its privileged pole (a phallic masculinity).

This brief account of what brings me to this forum calls into place another set of interarticulations. If the title of this anthology interarticulates feminist critical study with and against Jewish Studies, perhaps my inter-, anti-, or postdisciplinary situation in it is suggestive of some other crossings: the "intersecting analyses" of queer theory, critical race theory, Jewish cultural studies, feminist theory.[5] In this spirit, I want to ask, even if I do not have the time or space here to answer, the following questions: What does queer theory have to say to a Jewish Cultural Studies and vice versa? What does historical inquiry into nineteenth- and early twentieth-century constructions of Jewishness have to say to the history of sexuality and vice versa? Have some recent critical investigations of Jewishness as and at the gender, race, sexuality crossroads unwittingly reproduced the masculinist biases of the discourses they would scrutinize and unmask?

My own feminist critical research on the social construction of Jewishness in Freud's day is much indebted to the work of Daniel Boyarin, Jay Geller, and Sander L. Gilman. Like them, I have been particularly interested to trace the persistence and impact of a certain homology: Jew-as-woman. Perhaps the most infamous articulation of this virtual equation is Otto Weininger's 1903 best-seller *Geschlecht und Charakter* (English edition: *Sex and Character*).[6] From the time of its first publication, the book went through twenty-five printings in almost as many years. In the penultimate chapter of *Sex and Character*, "Judaism," Weininger joins the "woman question" to the "Jewish question." To repeat just one of his assertions: "The congruity between Jews and women further reveals itself in the extreme adaptability of the Jews, in their great talent for journalism, the 'mobility' of their minds, their lack of deep-rooted and original ideas, in fact the mode in which, like women, because they are nothing, they can become everything" (320). Relentlessly pursuing his "homology of Jew and woman" (309), Weininger represents the "eternal Jew" through the "eternal feminine" and thereby articulates the "racial" difference of "the" Jews through the "sexual" difference "man/woman." In this interarticulation, Jewishness becomes as much a category of gender as of race.

Weininger's curious fusion of anti-Semitism with misogyny did not come from nowhere. There is a rich and still-growing literature on Weininger, which attempts to read his reading of Jewishness in relation to the cultural predicament he shared with other male Jews.[7] Born into a middle-class Viennese Jewish household, Weininger converted to Protestantism on the same day he became a doctor of philosophy. *Sex and Character* is the revised version of his doctoral dissertation. Six months after the book's German publication, Weininger committed suicide.

The commercial success of *Sex and Character* was doubtless helped along by the notoriety surrounding its author's suicide. But this does not sufficiently explain the book's popularity among an "expert" and "lay" audience. Rather, it is necessary to look to the book's "productive" effects, to the ways it drew together and recirculated anti-Semitic and misogynist stereotypes. In the Vienna of Weininger and Freud, a stereotyped femininity underwrote representations of Jewish identity. Weininger took up, reworked, and reinforced popular and "scientific" images of Jewish men as perverse, effeminate, queer. In reinscribing Jew-as-woman, Weininger was also reflecting deeply held anxieties—and not his alone—about the increasing visibility of women and Jews in fin de siècle Austrian and, more broadly, central European public life. Rereading Weininger in context, in relation to the subject-positions open to him "as" a Jew and in relation also to the socially and historically available ways of thinking and representing Jewishness, is not to read away either his woman-hating or his Jew-hating. It is, however, to historicize their terms.[8] Historicizing Weininger's homology "Jew-as-woman" brings insight and examples for thinking gender, race, and sexuality together, for exploring the interarticulations of power and knowledge.

As helpful and thought provoking as I find much of the recent research on the construction of fin de siècle Jewish identity, however, I have also been troubled by the way some of this research tends to reproduce Weininger's blind spot.[9] For Weininger, "Jew" clearly means *male* Jew. He explicitly mentions the "Jewess" in only one passage in *Sex and Character*, and there, as Nancy A. Harrowitz and Barbara Hyams note, it is to indicate how the deficiencies of Jewish masculinity set the Jewish woman's possibilities of achieving full subjectivity even lower than that of her Aryan counterpart.[10] As I have asked elsewhere, what room does Weininger's intensely antisemitic and misogynist identification of male Jews with "woman" leave for Jewish women? If all Jews are womanly, are any women also Jews? The collapse of Jewish masculinity into an abject femininity appears to "disappear" Jewish women. Nor does this disappearance mark only Weininger's or, in another way, Freud's writings. It also seems to me to characterize some recent writings *about* Weininger and Freud.

The displacement of Jewish women from the scene of Jewishness seems to me an unfortunate and frequent side effect of some pathbreaking studies of race, gender, and Jewishness.[11] It is not, I want to make clear, the focus on Jewish masculinity that I find troubling. After all, *not* historicizing, denaturalizing, and deconstructing masculinity leaves it standing as femininity's ungrounded ground. Accordingly, investigating the social construction of Jewish masculinity is or can be a profoundly and queerly feminist project.[12]

Furthermore, I do not presume that any two researchers will approach the same materials with identical questions or commitments. We all pick and choose how much to expand and how much to narrow our research projects, selecting for what makes our research more manageable—doable—as well as for what will make our final product hold together for (other) readers. What does seem to me problematic, however, is a failure to attend to how the questions and modes of analysis we privilege (and I do not exempt myself from this failure) may unwittingly reproduce what and where we would critique. In other words, how can we narrow our range of research "objects" without contracting our angles of vision?

I want to know what impact the virtual nonappearance of the "Jewess" in *Sex and Character* may have had on Jewish women among that book's multiple reading publics. I also want to know whether and how stereotypes of the *belle juive* might complicate and enrich research into the interarticulations of gender, race, and sexuality.[13] I want to know how representations of Jewish men as womanly affected and effected stereotypes of Jewish women.[14] Finally, and this goes to the heart of my concern, I want to attend to the troubling ways our acts of interpretation may reinscribe relations of power-knowledge. If, as has been argued, Weininger's nonattention to Jewish women reproduces the centrality of men and male subjectivities in both Jewish and Christian cultures,[15] what does the virtual nonappearance of Jewish women in most contemporary criticism on Weininger reproduce? To what extent do these latter-day silences participate in and repeat these earlier silencings?[16]

I have asked more questions than I have offered answers. But I have done so in the spirit of this double challenge: first, to subject to historical scrutiny the interarticulation of Jewishness at the crossroads of gender, race, sexuality; second, to reflect critically on the intersecting aims and ambitions of the multiple and interdisciplinary sites from and through which we can begin to ask and perhaps to answer these questions.

Notes

Another version of this essay was presented as part of a panel discussion, "Disciplining Jewishness: Identity/Identification/Difference," at the 1995 annual meeting of the American Academy of Religion in Philadelphia. I want to thank the other participants in this panel for their continuing provocations: Daniel Boyarin, Sara R. Horowitz, Natalie Boymel Kampen, Laura Levitt, Miriam Peskowitz, Naomi Scheman, Susan Shapiro, and Liz Wiesen. I am also grateful to these other interlocutors, whose critical questions and comments were helpful in thinking through earlier drafts of this essay; they may not recognize this final version nor their part in it, but I recognize and appreciate the traces of their conversations here: Linda S. Garber, Rachel Fell McDermott, Carol Ockman, and Timea Szell.

1. This concern has an earlier (and ongoing) history in the criticisms leveled by feminists of color and working-class women and lesbians (who may, of course, also be "of color") against

the exclusions of a feminism and feminist theory whose exemplary objects and subjects of study were white, middle-class, heterosexual, and Christian. For important examples of such criticism, see *All the Women Are White, All the Blacks Are Men, But Some of Us Are Brave: Black Women's Studies,* ed. Gloria Hull, Patricia Bell Scott, and Barbara Smith (New York: Feminist Press, 1982); Elly Bulkin, Minnie Bruce Pratt, and Barbara Smith, *Yours In Struggle: Three Feminist Perspectives on Anti-Semitism and Racism* (Ithaca, NY: Firebrand Books, 1984); Elizabeth V. Spelman, *Inessential Woman: Problems of Exclusion in Feminist Thought* (Boston: Beacon Press, 1988); and *Making Face, Making Soul/Haciendo Caras: Creative and Critical Perspectives by Feminists of Color,* ed. Gloria Anzaldúa (San Francisco: Aunt Lute Books, 1990). For a recent collection of essays whose attempts to examine the intersections of gender, race, nationality, and sexuality critically cross the terrains of postcolonial theory, feminist theory, and lesbian and gay studies, see *Diacritics* 24.2–3 (Summer–Fall 1994), special issue: *Critical Crossings,* ed. Judith Butler and Biddy Martin.

2. Although I do not set quotation marks round the terms *gender, race, sexuality,* throughout this essay, I am referring not to ahistorical, transcultural essences of gender, race, and sexuality but to their social construction and real material effects.

3. Judith Butler, *Bodies That Matter: On the Discursive Limits of "Sex"* (New York: Routledge, 1993), 18.

4. I am here reminded of an interesting moment in Freud's 1920 "Psychogenesis of a Case of Homosexuality in a Woman," when he shifts from discussing the onset of his never-named patient's homosexuality—was it a late acquisition or a case of congenital homosexuality, he is wondering—to noting how the psychoanalytic method, with its movement from the present toward an ever-receding past, seems across the board to confront the analyst with this interpretive difficulty: "So long as we trace the development from its final outcome backwards, the chain of events appears continuous, and we feel we have gained an insight which is completely satisfactory or even exhaustive. But if we proceed the reverse way, if we start from the premises inferred from the analysis and try to follow these up to the final result, then we no longer get the impression of an inevitable sequence of events which could not have been otherwise determined. We notice at once that there might have been another result, and that we might have been just as well able to understand and explain the latter." See *The Standard Edition of the Complete Psychological Works of Sigmund Freud,* vol. 18, ed. James Strachey (London: Hogarth Press and the Institute of Psycho-Analysis, 1955), 167.

5. For the phrase "intersecting analyses," and an exposition of it, see Butler's and Martin's introduction to *Critical Crossings,* 3.

6. All quotations from this work are from the English edition: Otto Weininger, *Sex and Character,* authorized anonymous translation from the sixth German edition (London: William Heinemann, 1906).

7. See, for example, the essays collected in *Jews and Gender: Responses to Otto Weininger,* ed. Nancy A. Harrowitz and Barbara Hyams (Philadelphia: Temple University Press, 1995). For the cultural backdrop of Jewish masculinity, see especially Daniel Boyarin, "Freud's Baby, Fliess's Maybe: Homophobia, Anti-Semitism, and the Invention of Oedipus," *GLQ: A Journal of Lesbian and Gay Studies,* special issue, *Pink Freud,* ed. Diana Fuss, 2:1–2 (1995):

115–47; Jay Geller, "(G)nos(e)ology: The Cultural Construction of the Other," in *People of the Body: Jews and Judaism from an Embodied Perspective*, ed. Howard Eilberg-Schwartz (Albany: SUNY Press, 1992), 243–82; Sander L. Gilman, *The Jew's Body* (New York: Routledge, 1991); and Sander L. Gilman, *Freud, Race, and Gender* (Princeton: Princeton University Press, 1993). This bibliography is by no means exhaustive but marks important places to begin.

8. For this methodological and ethical difference, see Harrowitz and Hyams, *Jews and Gender*, 6.

9. This paragraph is largely paraphrased from my "Whiteface Performances: 'Race,' Gender, and Jewish Bodies," in *Jews and Other Differences: A New Jewish Cultural Studies*, ed. Daniel Boyarin and Jonathan Boyarin (Minneapolis: University of Minnesota Press, 1996). An expanded version of this essay appears in my *Performance Anxieties: Staging Psychoanalysis, Staging Race* (New York: Routledge, 1996).

10. See Harrowitz and Hyams, *Jews and Gender*, 4–5.

11. For a critique of Gilman's work, which also acknowledges his important contributions to thinking *male* jewishness through race and gender, see Pellegrini, *Performance Anxieties.*

12. That this is so is made eminently clear in Daniel Boyarin's contributions to this anthology and in his forthcoming project *Unheroic Conduct: The Rise of Heterosexuality and the Invention of the Jewish Man* (Berkeley: University of California Press, in press).

13. Gilman has offered a reading of the *belle juive.* See Sander L. Gilman, "Salome, Syphilis, Sarah Bernhardt, and the 'Modern Jewess,' " *German Quarterly* 66 (Spring 1993): 195–211. But compare the suggestions in John Hoberman, "Otto Weininger and the Critique of Jewish Masculinity," in Harrowitz and Hyams, *Jews and Gender*, 141–53, esp. 141–42; Carol Ockman, " 'Two Large Eyebrows à l'orientale': Ethnic Stereotyping in Ingres's *Baronne de Rothschild*," Art History 14.4 (December 1991): 521–39; Carol Ockman, "When Is a Jewish Star Just a Star? Interpreting Images of Sarah Bernhardt," in *The Jew in the Text: Modernity and the Politics of Identity*, ed. Linda Nochlin and Tamar Garb (London and New York: Thames & Hudson, 1995); and Pellegrini, "Whiteface Performances."

14. For one way into this question, see Jay Geller's contribution to this collection, "Circumcision and Jewish Women's Identity: Rahel Levin Varnhagen's Failed Assimilation."

15. This is an argument Harrowitz and Hyams make in their introduction to *Jews and Gender*. Nonetheless, I am disturbed by the way this argument justifies this otherwise admirable collection's inattention to Weininger's impact on Jewish women as distinct from non-Jewish women or Jewish men.

16. Judith Butler's observation that oppression works not simply through acts of overt prohibition but also, covertly, through refusals to recognize whole classes of persons as viable subjects is relevant here. See Butler, "Imitation and Gender Insubordination," in *The Lesbian and Gay Studies Reader*, ed. Henry Abelove, Michèle Aina Barale, and David M. Halperin (New York: Routledge, 1993), 312. See also Adrienne Rich's important early discussion of the enforcements of silence, which bears repeating: "Whatever is unnamed, undepicted in images, whatever is omitted from biography, censored in collections of letters,

whatever is misnamed as something else, made difficult-to-come-by, whatever is buried in the memory by the collapse of meaning under an inadequate or dying language—this will become not merely unspoken, but *unspeakable.*" Adrienne Rich, "It Is the Lesbian in Us . . ." (1976), in *Lies, Secrets and Silence: Selected Prose, 1966–1978* (New York: Norton, 1979), 199; emphasis in original.

Words and Radiators

Irena Klepfisz

I have always loved examining ideas. More precisely, I have always loved talking about ideas, about politics. Perhaps it is my rabbinic blood, for disputation and argumentation remain one of my greatest pleasures (my father came from a long line of Hassidic rabbis). Nothing is quite as satisfying as sitting with friends around a kitchen table or in a coffee shop and dissecting the exact implications of a political position or theory. The push-and-pull in these discussions, the interruptions, the sidetracking, the diversion of an irrelevant joke, the sudden exposure of an assumption or bias and identification of contradictions, the demand to return to the original subject—this free-associative, open-ended, unpredictable, and always unstructured process makes ideas alive and exciting. It grounds ideas in a common and familiar routine, shapes them according to the rhythms of our lives, smudges them with coffee stains, covers them with the dust of unclipped newspapers, endows them with the urgency emanating from a recent and off-the-wall article ("who would have believed a feminist could write anything that outrageous?"). It is in this everyday world where my voice mixes with those of friends and with the noise of clanging radiators and passing trucks that I like to test ideas and their worth. It is in this everyday world that I am certain ideas and theories matter, because with each dirty dish that I wash as I talk and listen, I experience how they affect my life.

When the Women Came to Shul

Karla Goldman

Much of my study of the place of women in the development of American Judaism focuses on the emergence of women's presence in the eighteenth- and nineteenth-century American synagogue.[1] I believe that this approach affords important insights into the experience of American Jewish women, but it also inevitably places the study of women within the context of a male-defined institution. Since my goal is to afford new perspectives on women's experience of nineteenth-century American Judaism as well as on American Judaism more broadly, I am apparently left with the problematic task of "adding" women to a story of which they have really always been a part.

Traditionally, the synagogue has been defined almost exclusively by male dominance and female marginality. Attention to women in the American synagogue, however, reveals that for acculturated nineteenth-century American Jews, the synagogue actually became an important and dynamic site for the expression of female religiosity. In the process, the centrality of women's absence from traditional definitions of the synagogue became both explicit and suddenly unacceptable. Non-Jewish visitors to eighteenth- and nineteenth-century North American synagogues often noted women's marginal presence at Jewish worship. In American social settings, religiosity and piety were seen as requisite female characteristics, and piety was customarily expressed in the public venue of the church. In this context, the gendered inflexibility of the synagogue was starkly exposed. For example, one non-Jewish visitor to New York's synagogue reported in 1744 that the women "of whom some were very pritty [sic], stood up in the gallery like a hen coop."[2]

Dissonance between the space given to women in the synagogue and the emerging Western thought about the appropriate religious status of women was not limited to America. Jewish leaders in western and central Europe also displayed an awareness that many of the gendered practices of traditional Judaism, including the ones that were exposed to public view in the synagogue, were not well suited to the expectations of a modern age. A committee of the 1846 German Rabbinical Conference, for example, observed that "the house of God was as good as closed" to a Jewish woman and demanded redress for this inequity. An 1846 questionnaire addressed to potential chief rabbis in France inquired what each candidate would do to assure women a more dignified and pleasant position in Jewish worship.[3]

What is striking about the American Jewish response to this sort of concern is the degree to which the physical structures of Judaism were changed in an effort to display greater respect toward women in the public sphere of religion. One little-noted, but widespread, modification of the design of the early American synagogue demonstrates this adjustment. The interior of the 1763 Newport, Rhode Island, synagogue, the second synagogue to be built in the thirteen colonies, was modeled after the design of the Spanish and Portuguese congregations of Amsterdam and London. The Newport building, however, distinguished itself from its forebears by omitting the grilled or lattice-work barrier that surmounted the balconies of their women's galleries.

The Newport example of a low balustrade without an additional obstructing partition became the model for the American synagogue; other than this modification, these buildings were constructed according to traditional models and designed for orthodox worship. An etching of Charleston's 1784 synagogue depicts open balconies.[4] Likewise, the 1817 building of New York's Shearith Israel was built with gallery fronts of "open work."[5] In contrast, open-galleried synagogues did not appear in Europe until 1818, when the Hamburg Temple was dedicated. In this case, the removal of the balcony's partition screen represented an ideological statement by a congregation attempting to distance itself from traditional orthodoxy. The Hamburg Temple's open gallery was only one of a series of radical departures from traditional Jewish practice effected by this community.[6] In contrast to the majority of the American counterparts, in the early nineteenth century, no orthodox European synagogue introduced open galleries for the use of female worshippers.

The other striking example of physical reconfiguration in the American synagogue with no parallel in European synagogues was the abolition of the women's gallery and the introduction of mixed male-and-female seating. The family-pew plan was first introduced in American synagogues in 1851. A number of strictly orthodox synagogues that had dispensed with the partition screens in front of the traditional women's galleries refused to do away with the women's gallery altogether. By 1869, however, family pews had become almost *de rigueur* in the new synagogues of acculturated American Jews.[7]

The rapid emergence of the open women's gallery and later, of family pews, was only the external marker of the changing status of women in American synagogues and in American Judaism. More striking than the actual physical changes was the fact that by the middle of the nineteenth century, and certainly by the end of the century, women had come to dominate attendance at the weekly Sabbath services of acculturated American congregations. Considered against the male-centered history of the synagogue, the incongruity of this reality raises significant questions about what it means to study the presence of women in traditional male institutions at a moment when, for whatever reasons, the familiar gender construction of Judaism was called into question.

Tracing the substantive arrival of women in the American synagogue exposes the conflicted process involved in creating and justifying new parameters for female religious identity. Much of the story here focuses on how a traditionally male-centered institution was stretched and reformulated in order to accommodate the presence of women. The study of women and the synagogue does examine how women were fitted into or added to a male sphere, but it is important to understand that ending the era of the almost exclusively male synagogue inevitably involved much more than just the addition of women. Synagogues filled with women were spaces profoundly different from synagogues filled with men. And the Jews associated with these spaces had inevitably become different kinds of Jews. If, for example, Jewish congregants had continued to assume the responsibilities usually incumbent upon worshippers in traditional Jewish prayer, women congregants with little formal Jewish education would never have been able to attain a status comparable to that of male worshippers. Men certainly retained control of both lay and religious leadership. Yet, as a site of gender-role redefinition for both men and women, the nineteenth-century American synagogue was itself redefined.

In the American context, a powerful middle-class gender ideology held that female religiosity was to be expressed in the church. This expectation obscured the centrality of the domestic religious responsibilities assigned to women in traditional Jewish life. At the same time, the evident marginality of women's presence in the synagogue came to seem increasingly at odds with prevailing bourgeois ideals of female religiosity. The gender divisions upon which the whole edifice had been balanced came to seem disturbingly out of kilter. Looking for stability on unfamiliar terrain, American Jews had to bring their structure into harmony with surrounding Christian institutions. For the Jewish synagogue, removal to the new and unfamiliar setting had exposed the "construction site" (to use Peskowitz's metaphor) underlying Jewish culture, with its confusing grid of gendered responsibilities and duties.

Jewish renovators worked earnestly to mask the suddenly exposed cracks in the foundations and walls of their culture. They strove to discern and emulate the ways in which gender had been constructed by those already occupying the avenue upon which they hoped to establish a home. Debates about women's place in the synagogue, shifts in the male : female attendance ratio at public worship, a reconfiguration of the place of the synagogue in Jewish life, knocking out the women's gallery, both figuratively and literally—all of these represented efforts to frame a workable blueprint for Jewish life in the United States.

As the essays in this collection indicate, many who observe Jewish experience at the end of the twentieth century are struggling to come to terms with a growing awareness of the fundamental role that gender hierarchies and assumptions have played in the structure of Jewish history and life. An examination of the evolution of female religious identity in relationship to the early American synagogue introduces us to earlier generations of American Jews who also had to confront the suddenly apparent awkwardness of gender arrangements that had long been taken for granted.

Whether at the end of the twentieth century or the beginning of the nineteenth, when women have come to recognize the inappropriateness of their absence or exclusion, they have responded by asserting their presence. The women who filled the pews of nineteenth-century synagogues were not overtly challenging Jewish tradition, but their presence carried its own radical implications. Each time an American synagogue moved in some new way to accommodate the presence of women, it moved toward a redefinition of itself and of the American Jewish religious culture of which it formed a part.

At times it may seem that the events of the past thirty years alone have finally pushed an indelibly patriarchal religion to respond to the evolving needs of acculturated Jewish women. Observers confidently predict that the full impact of female aspirations upon the remolding of the synagogue and American Judaism lies ahead of us.[8] However, a nuanced examination of the history of the early American synagogue suggests that gender has been a salient factor in shaping American Judaism from its earliest establishment in this country. When women came to shul, they began a transformation of Judaism that continues to this day.

Notes

1. Karla Goldman, "Beyond the Gallery: The Place of Women in the Development of American Judaism" (Ph.D. diss., Harvard University, 1993).

2. David Pool and Tamar H. de Sola, *An Old Faith in the New World: Portrait of Shearith Israel, 1654–1954* (New York: Columbia University Press, 1955), 453.

3. Protokolle der dritten Versammlung deutscher Rabbiner Verlag von F.E.C. Leuckart (Breslau, 1847), 264. For translation, see W. Gunther Plaut, *The Rise of Reform Judaism: A Sourcebook of its European Origins* (New York: Leuckart, 1963), 254; and Phyllis Cohen Albert, *The Modernization of French Jewry: Consistory and Community in the Nineteenth Century* (Hanover, NH: Brandeis University Press, 1977), 385–386.

4. For early American synagogue architecture, see Rachel Wischnitzer, *Synagogue Architecture in the United States: History and Interpretation* (Philadelphia: Jewish Publication Society, 1955), 11–22.

5. Shearith Israel, New York, *Board of Trustee Minutes*, vol. 3 (October 13, 1817), 373. Microfilm Collection #1, American Jewish Archives, Cincinnati.

6. Michael A. Meyer, *Response to Modernity: A History of the Reform Movement in Judaism* (New York: Oxford University Press, 1988), 54–55.

7. See Goldman, "Beyond the Gallery," 202–203. See also Jonathan Sarna, "The Debate over Mixed Seating in the American Synagogue," in *The American Synagogue: A Sanctuary Transformed*, ed. Jack Wertheimer (New York: Cambridge, 1991), 363–394.

8. See, for instance, Wertheimer, *American Synagogue*, 68, 106, 137.

Power / Knowledge / Gender: The Oranges-and-Grapefruit Debate

Tamar El-Or

It was the large basement of an apartment house in north Tel Aviv that was used as a meeting place for Emuna, the Zionist orthodox women's organization. When I entered the room, leaving behind a sunny February morning, it was already crowded with some sixty women who had come for their weekly lesson. Most of them were elderly. A few were wearing wigs, some had kerchiefs, but the majority did not cover their heads. We were about to discuss my book, *Educated and Ignorant: Ultraorthodox Jewish Women and Their World*, and I was nervous.

It had been easier, on other occasions, to present the book to a nonorthodox audience—people eager to hear the stories behind the long sleeves and under the wigs of ultraorthodox women. Some were disappointed when I related my refusal to look into very private, intimate matters, but they found comfort in other aspects sufficiently "exotic" to the unfamiliar ears of nonorthodox Jewish Israelis. During the discussions that followed these presentations, I usually found that their ears and hearts were never entirely alien to the subject. Many people in the audience had come from an orthodox background and were seeking to warm themselves near the rhythm and aroma of their "old world," contemplating again its relevance to their current lives. There were parents of *ba'alei teshuva,* who were brought to the subject by their children's choice, bouncing between anger, sorrow, and guilt, and seeking to understand. Others met ultraorthodox men and women every day as doctors, social workers, civil servants, or business people, and wanted to learn more about them. Most participants had good knowledge of Jewish history and Bible from their public school education. Nevertheless, talking to a nonorthodox audience meant conversing with people who conduct their lives outside the laws of halakha that govern orthodox life.

That morning in the dim basement I was to present my work to orthodox women in a very different subject position. I was curious to hear their reactions, especially to the "oranges-and-grapefruit debate." Although not ultraorthodox themselves, they were sure to feel resonances with my subject that other audiences did not.

A chapter of my book discussed the "oranges-and-grapefruit debate." Among the women in the Gur Hasidic community I had studied, this debate arose among a women's study group, during a session on *Laws of the Sabbath*. At this meeting, Tsipi, a twenty-one-year-old teacher at Beit Yaakov (a school for ultraorthodox girls) who was in charge of the study group, spoke about tasks forbidden on the Sabbath. She decided to focus on "sorting," explaining the prohibition and offering some solutions to potential problems, as her teacher, a rabbi, had taught her at the seminary for teachers she had attended.[1]

Tsipi said: "The act of sorting is to separate food from refuse. If I want to take oranges out of a bowl and there are grapefruits there too, the oranges are the food and the grapefruit are the refuse. You are permitted to take the oranges out of the bowl if you meet three conditions: the object is food, the task is done by hand, and the task is performed immediately. That means you take out what you want to eat with your hand and not with an implement, and you eat it now and not later" (123).

Tsipi's short presentation of both the problem and its solution raised an outcry in the room. The women were very upset by the use of the word *refuse*. It sounded like waste, like garbage, and they were curious to know what happens if later one wants to eat the grapefruit that previously had been declared refuse. Tsipi replied: "If you want the grapefruit, then it's food and whatever else is in the bowl is the refuse" (124).

This operational definition calmed the room, but Rachel said: "I don't understand, how can it be food one time and refuse the next time. Why call it refuse?" (124).

From that moment on a dialogue developed between those who tried to explain the "real meaning" of the term *refuse*, and those who refused to understand it. Hanna offered a parallel with the terms *primary* and *secondary*. Malka, the *ba'alat teshuva*, tried to explain that calling something "refuse" does not turn it into real garbage, but only defines it "as if it is waste in one case and as if not in another." Most of the women, however, were not comfortable with the terms and attacked them with a variety of examples from their everyday lives. The lesson ended with neither understanding nor acceptance.

Malka couldn't grasp the women's difficulty; she appeared amused but impatient, and her solution sounded as if she was mocking the difficulty the others were having in catching the point. I saw it as characteristic of the education of ultraorthodox women, which encourages earthbound thinking and rejects analytical or abstract thought. Malka and I, although on different "sides" (she is orthodox and I am nonorthodox), had no problem with Tsipi's terminology because of our common former education (remember, Malka came to orthodoxy as an adult after going through the secular school system). The rest of the women, I thought at first, simply could not make the abstraction.

The "oranges-and-grapefruit" debate chapter of my book had elaborated the above ethnography. I had explained the women's lack of abstraction both as confusion, and to some extent, as hesitation about the halakhic solution. Upon reading the book or hearing me read from it, the reactions of several audiences to this specific section made me realize that the women's debate—in all these contexts—was an intersection loaded with thematic traffic. I turn now to present a "thicker description" of the "oranges-and-grapefruit" debate, one that contains the perspectives of the audiences, and my reactions to their reactions. I lean on their responses, and in doing so, return the "oranges-and-grapefruit" debate to its "owners" enriched with meanings that they may or may not accept.[2]

When the organizer of Emuna meetings took time out to make a few announcements, including the birth of a granddaughter to one of the members, I took the opportunity to look at the women's faces, wondering whether they would laugh when I read "the debate." Nonorthodox people always laugh, and when they do, my reactions are mixed: I feel that I am doing my subjects a disservice by giving the impression they are stupid or ignorant, and that I am entertaining my listeners, who are eager to criticize the women. The laughter, I have learned, stems from the debaters' preoccupation with the details, with their literal decoding of the law, and with the specificity of the examples they raise.

I evoked a different kind of laughter years ago when I sent this section of my ethnography to a colleague studying in the United States. He wrote in the margins of my pages: "That sounds like a new sketch of the Gashashim, a popular Israeli comedy trio." The women's words became a game, a play acted *ad absurdum.*

The reading group I had set up to critique my thesis—four ultraorthodox women from the Gur sect, but not from the community I studied—also smiled at this section. Miriam, a senior teacher at Beit Yaakov, said: "Well, this is funny. Sure, I can see why people laugh, it could sound stupid. I'm not saying it didn't happen or that you're describing it incorrectly, but I'm sure we're laughing for different reasons. You're wondering whether they couldn't get it, but I know they did. I smile because I hear something familiar, understood, like meeting an old girlfriend. I smile because I know what was actually going on in their minds and hearts. You see it from your academic standpoint, I see it from our lives."

In the Emuna audience that day, some smiled, some laughed. Dora summed up their reactions: "It would never happen with us. We learn the reason, we are allowed to ask, to contemplate, to study the section you just read. It's a prime example of the ultraorthodox Haredi world. I know because I was raised that way, but I did not raise my children like that. My daughter is a very orthodox woman, but she's also a mathematician, and she studies Torah with her husband. Still, it's nice to hear that there is such naiveté amongst these women nowadays."

The superior laughter of the nonorthodox audience, the "emic" insider's smile of the ultraorthodox, the psychological interpretation of my colleague, and the empathic critique of the religious-Zionist women returned me to my original reading of the debate. At first, I did not think it was funny and was quite surprised to hear laughter from audiences. To me the debate was a sign of the women's inability to make abstractions, evidence of a possible "women's way of thinking." Second thoughts taught me that the women were indeed exercising their way of thinking, but at the same time trying to taste something new.[3] My reaction to the reaction of the audiences, and my feeling of insult when they laughed at "my women," pushed me toward this "thicker" view of the debate.

In *Power/Knowledge*, Foucault claims that knowledge/power relations are never personal or subjective; upper-middle-class men's knowledge merely allows the illusion of personal beholding, an illusion constituted through class and gender.[4] The Gur women's dialogue with the halakhic way of thinking, when they study on their own without a rabbinic teacher, shows their confrontation with the basic constituents of this knowledge. They recoil from the "easy solution" to sorting on the Sabbath (calling something refuse) not because of barriers in their thinking but as a sign of their resistance to, and even rejection of, that way of thinking.

When women negotiate men's literacy, that is, when women operate within the frame of male-defined constructs, they have roughly three possibilities: they can accept and internalize male-defined practices; they can reread, deconstruct, and read again; or, they can resist and reject them altogether. Ultraorthodox women traditionally have accepted and internalized men's knowledge a priori as *The Knowledge*, but they have done so without the benefit of exacting readings and study. Today, given their increased exposure to the texts, in ways that are unmediated by rabbis, these women might exercise other options. Rereading, deconstructing, and reading Jewish texts again is widely practiced by Jewish feminists, but ultraorthodox women lack the social legitimacy and intellectual preparation to do this. Thus, in the example that I narrated in *Educated and Ignorant*, the women are alienated by Tsipi's explanation of oranges, grapefruits, and the *Laws of the Sabbath*. The discussion that ensued in that example presents the halakhic way of thinking as a manipulation, as a juggling of "truths." In rejecting Tsipi's explanation, the women reject its very nature and its foundations. In this way they call into question the validity and reliability of halakhic knowledge per se as they know it. Their urge to ground the abstraction, to bring it down to earth with everyday examples, does not stem from stupidity or ignorance. It is, rather, a protest: a collective expression of loyalty to "straight talk." Because they cannot engage in rereading, deconstructing, and reading again, they work, instead, with a subtle resistance.

For a short time that day in the Emuna basement, the Gur Hasidic women I studied entered the passing traffic to mingle with different knowledges, unusual terminologies and syntax, novel logics, and the like. The intersection was relatively free of policemen, and they were almost free to direct the traffic themselves. During that brief episode, one could trace an effort to rearrange relationships of knowledge/power/gender: to check hierarchies, to test validities, and to determine the relevance for them of the canonical Jewish way of thinking. This disorganized and perhaps unself-conscious resistance created a chaotic situation, and chaos—especially when it's not your own—can provoke nervousness, anxiety, and laughter.

Notes

1. Tamar El-Or, *Educated and Ignorant: Ultraorthodox Jewish Women and Their World* (Boulder: Lynne Rienner, 1994), 122–128.

2. On "thin" and "thick" description, see Clifford Geertz, *The Interpretation of Cultures* (New York: Basic Books, 1973).

3. El-Or, *Educated and Ignorant*, 127.

4. Michel Foucault, *Power/Knowledge* (Brighton, Sussex: Harvester Press, 1980). See also Foucault, *The History of Sexuality*, vol. 1 (New York: Viking Penguin, 1986).

The Gender of the Angel

Jonathan Boyarin

Mein Flügel ist zum Schwung bereit
ich kehrte gern zurück
denn blieb ich auch lebendige Zeit
ich hätte wenig Glück

(My wing is ready for flight,
I would like to turn back.
If I stayed timeless time,
I would have little luck.)[1]

Well, there I was, walking past the United Nations of all places on a quiet Sunday afternoon, going uptown to retrieve the baby from his great-grandmother, enjoying the melancholy irony of my current situation, and trying to adjust my expectations toward starting *law school* of all things at this late date rather than toward finally becoming a professor. And the epigraph to the most famous moment in Walter Benjamin's "Theses on the Philosophy of History" came into my mind and out of my mouth, unresisted if somewhat garbled in my memory. In that famous "Thesis IX," Benjamin describes a solitary and unitary Angel of History struggling to resist the destructive storm of progress that constantly expells humanity from the Paradise of memory. Over the past decade or so, Benjamin's work on the poetics and politics of memory has inspired my own struggles with Jewish memory and identity. Before the great disaster of midcentury, Benjamin had suggested ways to articulate the power of generational memory that avoided the dangers of romantic or fascist mythification yet clearly saw through the liberal construction of the autonomous individual determined by nothing before her own birth. But what captured my imagination at that moment was the analogy between the image of the Angel and my immediate personal situation. Like the Angel, I'm poised now to change course (from trying to become a professor to becoming a student once again), and I'd love to turn back (to a critical practice that is "pure" in the sense that it expects rewards based on intellectual valuation). And like the Angel, I'm not sure I'd be successful there no matter how long I was able to stay (I could keep producing critical scholarship on Judaism and never be able to care for my family securely). Indeed.

Then I realized I was figuring myself *as* the Angel, and I felt a little silly. The Angel in Benjamin's text is a "he." But more than that—it struck me suddenly—he assumes a characteristically masculine style of lonely, melancholy, and heroic resistance. The style of the male Angel may be particularly seductive to marginalized male Jewish intellectuals.[2] The truth is that although I was indeed walking by myself, I was not quite facing the storm—Angel-like—at that moment. I was, rather, once again, *between* my work and my child. Once I reached him and his Nanny, I realized, my angel wings would certainly turn into a pair of arms to lift him into his stroller and push him all the way down Second Avenue back home.

Benjamin's "Theses" have come to stand, and not only for me, as a kind of last will and testament for prewar German Jewish critical thought. For me, the key moment of this testament comes with his renunciation of *hope for the future*, a renunciation that contains neither cynicism nor (at least in his writing) overt despair. A glance at the daily newspaper will reconfirm that today, as in 1939 when Benjamin was writing, there's not much to be hopeful about. But what choice do we have except to think of the future? What's most important in relating Benjamin's insights and their limitations to our own situation is to realize that whereas Benjamin implicitly links these two terms *hope* and *the future*, we need to learn how to separate them. It is something we are hardly accustomed to do.

Benjamin's conflation of *hope* and *the future* appears manifested at two main points in the "Theses." The first is Benjamin's insistence that the Angel of History faces only backward, as if any forward view would betray a trace of unwarranted faith in progress. The second moment of this collapse is Benjamin's insistence that true revolutionary efforts are fueled by the memories of "enslaved ancestors," not images of "liberated grandchildren." Both points are, of course, stated polemically, and their intended shocking effect has certainly been effective since the catastrophe. And both points leave us now in specific binds that can be briefly stated.

The Angel's desire to resist the oblivion of progress, his insistent, overriding concern for a redemption to be found in the past, may indeed provide us with powerful epiphanic "constellations" with which to transform the present. For Benjamin, "the critical historian grasps the constellation which his own era has formed with a definite earlier one" (263). But we cannot live out our daily lives in the *expectation* of surprising such constellations. They actually appear as unpredictable flashes of association, and if we assume a dependence on them, we turn "redemption through memory" into a hollow rubric, a kind of substitutionary faith analogous to the rejected hope and progress. If we try to read the "Theses" for daily practice—of family, community, institution—instead of in search of a revolutionary moment, we face a new problem. How is it possible to turn the Angel around without killing it, or fooling ourselves once again? Can we learn not to rely on "progress" but still allow ourselves to face tomorrow? And how can we be responsible toward life without hope?

The second pertinent moment in Benjamin's "Theses" is the valuation of grandparents over grandchildren. The polemical context is Benjamin's attack on the ultimately vacuous Social Democratic faith that things will get better one way or another. The critique certainly remains salutary, I suggest, especially for those progressive theorists who fondly refer to the present as "late capitalism." Yet, even without detailing Benjamin's family troubles, his formulation leaves another yawning gap when we try to use it rather than merely cite it: *What about* our descendants, our children, and (God willing) our grandchildren? Again, in the particular crisis out of which Benjamin was writing, issues of survival and continuity seemed less important than the how-to question of producing the revolution. That is, revolution seemed the necessary precondition for understanding, the prerequisite to any possible survival or continuity.

Yet we who come after survive (and thrive, in certain ways) without revolution. We continue to face the necessity of recognizing the tenuousness of any continuity, and the fragility of the momentary. At the same time, we face a possible global extinction that would exceed the narrative boundaries of the dialectic of oppressors and oppressed by obviating the conditions for human life on this planet.

Again, it might be argued (as if in "defense" of Benjamin, who needs no defense) that Benjamin was talking about ideology and not practice, about *imagined* grandchildren versus *remembered* ancestors. And indeed the limitations of the "Theses" that I've just identified needn't really become a problem for someone working in the post-Benjaminian vein where I often find myself. There is still much to be harvested from the "Theses" in theory, for at least two reasons. First, the legacies of "hope" are still so powerful that they need vigilant criticism if we are, in fact, to survive. Second, Benjamin's work in itself provides rich and powerful resources for a passionate life's work based on the resuscitation of the past, *regardless* of the future effects of this work on collective survival.

On the other hand, if you've got kids, as I do . . . but let me tell you just a bit about what my kids *are* like. I've got (we've got) two, and neither of them is ordinary. The older boy's "gifted"; the baby, it seems, is "special" (sure, that's a large part of the reason I'm going to law school; "special" is even more expensive than "gifted"). Both of them are my teachers, though I don't remember that as often as I should, and both place their own, stringent demands on me when it comes to the mitzvah of "choosing life": "I have set before thee life and death, the blessing and the curse; therefore choose life, that thou mayest live, thou and thy seed" (Deut. 30:19). The original context of that commandment identifies the choice of life with observance of the Torah. Torah is not just a book or list of precise actions set in advance. It subsumes the demand of appropriate responses to contingent situations, explicitly, some situations including children. Hardest of all about "choosing life" in regard to my children is remembering that even when they seem to be distracting me from critical discipline, they remind me what criticism might be for. Rarer yet, though still necessary, are the moments when criticism actually helps me respond to my children *in life*. Inasmuch as the commandment to "choose life" always threatens to collapse into a "dead" slogan of institutional rhetoric, unreflective fealty to it is, logically, impossible.

When criticism and personal practice are understood as ultimately inseparable, it becomes impossible to accept those limitations in Benjamin's "Theses" that are indicated by the collapse of the notions of "hope" or "progress," and "the future" into one. The limitations of this collapse must be confronted, or we remain content to understand Benjamin's anamnestics as an unusually rich intellectual aesthetics, but one without articulable bearing on the everyday, political aspects of our situation, those that pertain to personal, family, or collective survival, aside from any broader horizon of liberation.

What if these three scales of survival are incommensurate? What if I am wrong in thinking that somehow personal, family, and collective needs are all realized at my old-fashioned Lower East Side shul, where a gentle, unpretentious elderly European rabbi sustains a congregation made up primarily of elderly and isolated Jewish men and women? When I attempt to write critically about the shul, am I right to think that the shul's survival is somehow linked to the survival of the species, or am I really speaking just of a nostalgic kind of memory? And are the conflicts the shul presents really relevant to thinking about the future without hope?

The very marginality of the synagogue and its members can serve to mask the questions of power and identity that nevertheless are played out and replayed there. In my attendance, performance (reading the Torah), and writing about the shul, I am promoting and acting on a notion of anamnestic practice: the routines of my discipline are structured in part by a desire to sustain memory; they are intended to resist amnesia. Yet, I shrink from the perpetuation of a tradition founded in gender discrimination. I am not content to be Jewish only "in theory," and there is no everyday context available in which both of these conflicting values can simultaneously be acted on.

So I get in trouble when I try to celebrate, or at least identify, what I assert to be the shul's fragmentary answers to the desire for an impossible community. In its lack of pretense, the acceptance of anyone (that is, any adult Jewish male) who can make the minyan and keeping the congregation going, the shul keeps open a marginal traditionality. Meanwhile, the shul keeps women on its margins. Laura Levitt insists, fairly, that my redemptive critique is complicit with the shul's marginalization of women. But what is her demand, if not the desire for a resolution that is unavailable, either in theory or in practice? There is no formula for smoothing out the awkward gaps between resistant traditions and the equally pressing values of contemporary identity politics. Here, like the Angel, I am at an impasse; no matter how long I might consider this problem *in theory*, I could never find a solution in actual fact. I am diminished by this recognition even as I am nourished by my shul.

Even more: when Miriam Peskowitz points out that the shul might well be at once institutionally marginal and symbolically normative, it becomes clear to me that in writing about it, I produce an apology for the perpetuation of an inequity I would never dream of initiating. When I assert in writing that is critical and scholarly that the shul stand as a form of resistance to the homogenization of liberal suburban Judaism, I simultaneously reinforce the implicit idea that some form of Orthodoxy with its attendant sexist discriminations is "authentic" Jewishness. And even though one of my interests is the survival of the shul, I can find no good reason for thinking that my writing serves that particular goal. Perhaps the best thing would be for me to renounce the shul as unacceptable nostalgia, or instead, just practice and keep quiet.

I suspect not. The relation between questions of difference and questions of continuity-and-survival cannot be trumped. This relation must be thought and it must be lived, with constant attention to both the costs and the unexpected resources of resistant and fragmentary community. So I return to Rabbi Singer's shul, to a scene repeated almost every Shabbes morning for the past several months, and I watch my little boy learning to walk, a year and half behind schedule, around and around the *bimah* and back to the women's section, holding the hand of eighty-five-year-old Abie who can't really read Hebrew too well. Abie's not the Angel of History, any more than I am. But when he walks with Yeshaya, he helps to close the gap between the demands of memory and the demands of the future that sometimes threaten to pull me apart.

To close this way reinvokes the normative authority of the shul, *backed up* by its sentimental marginality, and if I had the whole afternoon free, maybe I could move beyond this momentary and inadequate safe point, but soon I have to take that same child to the clinic where they teach him to hear with his new hearing aids. At the end of the twentieth Christian century, there is never one way to choose life, hence almost no moments at which we can say to ourselves that we have unequivocally made that choice "truly." Maybe "choose life" shouldn't be counted as a mitzvah in itself if it's too large and too general to expect anyone to fulfill. But is there any alternative?

Notes

1. Gershom Scholem, "Gruss vom Angelus/Greeting from the Angel," cited as the epigraph to Thesis IX of Walter Benjamin's "Theses on the Philosophy of History," in *Illuminations*, ed. Hannah Arendt, trans. Harry Zohn (New York: Schocken Books, 1969), 257.

2. Indeed, the "Theses" are shot through with masculinism: "The kind of happiness that could arouse envy in us exists only in . . . women who could have given themselves to us" (254); "The historical materialist leaves it to others to be drained by the whore called 'Once upon a time' in historicism's bordello. He remains in control of his powers, man enough to blast open the continuum of history" (262).

Other Tales: Museum Objects, Women, and Jewish Knowledges

Paula Chaiken

"What can you tell me about this object?" I asked the group of high school students visiting the Spertus Museum[1] from a Reform congregation in Chicago's northern suburbs, as we stopped in front of an eighteenth-century North African Torah scroll.

A student described the Torah's appearance, explained its contents, and discussed how it may have been used in communal worship long ago.

"And what is special about the way in which a Torah is produced?" I asked.

The students explained that a Torah is written with a quill and naturally produced ink on parchment made from the hide of a kosher animal by a *sofer*, a professional scribe.

I elaborated, "The scribe works for a very long time to create a Torah. He may spend years working on one because it has to be perfect."

One boy looked puzzled. He was upset by my choice of pronoun and asked, "Does the scribe have to be a man?"

"Well," I hesitated. "Traditionally, the *sofer* is a man. Though there are many talented female scribes who write *ketubbot* (marriage contracts), I don't know of any recorded instances of a Torah's having been written by a woman."

His question sent us on a new journey. We had not set out to talk about the roles of men and women in Judaism, but the museum experience made it possible. We continued our tour guided by the question.

We came to a case containing another Torah from Westphalia, Germany, produced in the late nineteenth century. There was no synagogue there, so Moses and Zipporah Pagener had housed the community Torah in their home. I explained how Zipporah Pagener had wanted to keep the Torah in a special place so she donated the finest cloth available, her wedding dress, to serve as a *parokhet*, a Torah ark curtain. The students heard this story while they looked at the piece of wedding dress.

As we admired the *parokhet,* one student asked, "How do we know Mrs. Pagener wanted to donate her dress?"

"We don't," I answered honestly. And I thought to myself, "This is the difficult part. As museum visitors, we have the power to make the objects tell stories, which means we generally make them tell the stories we want to hear." I preferred to believe that Zipporah had chosen to give her dress out of love and commitment to the Jewish community, because I don't want to believe that someone else made the choice for her.

As a group, we pondered the question: Did Zipporah choose happily to give up her finest dress to cover the Torah, did she watch passively as her husband decided the Torah ought to be dressed better than she was, or did she argue passionately to save the dress so that she might wear it to future special events?[2]

As we arrived in front of the case filled with objects used on Shabbat, the students felt confident that they understood women's obligations concerning the Jewish day of rest. "My mom lights the Shabbat candles every Friday," one girl called out.

I told her that her mother is observing one of three *mitzvot* (commandments) that women perform: lighting Shabbat candles, taking *hallah* (setting aside and burning a piece of the dough as a reminder of providing sustenance for the Temple priests), and going to the *mikveh.*[3]

Her friend commented that all of the pairs of candleholders in the case—from Poland, Israel, England—probably held candles that were lit by women in Jewish communities throughout the world. "And polished by them, too," I commented as we noticed the brass and silver.

We arrived at the life-cycle section of the museum and the students realized that, traditionally, males have more rites of passage than females. We looked at some objects associated with the *brit milah* (ritual circumcision)—an eighteenth-century Persian circumcision coat, a silver tray from central Europe, and a set of eighteenth-century circumcision implements from Germany—and discussed alternatives to the *brit milah* to welcome a baby girl into the community. The kids spoke of naming ceremonies that they have seen in their synagogue or attended at relatives' homes. The girls said they did not feel bad that they were traditionally excluded from entering the covenant; they preferred naming to cutting. As for me, I couldn't help but feel marginalized; I had not been welcomed in any ritual way into the Jewish community. I still have no Hebrew name.

At the next display we met an elderly woman, a museum visitor, who was moved by the objects used for daily prayer. She told us how *tefillin* (phylacteries) reminded her of a painful childhood experience. She recalled peeking from behind the study door to watch her father patiently teaching her younger brother how to wrap the leather straps. When she asked what they were doing, her father shooed her into the kitchen. As she shared this story with the students, they told me that they had seen *tefillin* only in the paintings of Marc Chagall and that the story meant nothing to them.

We arrived at the wedding display and one of the girls seemed excited as she pointed out that here at last was a ritual centered around women.[4] And while I agreed that being the bride is an exciting role to play, I pointed out that traditionally, a Jewish woman speaks no words at her wedding. A woman traditionally is not allowed to act as a witness or sign the *ketubbah*, either.

I read the students the text of a traditional *ketubbah* and asked them if they would use a traditional *ketubbah* if they were married one day. They expressed mixed feelings. Some were put off by the purchase of the bride described in Aramaic and said they would use more egalitarian language; others liked continuing the tradition of the ancient text of the *ketubbah*. "And it's not like you're really going to live the way it says," one girl remarked.

Another girl added, "I'm not going to be bought for two-hundred *zuzim*."[5]

Finally, we looked at the objects associated with death, the other life-cycle event in which women cannot be ignored.[6] We considered that this might be the only ceremony in which women and men—or at least their bodies—are accorded equal treatment. It is, after all, the first time in a traditional religious setting that men and women are side-by-side. But even at this final moment, we had to acknowledge women's inferior status. Traditionally, Jews prohibit women from reciting the *kaddish*, the mourners' prayer. Honoring the dead is a job for the men.

The students and I discovered that museums allow us to experience objects from the past; they enable us to shape new questions and ask old questions in new ways; they empower us to slow down, to stop, and to look long and hard. We experienced the ways in which "museums can put minds in motion without pre-determining their destination."[7]

Sometimes, as in the tour we took, the destination proves to be one of learning about the roles of men and women in Judaism. As we moved through the collection, we looked at, thought about, and discussed the artifacts on display, giving voice to the once-silent objects.[8] With the help of the museum-goer, a Torah ark curtain or a candle holder or a painting remains silent no longer.

On this particular visit, the students and I enabled the objects to speak about another group: women.[9] Historically, their tales have been ignored by those who have written Jewish history. But some of the objects in the museum had been created or used by women. By observing those objects, reading their labels, and thinking creatively, museum visitors can recover pieces of women's history, imagining the stories of the women whose hands may have touched these objects. In this way, we can both dispel the silence of the objects and vocalize the unvoiced history of Jewish women.[10]

We must be responsible when we project our voices onto objects. Silent objects do not have the power to censor our stories, and stories are limited only by our imaginations. We may invent romantic tales of women's contributions to Jewish life or we may imagine their quiet and unrecorded suffering. Either way, the objects can only direct our questions. They cannot correct our misconceptions and they cannot provide us with their historical truths, especially when we're trying to recall histories as frequently unwritten as those of Jewish women.

Because we have only begun to recall Jewish women's experiences, we must use whatever resources we have at hand to recover the histories of Jewish women. Using museum objects, we can piece together stories about the women who may have used, seen, or lived with them. As we look at artifacts like those in the Spertus Museum, we can capture at least fragments of their lives. Although museums currently do not tell the stories of Jewish women, someday, as more feminists assume leadership roles in the museum world, as curators, directors, board members, and donors, and as visitors insist on objects telling women's and men's stories, the lives and experiences of women will be presented more fully.[11] But until then, those who walk through museums halls and displays can notice these absences and begin to use their own eyes, voices, and imaginations to produce other tales.

Notes

1. The Spertus Museum in Chicago, is the largest Jewish museum in the Midwest. Its Judaica collection includes objects from several thousand years of Jewish life, as well as the Bernard and Rochelle Zell Holocaust Memorial; the Paul and Gabriella Rosenbaum ARTiFACT Center, a hands-on children's archaeological museum; and temporary exhibitions illustrating Jewish art, history, and culture.

2. At this time and place, wedding dresses were dark colors. Women would wear them for the first time to their own wedding and then over and over again to other occasions. Zipporah Pagener's dress was midnight blue.

3. "The third of the *mitzvot, mikveh,* is an important part of a ritually observant woman's life. However, it remains unnoted in this exhibition." Kathi Lieb, "Ceremonial Art and Women: Giving Voice to the Silence," gallery lecture, Spertus Museum, Chicago, June 1991.

4. Ibid.

5. The purchase price for a virgin, according to Mishnah.

6. Lieb, "Ceremonial Art and Women."

7. Alan Gartenhaus, *Minds in Motion: Using Museums to Expand Creative Thinking* (San Francisco: Caddo Gap Press, 1993), 28.

8. I thank Kathi Lieb, the former Education Curator of the Spertus Museum, for this expression; for the many facts and stories I learned from her gallery lecture "Ceremonial Art and Women: Giving Voice to the Silence"; and for her guidance and friendship in our work together.

9. An exhibition dedicated to recalling the experiences of the female Jewish immigrant is "Becoming Jewish Women: Clothing and the Jewish Immigrant Experience, 1880–1920." Organized by the Chicago Historical Society: Chicago Historical Society, March 6, 1994–January 2, 1995; Ellis Island Immigration Museum, New York City, March 15, 1995–July 16, 1995; National Museum of American Jewish History, Philadelphia, September 10, 1995–December 31, 1995; Skirball Museum, Los Angeles, April 21, 1995–August 25, 1996; The Detroit Historical Museum, Detroit, November 1, 1996–March 27, 1997. For the exhibition catalog, see Barbara A. Schreir, *Becoming American Women* (Chicago: Chicago Historical Society, 1994).

10. For an examination of the noninclusion of women's contributions to Jewish life at Beit Hatefusot, the Museum of the Jewish Diaspora, in Tel Aviv, Israel, see Dafna N. Izraeli, "They Have Eyes and See Not: Gender Politics in the Diaspora Museum," *Psychology of Women Quarterly* 17 (1993): 515–523. See also Jane Glaser and Artemis Zenetou, eds., *Gender Perspectives: Essays on Women in Museums* (Washington, DC: Smithsonian Museum Press, 1994).

11. This does not begin to address the many changes that need to occur in order for women's lives and contributions to be documented fully, or even adequately, in exhibits.

American Jewish Culture Through a Gender-Tinted Lens

Riv-Ellen Prell

In the first decades of this century European Jews, to a greater extent than many other European immigrants, represented their experience to one another and to the larger society. Through fiction, poetry, drama, journalism, music, and, later, film, they narrated the process of becoming American Jews. At the center of these portraits was the family, in both its Old World and New World manifestations. For much of this century images of the Jewish family have continued to serve as metaphors for Jews' relationships to the larger culture. Generational conflict, intermarriage, and relations between sons, mothers, fathers, and daughters have usually revolved around the solidity and solidarity of the family and the ability of the younger generation to move into the broader society.

Consider, for example, "His People," Edward Sloman's popular 1925 American film. This film portrayed the Cominsky family's Americanization in terms of its two sons' choices of occupations, brides, and relationships to their parents. Only when the scholarly and ineffective Old World father could accept the right of a son to be a boxer, and when the social-climbing lawyer son atoned for abandoning and denying his family in order to wed a wealthy German Jewish woman, could generation conflict find resolution.

On the face of it, these portraits seem to be no more than ephemeral images, products of the psychological tensions of a temporary period of cultural adjustment and its inevitable effect upon a family undergoing dramatic transformations in the New World. But even with Jews' successful acculturation, these images and conflicts do not fade. In popular culture created by Jews, families, marriages, generational tensions, and other forms of emotional connection continued to be used as media for exploring Jews' relationships to American society. For example, the Jewish-American Princess has been one of the most powerful stereotypes that Jews have generated about one another since World War II. The JAP stereotype is as clear an announcement of Jews' ongoing concerns about future generations, success, and fitting in as were the previous generations' more crude portrayals of immigrant life and the immigrant family.

These pervasive images and metaphors point us toward salient questions about American Jewish life, questions that will allow us to understand how—in various decades and under changing conditions in the United States—Jews have understood themselves as Jews. Gender and family play a crucial role in Jews' self-representations and, hence, in the negotiation of American Jewish experience. Differences between Jewish men and women, attributing blame and virtue systematically to each, are a prominent feature of Jewish self-reflection.[1]

When Jews describe what they consider uniquely Jewish—the family, the kitchen, celebrations, and why or why not Jews are attracted to, marry, and raise children with one another—they invariably focus on private life. Indeed, Liebman and Cohen argue that "familism" is the defining characteristic of American and Israeli Jewishness.[2] Jews see one another as members of a family and most often represent their experience through the family. Taking into account an ideology of "familism" as we consider Jewish cultural representations of family, we reach a new understanding of American Jewish ethnicity. At the same time, we raise questions and concerns that social scientists who study ethnicity have systematically overlooked.

We have known American Jewish identity or ethnicity through the life course of the male. For more than half a century his education, occupations, religious attitudes, synagogue participation, and institutional life have been a matter of great interest to social scientists. He is the primary agent of cultural life or change, and his family follows behind, hoisted by him up the ladder of economic success.[3] Women, children, and life outside work and the public sector are not pursued as relevant to the understanding of American Jews' economic success, or to the meanings of being a Jew in the United States.

It is not that sociologists are reluctant to measure women's education or ritual practice; rather, they believe that at the present time men and women behave the same (in ways that are statistically measurable). Therefore, gender becomes irrelevant, and social science continues to focus on men as the norm.[4] In defining Jews as men, social scientists have failed to ask what a gendered American Jewish experience looks like. Instead of exploring what the category "Jewish" means to the people who identify themselves as such, social scientists have represented Jews as an ethnic group modeled on the notion of an "interest group." Internal stratification, whether by class or gender, is thus seen to be less compelling than the way that Jews—as a group—are different from other groups.[5]

In contrast, by following the lead of Jewish cultural self-representations (of immigrants and fully acculturated Americans, both), we can see that relationships between the sexes and the generations have been one of the most powerful images through which Jews have attempted to understand their sojourn in the United

States. Both "popular" and "high" culture—from immigrant music that evoked "home" to the postwar novels that used the "Jewish Mother" to symbolize American success and materialism—tell us that the cultural category of jewishness requires careful unpacking and sophisticated interpretation. If jewishness is a gendered and relational category, then Jewish men and women have not experienced their lives in identical ways. Immigration had different effects on men and women. The American Jewish synagogue was shaped by gender difference, as Jewish religious practice was transformed by the presence of men and/or women. And economically, when Jewish women entered the work force in large numbers, this too had a significant effect on how Jewish men understood themselves and their relations to potential marriage partners.[6]

Through these and other emerging issues, points, and questions, "Judaism" and "jewishness" become categories, and gendered categories at that. The study of Jewish life in the United States depends on gendering subjects, and, as Peskowitz argues, understanding those subjects depends on studying their social constructions. "jewishness" and "Judaism" are more than a series of beliefs and activities; they are a matrix of issues through which self-definition is actually constructed.

Notes

1. In her work on emancipation in the nineteenth and early twentieth centuries in the United States and Europe, Paula Hyman discusses why women are portrayed as first parochial and then irresponsible in handling their sons' Jewish socialization. See *Gender and Assimilation in Modern Jewish History: The Roles and Representation of Women. Gender and the Project of Jewish Assimilation* (Seattle: University of Washington Press, 1995).

2. Charles S. Liebman and Steven M. Cohen, *Two Worlds of Judaism: The Israeli and American Experiences* (New Haven: Yale University Press, 1990).

3. For a recent review of sociological studies of Jews, see Gerald L. Showstack, "Perspectives in the Study of American Jewish Ethnicity," *Contemporary Jewry* 11 (1991): 77–90.

4. More recent historical studies have dealt with gender, although they assume that "Jewishness" does not require investigation; it is simply group membership. For examples, see Susan Glenn, *Daughters of the Shtetl* (Ithaca, NY: Cornell University Press, 1990); Andrew Heinze, *Adapting to Abundance* (New York: Columbia University Press, 1990); and Judith Smith, *Family Connections* (Albany: SUNY Press, 1985). Charlotte Baum, Paula Hyman, and Sonya Michel, *The Jewish Woman in America* (New York: Plume Books, 1975), was the first interdisciplinary attempt to tell the story of Jewish women in the United States. Sylvia Barack Fishman's *A Breath of Life: Feminism in the American Jewish Community* (New York: Free Press, 1993) is a sociological study of contemporary American Jewish women's lives and their impact on Judaism.

5. In "Landscape of Enchantment: Redaction in a Theory of Ethnicity," *Cultural Anthropology* 4 (1989), Phyllis Chock calls for an anthropology of ethnicity in the United States that

locates "scholarly discourse on ethnicity in its relationship with indigenous discourse" (163). In discussing a seminal work on ethnicity and interest groups, she writes that in *Beyond the Melting Pot*, Glazer and Moynihan focus on the "interests of the ethnic group as an heuristic device to locate all ethnics within a single containing landscape. The marketplace model diminishes all social differences" (177). This model erases internal Jewish differentiation as well.

6. These and other ramifications are discussed more fully in Riv-Ellen Prell, *Fighting to Become American: Jewish Women and Men in Conflict in the Twentieth Century* (New York: Basic Books, forthcoming).

Gender, Colonialism, and the Representation of Middle Eastern Jews

Joëlle Bahloul

The alleged irrationality of the Middle Eastern Jewish world is a widespread assumption in both popular and scholarly discussion.[1] I first encountered this paradigm in the early 1970s, when I was in the preliminary stage of my doctoral research, looking for bibliographic sources on the social and cultural history of the Jews of North Africa. A doctoral thesis in medicine, defended in 1902 in Montpellier (France), proposed an analysis of the spread of psychosis among the Jews of Algeria.[2] The author, V. Trenga, based his argument on the hypothesis that "race" is an important factor in the etiology of certain diseases, and that, de facto, the Jews make up a specific "race." Trenga's thesis attempts to answer the question, "Are the Jews predisposed to psychosis?" He makes use of a survey (conducted among the Jews of Algiers between 1898 and 1901) that shows that the Jews are more often subject to hospitalization for mental disease than any other population. Several reasons are put forward to explain this observation: (1) the morbid nature of the Jewish psychological heritage and the obsession with persecution; (2) the extension of consanguineous marriages among Jews; (3) the Jewish predisposition toward exaltation and passion; (4) the popularity of superstitions and irrational beliefs; (5) the constant drive for migration among Jews; (6) the alleged drive for alcohol consumption; (7) the abusive sexual activity among Jews, as "Oriental people"; and (8) the insufficiency of meat in the Jewish diet.

The major point in this etiological discussion is that women are the most frequent patients and that their predisposition toward mental disease is correlated to their strict adherence to various forms of superstitions and obscure rituals such as chicken sacrifices and magical beliefs. Women are portrayed as the most irrational element within the Jewish community of Algiers, and an element pushing Jews closer to the local Arabs than to the Jews of Paris or Berlin. It is as if women were the archetypical identity factor in the construction of the pathological Jew. And although the author does not identify the subjects of his enquiry as Sephardic Jews, he clearly characterizes them as "Oriental," which in French equals "Levantine," and as different from northern European Jews.

Trenga's analysis is best understood in the context of a colonialist and traditionally antisemitic worldview. Colonialist ideology was at its peak in the European community of early twentieth-century Algeria, and it was often associated with the antisemitic propaganda that flourished in both Europe and the colonies of that day. Trenga emphasizes the Algerian Jews' nativeness and refers to their culture as part of the indigenous Arabic-speaking culture, but Algerian Jews had been French citizens for half a century. In his discussion of their drive for passion and exaltation, as well as their overactive sexuality, the author articulates a typical colonialist discourse. Algerian Jews appear as an archetype of gemeinschaft,[3] and the females are presented as an unevolved subgroup that pulls the community into backwardness.

A Geo-ideological Paradigm

As I continued my research in Sephardic history and culture, I was surprised to encounter the "primitive" paradigm in more recent academic literature. Academic and popular discourses on Sephardic culture have continued to maintain this perspective, even as North African Jewish communities experienced the historical upheavals associated with migration and integration into Western cultures. In post–World War II academic production, the social scientific description of Sephardic life perpetuates most of the ideological biases that Mediterranean ethnography had suffered for decades.[4] Scholars continue to view the Sephardic world as "archaic" and nonprogressive, in large part because of its treatment of women and the extensive sexual discrimination found in it. Goitein's *Mediterranean Society* proves an exception to this rule. His unusually nuanced picture of Jewish women in Mediterranean society describes them as a "world within a world."[5] However, using evidence from the *Geniza*, he informs us about the presence of women in public affairs and business as well. Yet in most scholarly literature, even that which demonstrates some sympathy with feminism, the representation of Sephardic women as passive and oppressed is widespread.[6] In Goitein's leading historical scholarship, Mediterranean Jewish society was characterized as a diverse social world with a number of commercial, cultural, and social exchanges. In contemporary Sephardic studies, it is theoretically and ideologically constructed as a socio-cultural identity defined by patriarchy and gender inequality.

A Question of History

Ultimately, the paradigm of female inferiority as evidence of the *gemeinschaft* nature of Sephardic culture serves to deny the latter a place in modern Jewish history. Sephardic identity is generally viewed as "traditional" by nature,[7] as a "people without history."[8] Its alleged discriminative treatment of women is analyzed as pertaining to an outdated premodern history in which the former Arab neighbors of most Sephardic communities are believed to have remained. Gender inequality in Sephardic culture is conceived of as a handicap to modernization, emancipation, and Westernization. Thus Sephardic women are ideologically "left behind," in the Levantine world, at the margins of the geo-historical Jewish modernity located in northern Europe.

Even when it is presented as a feminist argument, the emphasis on the discrimination against women in Sephardic culture and society is nothing less than *ethnocentrism.* Such an ideology, like early evolutionist essentialist anthropological literature, tends to identify northern European (Jewish) culture as the most advanced stage of modernity. This scholarly blindness typically ignores the Sephardic female yearning for modernity and the fact that women did become "modern" through the complex discursive forms of narrative, domestic, and family practices, and through professional emancipation.[9] For North African Jewish women in the first half of the twentieth century, to be a "modern" woman was a personal "vocation," a contribution to their community's modernization and emancipation. Becoming "modern" meant gaining a greater degree of dignity and independence. It also meant that one would be distinguished from Moslem women, whose emancipation is still contested. The "modern woman" was an ideal, a goal to achieve. North African Jewish women were indeed very successful in achieving this goal, and they often modernized even before most of the men in their communities. Since the beginning of the twentieth century, a significant number of these women acquired secular education. And, after they married, these same women encouraged their children, notably the generation born after World War I, to pursue secular education. Sephardic women were thus instrumental in the process of modernizing their communities,[10] even as Trenga wrote his thesis.

Because very few historical or ethnographic accounts of the modern North African Jewish experience deal with women's various private strategies of modernization, women continue to be characterized in terms not unlike Trenga's. The accomplishments of these women remain outside the parameters of most social scientific discourse, much less popular representations of Sephardic culture.

Notes

1. For an extensive analysis of the discursive debate dealt with in this essay, see my article "The Sephardic Jew as Mediterranean: A View from Kinship and Gender," *Journal of Mediterranean Studies* 4.2 (1994): 197–207.

2. V. Trenga, "Sur les psychoses chez les juifs d'Algérie" (Ph.D. diss., Montpellier, 1902).

3. This concept was introduced by the German social thinker F. Tönnies (1855–1936), in his magnum opus *Gemeinschaft und Gesellschaft* (1887). *Gemeinschaft* characterizes a type of social organization that is homogenous and based on kinship ties. Traditionally translated as

"community," *Gemeinschaft* has been opposed to *Gesellschaft*, a more "evolved" type of social organization in which social relations are governed by individualism and the complexity of the division of labor.

4. See the development of the debate in M. Herzfeld, *Anthropology Through the Looking-Glass: Critical Ethnography in the Margins of Europe* (Cambridge and New York: Cambridge University Press, 1987); J. (de) Pina-Cabral, "The Mediterranean as a Category of Regional Comparison: A Critical View," *Current Anthropology* 30.3(1989): 399–406; D. Gilmore, ed., *Honour and Shame in the Unity of the Mediterranean* (Washington D.C.: American Anthropological Association, 1987); R. Banfield, *The Moral Basis of a Backward Society* (Glencoe, IL: Free Press, 1958).

5. S. D. Goitein, *A Mediterranean Society*, vol. 3, *The Family* (Berkeley: University of California Press, 1978), 354.

6. D. Bensimon-Donath, *Immigrants d'Afrique du Nord en Israël* (Paris: Anthropos, 1970); *L'intégration des Juifs Nord-Africains en France* (Paris: Mouton, 1971); D. Schnapper, *Jewish Identities in France* (Chicago: University of Chicago Press, 1983).

7. Sh. Deshen and W. P. Zenner, eds., *Jewish Societies in the Middle East: Community, Culture and Authority* (New York: University Press of America, 1982), 8.

8. Eric Wolf, *Europe and the People Without History* (Berkeley: University of California Press, 1982).

9. See J. Bahloul, "Stratégies familiales et reproduction socio-culturelle: parentèles juives nord-africaines en France," *Pardès* 1.1(1985): 31–61; "La famille sépharade dans la diaspora du XXème siècle," in *La Société juive à travers l'histoire*, sous la direction de Shmuel Trigano, vol. 2 (Paris: Editions Fayard, 1992), 469–495; *The Architecture of Memory* (Cambridge and New York: Cambridge University Press, 1996).

10. See Bahloul, "La famille sépharade," and *Architecture of Memory*.

Boys of the *Wissenschaft*

Robert J. Baird

An Experiment in Phil-History

Early in Miriam Peskowitz's "Engendering Jewish Religious History," she characterizes a "traditional scholarship" that is blind to the ways it has been shaped by a masculinist and colonialist European Enlightenment inheritance. In an almost passing way she goes on to note that this inheritance "veils a specific christian-ness behind its claims to the universal." Although it is fairly common these days to speak of the impact (pro or con) of the Enlightenment on scholarship, I was arrested by Peskowitz's reference to a specific christian-ness hidden in Enlightenment universalism. That same veiled "christian-ness" reveals itself as well, I would say, in the efforts of the maskilim and the *Wissenschaft des Judentums* to invent a "modern Jewish Studies." In this essay I link my genealogy of the "christian-ness" inherent in Enlightenment thought to the masculinism which is the central focus of "Engendering Jewish Religious History."

One outgrowth of the *Wissenschaft* school was the prominent nineteenth-century discourse of *Jewish renewal through Enlightenment.* Emboldened by a hypertrophied notion of reason, *Wissenschaft* thinkers created a new appropriation of the past designed to purge Judaism of its rabbinic traces and correct the Gentile world's venomous misunderstandings of Jewish culture and life. Modern Jewish studies was to be a separate, autonomous, *Jewish* discipline. It was interpreted as an expression of rebirth and pride, as an early nineteenth-century attempt to offset Judaism's cultural and historic tutelage to Christianity. At the same time, certain key conceptual and metaphoric moves, which were central to the *Wissenschaft*'s invention of Jewish studies, seem distinctly predicated (and dependent) upon *Christian* philosophical resources.

This conceptual reliance, a veiled christian-ness of the *Wissenschaft des Judentums,* provides the starting point for the genealogical argument I will develop.[1] But

invent of J. Studies

even this formulation of a "conceptual reliance" between Christianity and Enlightenment reason puts it too weakly, for in the sense of christian-ness I want to flesh out, *Wissenschaft* thinkers did not *choose* to be Christian, nor did they explicitly attempt to inflect their thought with Christian motifs. The meaning of "veiled christian-ness" I have in mind is not even captured in the widely acknowledged influence, active and passive, of regnant Christian norms on a variety of traditional forms of Jewish piety and education. Instead, christian-ness is seen as part of the ethos of the Enlightenment and, by extension, the ethos of the *Wissenschaft*. This historically undeniable statement becomes interesting only when we realize that the Enlightenment, to speak in broad strokes, was premised on the overthrow of Christian revelation as a mode of human authority. I am asserting that two "irreconcilable" nodes of the Western imaginary—Christianity and the Enlightenment—are married in the modern European ethos and imbricated with a dominant masculinism.

By invoking the concept of ethos, I am underlining the degree to which an ethos works precisely because it does not depend on voluntary choice. Rather, it tacitly directs and shapes the options in which a contemporary reality is imagined or lived out. Christian-ness "manifests" itself in the Enlightenment ethos, yet is simultaneously effaced as a piece of positive knowledge and therefore veiled to modernity. Enlightenment and modernity did not, as anti-hegemonists everywhere tell us, define and name everything like Adam on a rampage but were themselves "defined" as they traded upon preexisting structures of Christian thought and practice. Renewal through Enlightenment—the project of crafting "jewishness" in the *Wissenschaft des Judentums*—by no means made Judaism immune to this structuration, in fact just the opposite.

Specifically, *Wissenschaft* thinkers' strategy of creating in modern Jewish studies a consistent, core, unchanging meaning of "jewishness"—an identity resistant to historical change—strikes me as a problematic way of rejecting Christianity's cultural hegemony. In short, can one throw off the yoke of Christianity when the conditions for the possibility of imagining and enacting "liberation" are firmly rooted in discursive formations specific to seventeenth- and eighteenth-century Christian traditions? To put this another way, positing a philosophical essence to modern Jewish studies—essentializing Judaism—as a mode of emancipation for Jews in nineteenth-century Germany reinscribes what Michel de Certeau calls "the formality of Christian practices" back into the center of Judaism—albeit veiled behind Enlightenment universalism. This is the crux of the genealogical argument to be developed below.

In the spirit of Miriam Peskowitz's "Engendering Jewish Religious History," my essay is offered as a thought experiment in which I imagine historical moments as already imbricated with philosophical and gendered meanings and the conditions for the possibility of philosophy as nascent in the exigencies of history. This reading and reconstruction of the imaginative resources[2] of the *Wissenschaft des Judentums* strikes me as much more useful than would be a confident deconstruction of its philosophical grounds. We are too familiar with the ways in which philosophical and cultural analysis can be applied like a vise to flatten complex historical moments into breezy schematizations.

A Genealogy of the *Wissenschaft des Judentums*

More than fifty years before the scientific study of religion was conceived as a formal academic discipline in England and Germany,[3] seven Jewish students in Berlin formed the Society for Culture and Scientific Study of the Jews (*Der Verein für Cultur und Wissenschaft*). It was November of 1819 when this small group, threatened by a resurgent antisemitism expressed in the vitriolic, anti-Jewish "Hep! Hep!"[4] riots of that year started meeting regularly with no clear aims other than simply to foster "the improvement of the situation of the Jews in the German federated states."[5] The emancipatory environment for Jews in early nineteenth-century Germany was rapidly deteriorating. The members of the Society had been galvanized by Napoleon's defeat at Waterloo and the refusal in 1815 of the Congress of Vienna to universalize Jewish emancipation in Germany. They saw in these events, along with increasing levels of violence against Jews, progressive signs of German/Christian culture's rejection of Jewish assimilatory claims.

But retrenchment on Jewish emancipation was not the sole factor in the formation of the Society. Members were equally if not more motivated by a profound need to rethink Judaism at its core, not only to defend it against external attack but to reform it from within by aligning it with the regnant philosophical and cultural norms of nineteenth-century modernity. Isaak Markus Jost, Leopold Zunz, Joseph Hillmar, Joel Abraham List, Isaac Levin Auerbach, Eduard Gans, and Moses Moser, founding members of the Society, although theologically at odds, were united in the belief that Judaism itself was impeding the assimilation process. Legislative and political reforms, they were convinced, were not sufficient to the task of upholding two decades of increasing liberation. If increasing numbers of Jews were to assimilate into the norms of "cultivated" German culture, continued adherence to Jewish faith and Jewish law needed to be reconceptualized.

The members of the Society, who were later to form the nucleus of the *Wissenschaft des Judentums*, came from Jewish homes in which their own education had been based on a rabbinic tradition they loathed. Increasingly, they were struck by the stark contrasts in their own imaginations between this formative background and the historical, empirical, and critical modes of scholarship they were encountering in German universities. Therefore, the task of fashioning Judaism into a phenomenon palatable to modern sensibilities was more than an intellectual dilemma for the thinkers of the *Wissenschaft*. "The deghettoization of the Jewish community,"[6] to quote Michael Meyer, was tied directly to the viability of a scholarly Jewish studies. To put it emphatically, the *Wissenschaft des Ju-*

dentums was the recognition that the deghettoization of the Jewish community, socially and politically, was inextricably linked with a fundamental reimagining of Judaism itself.

The scientific study of Judaism would, in Heinrich Heine's conception, "reconcile historical Judaism with the modern science which, one supposed, in the course of time would gain world dominion."[7] Heine's short-lived triumphalism (he converted to Christianity in 1825) underscored the deep alliance between the Wissenschaft's construction of Judaism and Aufklärung. Through its merger with critical thought, the thinkers of the *Wissenschaft* attempted to reconceptualize Judaism as a new historical object. Articulated by Zunz, Ganz, and Immanuel Wolf, *Wissenschaft* created the conditions for the possibility of a new and distinctive appropriation of Judaism *as history, as fact, as a positive science,* and not as eternal, religious revelation. The conceptual space for something called "modern Jewish studies" was now, for the first time in western European history, to be carved out in Christian-dominated universities, schools, and modes of scholarship. This sense of the formation of a new discipline is clearly conveyed in the essay that Wolf wrote to introduce the *Wissenschaft*'s journal and outline the project of a scientific study of Judaism.

> What Jewish scholars have achieved, especially in earlier times, is mostly theological in character. In particular, they have almost completely neglected the study of history. But Christian scholars, however great their merit in the development of individual aspects of Judaism, have almost always treated Judaism for the sake of a historical understanding of Christian theology, even if it was not their intention to place Judaism itself in a hateful light, or, as they put it, to confute Judaism. . . . But if Judaism is to become an object of the science in its own right and if a science of Judaism is to be formed, then it is obvious that quite a different method of treatment is under discussion. But any object, no matter of what type, that in its essence is of interest to the human spirit, and comprehensive in its diverse formation and development, can become the object of a special science.[8]

The science of Judaism in Wolf's text is clearly linked to the overthrow of Judaism's secondary status. Science, which Wolf describes as "universality" and "infinity," is naturally affiliated with "the human spirit whose nobler nature rejects any limitation, any rest, any standing still";[9] in short, science and spirit transcend the merely human. Wolf continues:

> The Jews must once again show their mettle as doughty fellow workers in a common task of mankind. They must raise themselves and their principle to the level of a science, for this is the attitude of the European world. On this level the relationship of strangeness in which Jews and Judaism have hitherto stood to the outside world must vanish. And if one day a bond is to join the whole of humanity, then it is *the bond of science, the bond of pure rationality, the bond of truth.*[10]

If Judaism is to overcome its "relationship of strangeness" to the "outside world," then its essence must unite with the essence of science, which is pure rationality and truth. To use Peter Van Der Veer's apt phrase, Judaism is "converting to modernity,"[11] but doing so through Enlightenment resources that have not abandoned their relationship to Christianity. "Joining the whole of humanity" (Wolf) or to speak of integrating the science of Judaism "into the whole of human knowledge" (Gans) as a means of effacing centuries of difference, hatred, and violence carries, to say the least, missionary or soteriological overtones. The *Wissenschaftlers* were engaged in a civilizing mission, exhorting Jews to realize their essential nature by converting to the regnant philosophies of the day. But beyond the simple messianic and evangelist motifs of this Enlightenment gospel, the *Wissenschaft* discourse was also truly Christian in other ways.

Natural Religion

Certainly there was an acknowledged Protestantism that affected the structure of everyday Jewish education, the nature of liturgy, and the formation of the rabbinate in nineteenth-century Germany, but Geiger and other Wissenschaftlers were already railing about this in the late 1860s. The veiled christian-ness of Jewish renewal is to be found, I believe, in the *Wissenschaft's* deployment of "Jewish essence"—a notion that has a specific Christian history in seventeenth- and eighteenth-century debates about natural religion. Essentialized definitions of religion emerge in what Richard Popkin calls the seventeenth-century "inundation of data" about the diversities of human belief, ancient and modern, uncovered by contemporary linguists, missionaries, and explorers.

Scholars were attempting to find rational patterns for the religions of antiquity, those of Greece, Babylon, and Persia and the newly discovered religions of the Americas, the South Sea Islanders, the Africans, and the Laplanders, to name a few. Similarities and differences were drawn between these New (and Old) World religions and Judaism and Christianity, sometimes for the purpose of attacking the historic dominance of the latter, or sometimes for promoting the superior truths of the Western revealed religions over these "strange" beliefs and practices. As Popkin comments, "The data indicating that the varieties of mankind could not be encompassed within Biblical history, chronologically or geographically, and that the varieties of human belief could not be squared with the Biblical account raised most serious problems about the then generally accepted Jewish and Christian framework."[12] Besides the obvious questions that this pluralism prompted about the causes for and origins of these new religions, the proliferation of different beliefs created a verificatory line of questioning: Which religion was the *true* one, which religion could ensure man's salvation? To put it very simply, religious salvation was being conceptualized in terms of saving *knowledge, correct belief, and rational justification* instead of by a pervasive (Christian) faith that did not need to know itself as "faith."

Without entering into the complexities of debate surrounding the fragmentation of Christendom into competing Protestant sects in post-Reformation England, we may locate the response to religious pluralism most directly in the theories of seventeenth- and eighteenth-century English theologians, from the Cambridge Platonists, including Benjamin Whichcote, Ralph Cudworth, Henry More, and Nathaniel Culverwel, to the Deists, such as Herbert of Cherbury, Charles Blount, John Toland, and Matthew Tindal. Both movements, as different as they were, sought to "establish some final court of appeal on matters of religious doctrine"[13] in order to quell religious violence and persecution brought about by advocates of opposing religious dogmas. Herbert of Cherbury proposed that Christianity could be reduced to its lowest common denominator through the acknowledgment of a natural religion consisting of generic beliefs, practices, and ethics. The motivation behind Herbert's "Common Notions Concerning Religion"[14] was to establish a "standard of discrimination" to determine the true religion from among competing revelations.

What is significant here is that within the Christian response to seventeenth- and early eighteenth-century pluralism, "religion" is reconceptualized on a radically new axis, that of transhistorical and transcultural beliefs. The emphasis on reconstructing religion as *generic belief* means that religion could be imagined to consist solely of a set of coherent propositions to which believers gave assent. Accordingly, different religions could be compared, and generic religion could be judged against natural science.[15] This notion of a universal or natural form of religion emerges as part of a Christian theological response to the question provoked by pluralism: Which religion is more fundamental than these competing religions? The answer is obviously a natural religion, whose essence is stable, which can be identified across ages, and which defines what constitutes "the religious dimension" of life.

Veiling

The effacement of Christianity within the notion of natural religion does not negate (but only veils) the relationship natural religion maintains with its site of conception—Christian polemics. From natural religion we are only one conceptual and metaphorical step away from the fully essentialized notion of religion found in Kant and in the *Wissenschaft des Judentums*. The movement from naturalizing to essentializing religion is perfectly captured in Kant's *Perpetual Peace: A Philosophical Sketch*:

> Religious Differences—an odd expression! As if we were to speak of different moralities. There may certainly be different historical confessions although these have nothing to do with religion itself but only with changes in the means used to further religion, and are thus the province of historical research. And there may be just as

> many religious *books* (the Zend-Avesta, the Vedas, the Koran, etc.). But there can only be *one religion* which is valid for all men and at all times. Thus the different confessions can scarcely be more than the vehicles of religion; these are fortuitous, and may vary with differences in time or place.[16]

Reading Kant, I am reminded of Immanuel Wolf's reconstruction of Judaism as a universal essence that unfolds in "diverse formation." The claim of the Wissenschaftlers that "jewishness" persists, that it is an "eternal inner substance" (to quote Ismar Schorsch) that should not be confused with its historical forms, should, by now, have a familiar ring. In that vein, Ismar Elbogen in "A Century of Wissenschaft des Judentums" retells the story of Heinrich Grätz's first meeting with Zunz. When Grätz was introduced to Zunz as the author of a scholarly work in Jewish history, Elbogen reports that the latter stated in exasperation, "What, another Jewish history?" Whereupon Grätz immediately responded, "Indeed, but this time a *Jewish* one."[17] Jewish historical scholarship, if we are to draw any methodological import from Gratz's pithy retort, is meaningfully amassed for the Wissenschaftlers only in the service of reinforcing an essential *jewishness* that is discernible in the Judaism of all ages and all countries.

It seems to me to be the same conceptual and metaphorical environment that gives rise to Kant's distinction between "one religion" and "different historical confessions" and the Wissenschaft's recuperative project of conceptualizing an integrated and whole "Jewish world" characterized by an unchanging essence in the midst of a stream of historical change. The Christian origins of nineteenth-century Jewish essentialism have a certain sad irony about them. They are constitutive of the very moment and appear in the very movement through which these scholarly Jewish men attempted to revivify Judaism and legitimate their own place in the modern world. Twentieth-century studies of Judaism have been based in these very same veiled and essentialized terms. This brief thought experiment may clear imaginative space for alternate studies to emerge.

Notes

1. By emphasizing "christian-ness" I have no interest in invoking an orthodox critique of the *Wissenschaft des Judentums* as an anti-traditional capitulation to humanist and Christian norms. There the attempt to shed distinctive Jewish practices or the strategy of abandoning "particularist" features of Jewish ways of life is portrayed as kind of bargain with the devil: the loss of jewishness in exchange for civil equality with Christians. This critique, which gained currency through the *Haskalah* and *Wissenschaft* movements, is drawn from a wider discourse concerning the diminution of "Jewish tradition" through contact with critical thought. The end result of this acculturation process is of course conversion to Christianity. Underlining this point, Werner Mosse points out that Jewish conversion in mid-nineteenth-century Germany was advocated more on civic than religious grounds. But how independent are the cat-

egories of "civic" and "religious" in this mode of analysis? Quoting from Jacob Katz's *Out of the Ghetto,* Mosse retells a story of conversion: "It is not baptism that counts," an opponent of Judaism declared, "but that the Jew, by saying 'Baptize me,' says at the same time: I obey the laws of the country, I submit myself to the institutions you have created, I fulfill all the obligations laid upon me at all times." An imbrication such as this of Christianity and the state undermines any easy distinction between the religious and/or civic meaning of conversion. In this sense, at this particular historical moment, secularization does equal Christianization. In Werner E. Mosse, "From 'Schutzjuden' to 'Deutsche Staatsbürger Jüdischen Glaubens': The Long and Bumpy Road of Jewish Emancipation in Germany," in *Paths of Emancipation: Jews, States, and Citizenship,* ed. Pierre Birnbaum and Ira Katznelson (Princeton: Princeton University Press, 1995), 82–83.

2. I use "imaginative" outside the normative binary opposition in which "the imagination is pitted against "reality" or some other equally hard-nosed word to indicate "the actual." In my usage, the imagination is productive of the real, and the real is coextensive with the imaginary.

3. F. Max Müller is typically credited with launching the discipline of the history of religions. His role as the father, along with the anthropologist E. B. Tylor, of the modern scientific study of religion or *Religionswissenschaft* is undisputed in the contemporary field of comparative religious studies. Interestingly, what seems to have escaped notice in this scholarship is the role played by the *Wissenschaft des Judentums* in inaugurating the analytic and scientific study of religion. After all, the significant writings of Ganz, Zunz, and Wolf preceded Müller's, Tylor's, and Monier-Williams's by approximately fifty years. Why is there no mention of the scientific, philologically based, scholarship of the *Wissenschaft* thinkers in the origins of the discipline of the history of religions? Why, in fact, do we find accounts and narratives of the *Wissenschaft des Judentums* only in provincial histories of the Jews or Jewish studies, whereas the discipline of *Religionswissenschaft* is portrayed as generic and universal in its hermeneutic power? One might argue, as I do, that the latter's claim to universality is importantly linked with its provincial origins in the Christian Enlightenment.

4. These so-called Hep! Hep! riots drew their name from an antisemitic rallying cry supposedly dating back to the Crusades. "Hep" was formed acrostically from the initials of the words *Hierosolyma est perdita* ("Jerusalem is lost").

5. Cited in Eduard Gans, "A Society to Further Jewish Integration," in *The Jew in the Modern World,* ed. Paul Mendes-Flohr and Jehuda Reinharz (New York: Oxford University Press, 1980), 192.

6. Michael Meyer, *Response to Modernity: A History of the Reform Movement in Judaism* (Detroit: Wayne State University Press, 1988), 74.

7. Cited in Michael A. Meyer, *The Origins of the Modern Jew* (Detroit: Wayne State University Press, 1967), 173.

8. Cited in Immanuel Wolf, "On the Concept of a Science of Judaism," in Mendes-Flohr, and Reinharz, *Jew in the Modern World,* 194.

9. Ibid., 195.

10. Ibid.

11. Peter Van Der Veer, ed., *Conversion to Modernities: The Globalization of Christianity* (New York: Routledge, 1995).

12. Richard Popkin, "Polytheism, Deism, and Newton," in James Force and Richard Popkin, eds., *Essays on the Context, Nature, and Influence of Isaac Newton's Theology* (Dordrecht: Kluwer Academic Publishers, International Archives of the History of Ideas, 1990), 27.

13. Peter Harrison, *"Religion" and the Religions in the English Enlightenment* (Cambridge: Cambridge University Press, 1990), 28.

14. Lord Herbert believed the teaching of the true *Catholic Church* is contained in the following five propositions, which he outlined in *De Veritate*: (1) that there is a supreme God; (2) that God is to be worshipped; (3) that virtue and piety are the most important part of religious practice; (4) that we must repent our wickedness; (5) that there is reward or punishment after this life. (Harrison, *"Religion,"* 66–67).

15. I am grateful to Peter Harrison for this insight; cited in Harrison, *"Religion."*

16. Cited in Talal Asad, *Genealogies of Religion: Discipline and Reasons of Power in Christianity and Islam* (Baltimore: Johns Hopkins University Press, 1993), 42.

17. This story is cited in Ismar Elbogen, "A Century of Wissenschaft des Judentums," in Alfred Jospe, ed., *Studies in Jewish Thought: An Anthology of German Jewish Scholarship* (Detroit: Wayne State University Press, 1981), 34.

Toward a Postzionist Discourse

Laurence J. Silberstein

One of the most significant cultural effects of Zionism has been to displace the previously dominant religious notions of Jewish culture and identity.[1] Challenging the basic assumptions of a European Jewry that understood its collective identity in religious terms, Zionism constructed the discourse that enabled a secular Jewish identity. "The new Hebrew," a product of the secular cultural discourse of a community living in its own land, replaced "the Jew," now viewed as a product of the religious discourse of exile. Judaism itself was transformed by the new discourse of Jewish nationalism from a divinely ordained body of beliefs, norms, and practices into a humanly created, secular-national culture.[2]

Eschewing an identity derived from religious beliefs and practices, the Zionists constructed a notion of "the Jewish people," Jewish history, and Jewish identity. This identity was, in turn, grounded in the new secular construct of Jewish peoplehood and the secularized narratives of the Jewish past. Thus, the zionist theorist Ahad Haam valued "the Jew who loves his people, its literature, and its cultural heritage and yearns for its renewal, but who is a free thinker in the full sense of the term" more highly than the religious believer who lived his or her Jewish life as a divine commandment.[3] In contrast to other formulations of Jewish identity, Zionism's notion of identity was rooted neither in genetics nor in religious beliefs and practices but, rather, in one's relation to the Jewish past and to cultural values and practices that were designated as "Jewish."

Within zionist discourse, the constructed entity known as "the Jewish people" or "the Jewish nation" was conceived of as something natural. As a "natural" entity, in the terms of nineteenth-century European knowledge production, "the Jewish people" was imagined as having an "essence." The basic characteristics of this people could be isolated, identified, and described. This notion of an essential jewishness included the assumption of a unified, cohesive entity that had a continuous existence in history, and whose basic characteristics did not change. This notion, informing virtually all contemporary writings on Jewish identity and Jewish history, is represented concisely in the official Proclamation of the State of Israel:

> The Land of Israel was the birthplace of the Jewish people. Here their spiritual, religious and national identity was formed. Here they achieved independence and created a culture of national and universal significance. . . . Exiled from Israel, the Jewish people remained faithful to it in all countries of their dispersion.[4]

In the context of this discourse, Judaism, the Jewish people, Jewish culture, and Jewish society all appear as coherent and identifiable objects.[5] And although many Zionists had (and have) diverse and sharply contested conceptions of Jewish identity and culture, they all spoke of it in terms of a common set of cultural characteristics. In other words, the identity and culture of "the Jewish people" (or nation) were imagined to have an essential, unchanging core.

In recent years, this essentialist approach to identity has been rendered problematic by feminists and other cultural critics. Zionist discourse, like other nationalist discourses, has been has been the subject of a two-stage critique.[6] First, critics question these conventional notions of identity, and seek to deconstruct the assumptions upon which such notions of identity are founded. Second, they seek to formulate an alternative, nonessentializing discourse of identity and community, one that attends to the conflicts in and discontinuities of communities and cultures. As feminist critic Linda Alcoff notes, identity can be understood "relative to a constantly shifting context, to a situation that included a network of elements involving others, the objective economic conditions, cultural and political institutions, ideologies, and so on."[7] The significant political implications of our notions of identity have been highlighted by advocates of this new, anti-essentializing discourse. As Virginia Dominguez observes:

> How we conceptualize ourselves, represent ourselves, objectify ourselves, matters not just because it is an interesting example of the relationship between being, consciousness, knowledge, reference, and social action, but at least as much because it is a statement about power. Social representations are dually constituted. They are simultaneously descriptive and prescriptive, presupposing and creative.[8]

The production of identity—of notions of who we are and how we differ from others—necessitates excluding or closing ourselves off from certain discourses and narratives; in other words, the production of identity entails acts of power. This is particularly evident in how we designate as "other" those individuals and groups whose discourse and narrative we reject as alien to "us." In the case of Zionism, European Jews constituted the "we." The exercise of power that created multiple "others" is evident in the exclusion of Palestinians and in the marginalization of Jews of Middle Eastern origin.[9] However, as Dominguez points out, rather than acknowledge the political implications of identity construction, we have conventionally treated it as a benign process. To recognize that the construction of our own group identity entails the power to constitute "others" is to acknowledge having more power than we may wish to have or be comfortable having.[10] Consequently, most discussions of Jewish identity avoid the issue of power.

The critique of essentialist notions of identity and the resulting efforts to formulate alternative conceptions have much to contribute to a postzionist critique of zionist formulations of identity, and to a rethinking of Jewish identity in general. Moreover, the significance of this critique extends beyond the borders of Israel and applies as well to Jews in the diaspora, where the influence of zionist discourse remains strong. As one observer, David Biale, recently commented: "Zionism, more in its contemporary Israeli incarnations than in its classical form, has become the underlying ideology of the diaspora Jews."[11]

As certain feminist critics effectively argue, essentialist notions of identity are grounded in outmoded assumptions about language, experience, and culture. As a result, these notions occlude the complex realities and effects of identity formation. As our discourses shift and as our social and cultural contexts change, so do the ways in which we perceive and position ourselves vis-à-vis these designations. We do not passively assume or accept an identity. Instead, through the narratives we relate and the actions we take, we participate in the production of our identities.[12]

When we apply these ideas to the case of Zionism and Jewish idenitity, we come to recognize that rather than view identities such as "zionist," "feminist," or "Jew" as natural givens, we should treat them as the products (or effects) of the social and cultural processes through which they are produced, disseminated, and maintained. Thus, rather than accept references to "the Jewish people" or "the Jewish nation" as natural and given, a postzionist critique emphasizes that Jewish identities have been fluid. It also shows how constructed categories such as "peoplehood" or "nation" have their own specific histories. In addition, to formulate a postzionist critique is to show that prevailing zionist notions have been shaped through a contested process.[13]

To engage in a postzionist critique also involves rethinking the processes that have produced certain unnatural distinctions, such as insider/outsider, self/other, Jew/non-Jew. These distinctions, which seem so naturally a part of the current cultural and political terrain, are in fact constructs. They are also the product of ongoing contestation. Recognizing this constructedness and contestation draws our attention to the processes by means of which Jewish discourse constructs "others," reifying, marginalizing or excluding them, both within and outside the Jewish community.

From a postzionist perspective, Judaism would be viewed not as a core of essential ideas or practices but as a dynamic, inherently conflicted discourse and practice in a continual state of flux. Rather than assume the coherence of a zionist construct of jewishness and Jewish history, we are led to examine critically the processes, political as well as cultural, that have generated, disseminated, and perpetuated that which we understand through a zionist frame to be "Jewish." Insofar as the "meaning" of Zionism and its conceptions of Jewish identity change with shifting discursive frameworks and cultural contexts, it might be preferable to speak of Zionisms and Judaisms.

However, this is not the prevailing way that issues of jewishness, Zionism, and Jewish identity are usually presented. Rather than focus on the constructed, contested, contingent character of zionist discourse, contemporary scholarship, media, and popular discussion commonly treat Zionism as the "true" interpretation of the political, social, and cultural conditions of modern Jewish life. Rather than situating Zionism as one among many competing discourses that define Judaism, Jewish identity, and Jewish history, most contemporary studies tend to treat Zionism as the natural outgrowth of Jewish historical experience, and as the realization of an essential vision or idea. But this is teleological; in point of fact, writing this kind of essentialist history is possible only within an already essentializing discourse such as the discourse that constructs "the Jewish people." Thus, the historical narrative in which Zionism (and its view of the specific Jewish relation to the "homeland") is the inevitable outcome of Jews' experiences is itself a product of the discourses from which Zionism was constructed.

The ongoing debates and struggles to define the limits of Jewish discourse and identity are the subjects for a postzionist discourse. The way is now open for discourses that are oppositional or counter to zionist discourse to be seen not as deviations or anomalies but as legitimate options. Such an approach also focuses on the social, cultural, and political processes by means of which certain zionist claims have come to be perceived as "natural," "given," "commonsensical," and "self-evident."

Actual and potential critics among Jews and Zionists may worry that the approach I advocate will undermine the stability and threaten the continuity of "the Jewish people." To critics of postzionism, the deconstruction of essentialist conceptions of Jewish culture, history, and identity contributes to the erosion of the collective life of the Jews. Although I understand such concerns, they are themselves grounded in the essential (or foundational) understanding of Jewish identity that has been the subject of my analysis. Criticisms such as these resemble those of some feminists who responded to the deconstruction of stable categories such as "woman" with concerns about the disruptive effects of this approach on feminist group action. In making this temporary analogy between Jews and women, I find the response of the philosopher Judith Butler helpful. Butler shows the fallacy in the claim that deconstruction is destructive. She argues that problematizing the prevailing concepts of identity does not mean that we can no longer claim specific positions, whether feminist, zionist, or Jewish:

> To deconstruct the subject is not to negate or throw away the concept; on the contrary, deconstruction implies only that we suspend all commitments to that to which the term "the subject" refers, and that we consider the linguistic functions it serves in the consolidation of authority. To deconstruct is not to negate or dismiss, but to call into question and, perhaps most importantly, to open up a term, like the subject, to a reusage or redeployment that previously has not been authorized.[14]

"To deconstruct is not to negate or dismiss, but to call into question." Calling into question the familiar zionist constructs of Jewish identity means opening up Jewishness to new prospects and politics. Following Butler, I argue that deconstructing essentialistic notions of Jewish identity and culture need not pose a threat to the survival of Jews. Instead, like Butler, I regard a deconstructive analysis of Zionism as a positive process that can have the effect of clearing space for new and more adequate formulations of Jewish identity and culture. Through "a reusage or redeployment that previously has not been authorized," a postzionist discourse will open up new possibilities for imagining and enacting Jewish identities.

Notes

1. The ensuing analysis is a preliminary effort at formulating an approach. It will be incorporated into a larger study of postzionist discourse in which I am currently engaged. In that study I shall draw from cultural studies and postmodern theory in an effort to frame recent debates in Israel about postzionism. At the same time, as this article reflects, this theoretical framework serves as the basis for an alternative approach to the interpretation of Zionism and its history.

2. Among the key figures shaping the new, secular conception of Jewish identity were Ahad Haam, Micah Yosef Berdichevski, and Yosef Haim Brenner. On the conceptions of the "new Hebrew" and the "new Jew," see Amnon Rubinstein, *The Zionist Dream Revisited* (New York: Schocken Books, 1984), chaps.1–2; and Amos Elon, *The Israelis: Founders and Sons* (New York: Holt, Rinehart & Winston, 1971), chap. 6. A discussion in Hebrew of the contrasting views of Ahad Haam, Berdichevski, and Brenner with an accompanying selection of relevant sources is found in Menahem Brinker, "Ahad Haam, Berdichevski, and Brenner: Three Secular Approaches to Obligatory Jewish Texts," *Kivunim: A Journal of Zionism and Judaism* 2 (1990): 7–24.

3. See Ahad Haam, *Kol kitve Ahad Haam* (Tel Aviv: Devir, 1947), 291–292. Ahad Haam also contrasted the "new Jew," who predicated his or her Jewishness on national feeling, with the "religious Jew," who predicated his or her jewishness on religious faith (308).

4. "Proclamation of the State of Israel," in *The Jew in the Modern World: A Documentary History*, ed. Paul R. Mendes-Flohr and Jehuda Reinharz (New York: Oxford University Press, 1980), 477. One of the few efforts to formulate an alternative, nonessentialist approach to the problem of Jewish group identity is Virginia Dominguez, *People as Subject, People as Object* (Madison: University of Wisconsin Press, 1989). Rather than taking concepts such as

people and peoplehood as natural givens, Dominguez problematizes them: "What is peoplehood? In what ways is it a representation, an objectification? How is it shaped, molded, altered, and perpetuated? And how can it help us learn about the very processes of objectification in which we all participate" (19). Dominguez's assumption is that "collective identities are conceptual representations masquerading as objects (positivities in Foucault's sense) and that they are in perpetual need of nurturing" (189). Other recent works that treat nationhood and peoplehood as socially constructed and culturally imagined include Benedict Anderson, *Imagined Communities* (London and New York: Verso, 1991); E. J. Hobsbawm, *Nations and Nationalism Since 1780* (Cambridge: Cambridge University Press, 1990); and Anthony D. Smith, *National Identity* (Reno: University of Nevada Press, 1991).

5. On the constitutive function of national discourse, see Homi K. Bhabha, "DissemiNation: Time, Narrative, and the Margins of the Modern Nation," in *Nation and Narration*, ed. Homi K. Bhabha (London and New York: Routledge, 1990), 291–322.

6. See Judith Butler, *Gender Trouble: Feminism and the Subversion of Identity* (New York: Routledge, 1990); Dorinne K. Kondo, *Crafting Selves: Power, Gender and Discourses in a Japanese Workplace* (Chicago: University of Chicago Press, 1990); and Joan Wallach Scott, "Experience," in *Feminists Theorize the Political*, ed. Judith Butler and Joan W. Scott (New York and London: Routledge, 1992), 22–40. A seminal treatment in the field of cultural studies is Stuart Hall, "Cultural Identity and Diaspora," in *Identity, Community, Culture, Difference*, ed. Jonathan Rutherford (London: Lawrence & Wishart, 1990), 222–237. An important postmarxist effort to formulate a nonessentialistic conception of community and identity is found in Ernesto Laclau and Chantal Mouffe, *Hegemony and Socialist Strategy: Towards a Radical Democratic Politics* (London: Verso, 1985). See also Laclau and Mouffe, "Post-Marxism Without Apologies," in *New Reflections on the Revolution of Our Time*, ed. Ernesto Laclau (London and New York: Verso, 1990), 3–40.

7. Linda Alcoff, "Cultural Feminism versus Post-structuralism: The Identity Crisis in Feminist Theory," *Signs: Journal of Women in Culture and Society* 13 (1988): 433.

8. Dominguez, *People as Subject*, 190.

9. Ibid., 70–191. For an overview of the treatment of these "others" in recent Israeli sociology, see Uri Ram, *The Changing Agenda of Israel Sociology: Theory, Ideology, & Identity* (Albany: SUNY Press, 1995), 97–117. Ram is one of the leading proponents of postzionism in Israel. One of the most powerful voices of the "other" in Israeli society is that of the Palestinian writer Anton Shammas. For a discussion of Shammas and reference to his writings, see my "Cultural Criticism, Ideology, and the Interpretation of Zionism: Toward a Post-Zionist Discourse," in *Postmodern Interpretations of Judaism: Deconstructive and Constructive Approaches*, ed. Steven Kepnes (New York: New York University Press, 1995)

10. Dominguez, *People as Subject*, 191.

11. David Biale, *Power and Powerlessness in Jewish History* (New York: Schocken Books, 1986), 190.

12. B. Honig argues for a performative conception in which identity is seen as constructed through the actions we perform. According to Honig, the self is an "agonistic, differentiated,

multiple, nonidentified being that is always becoming, always calling out for augmentation and amendment." See B. Honig, "Towards an Agonistic Feminism: Hannah Arendt and the Politics of Identity," in Butler and Scott, *Feminists Theorize the Political,* 232. Converging with the argument presented in this article, Honig argues that the performative notion opens up new possibilities and could lead to "the empowering discovery that there are many ways to do one's Jewishness" (231).

13. The most comprehensive attempt thus far to formulate a postzionist approach to Zionism and Jewish history, only recently available in English, is Boas Evron, *Jewish State or Israeli Nation* (Bloomington: Indiana University Press, 1995). This is a revised version of the Hebrew original, *HaHeshbon HaLeumi* (Tel Aviv: Devir, 1988). It should be noted, however, that Evron does not base his approach on the theoretical literature discussed here.

14. Judith Butler, "Contingent Foundations," in Butler and Scott, *Feminists Theorize the Political,* 15.

Finding a Language for Memories of the Future

Ammiel Alcalay

> The question is not linear, but spherical. The problem concerns the explosive impulses of the individual. Violence shoots its thousand arrows and pierces all that it encounters. It is no longer a question of clarifying the distinction between the feminine and the masculine, but of redefining the human species.
>
> Etel Adnan, *Of Cities and Women*

Beforehand

One summer on my way to the airport (New York/Paris/Tel Aviv), the driver from New Jerusalem Car Service, a native of Nablus, told me that after getting his American visa he stopped over—en route—in Jordan, Saudi Arabia, Iraq, and Syria (where his brother had finished electrical engineering at Damascus University). Now he was moving to Oregon. "For the girls," as he put it. His family ran a pastry shop in Nablus, but he gave the address of another, Abu Seer, on Granada Street, that he said was even better. As I got off the connecting bus in Paris, an extended Palestinian family, each by its own generation, made their way to the departure gate: three young boys with a huge boom box discussed its various features in the King's English; a sister, covered in a pale green head scarf, wore a Boyz 'N the Hood t-shirt; an older sister, wearing jeans, occasionally looked at a copy of the *Jerusalem Post* she was holding; the matriarch, a real villager, looked on, directing all to their respective duties. The relations between a family of Arab Jews, speaking French, Arabic, and Hebrew all at once, seemed just as precise and confused as both the language they were speaking *and* the Palestinian family working their way into the line before them. Once in the plane I notice a headline in the *European*, held by the larger half of a very large American couple: "The Terrible Price of a Joke Against Islam." I am reading *Woman's Body, Woman's Word: Gender and Discourse in Arabo-Islamic Writing.*[1] As the food comes, the other half of the couple turns to me, saying: "I couldn't resist, but you can't expect to sit next to a woman and not have her ask you about what you're reading." She proceeds to ask from "what point of view" the book is written and I explain that the author takes classical medieval texts and juxtaposes them to contemporary Arab feminist writers. With a conspiratorial smile, she says: "But isn't that an oxymoron?" We're somewhere over the Alps. I put down the food, feeling queasy. It's not until we're over Elba that I start to feel better.

1. Ghosts

The inherent push and pull of a process that includes the struggle of redefinition and changing space—personal, cultural, geographic, social, political—often leaves language by the wayside, as if the work that needs to be done were that easy and you could simply rely on hand-me-downs. Yosef Ibn Chikitilla, a Jewish mystic born in Castille in 1248, wrote:

> A person must understand and know that from the earth unto the firmament there is no free space, but it is all filled by a multitude of hosts; those that are pure, possessing kindness and mercy, and below them the impure beings, harmful and accusing, but all of them contingent, about to materialize. And there is no free space from the earth unto the firmament, but it is all filled with multitudes, those for peace and those for war, those for good and those for evil, those for life and those for death.[2]

As unfashionable as it might be to pronounce, language is substance, the very thread and texture of historical material. Not only does it fill space as "a multitude of hosts" (in the language of "then"), but these very multitudes make up the roads not taken, the antithetical, oppositional, and alternative readings that are the unexorcised ghosts of contingent meaning.

2. Looking Back

The first fable involves the pain of childbirth and expulsion from the garden, the central human story of exile from the womb and birth into the world, uncovered, revealed, and exposed, our first diaspora, singular but part of the race's collective experience. And we all know the price exacted for turning to look back; as the Israeli poet Bracha Serri writes: "I am the daughter of Lot. / Silent like my mother who became a pillar of salt / a pillar of remembrance."[3] But such "memorials" can also open new space within the dense multitude of hosts.

In the contemporary Israeli poet Shelley Elkayam's poem, "Yes Indeed I'll Answer God," the narrator (identified only as "I will ever be what I now am") switches gender within the body of the text. The woman who has invited readers into the garden of poetry (where poetry is identified as part of the covenant between Moses and the Hebrews, when the Lord specifies that the Law, "this poem may be a witness for me against the children of Yisra'el"),[4] suddenly "remembers." Such remembrance extracts the root of the word (*ZaKHaR*) and binds it to male experience:

Therefore, for the sake of the liberty you gained:
All ceremonies of the covenant
are memorial.
In Remembrance, of course.
Like a garden bell. Accordingly, say,
I forgive my father for doing things without questioning my desire.
Look, after all, the ledger's open.
Ceremonial testaments inscribed in the body.
A man and his covenant
carved in his form.

The implications of this are many: perhaps the very nature of "remembrance" has been dictated and defined by the constituent elements that make up its "male" version. This includes, most obviously, the powerlessness of a baby being subjected to a ritual wound. Thus, the very nature of what we have come to consider or accept as "memory" is also inscribed within the body of language and must be judged, for as Elkayam's poem begins, "And this is the judgement."[5]

In an essay called "The Contemporary Logos," the American poet and novelist Fanny Howe writes:

> Just as, in one sentence, *you* cannot turn into *she*, *run* cannot turn into *ran*, you can't, in your desire to be free of a certain moment, be somewhere else immediately. This is the judgement of time, history and gender as it is reflected in any written line.
>
> And just as the sentence contains only as much language as it can bear, so can it be viewed as an image of the pressure of temporality. The facing of what is in front of you, by sorting out what is behind, goes into the careful syntactic processing of a sentence. Law and grammar must coexist in that cell. This coexistence requires the exaction of judgement.
>
> Poetic language goes to the extreme with this exaction, and the more extreme it is, the more otherly it becomes. It transforms the state of being lost into that of being free, by making judgement on judgement itself.[6]

Here we can see the power of possibility in ringing changes ("Like a garden bell") upon the multitude of ghosts that not only inhabit the spaces we traverse but also are the very building blocks determining both our perceptions of that space and the routes through it we deem navigable. We work our way back through texts and memories, retracing Hagar's footsteps in the sand, looking under bushes that never burned, thinking we were one place before finding out we were another. To want to retrieve or recuperate memory (*kids with schoolbags running after a trolley in Cairo, late afternoon; cutting curves on the way to Abu George's in Bethlehem, past midnight, after a show at al-Hakawati; Easter in Athens*), would be to concede defeat. As al-Ghazali wrote: "There is no hope in returning to a traditional faith after it has once been abandoned, since the essential condition for holders of a traditional faith is not to know they are traditionalists." An old story: if those who can grasp things (the "masses," the "crowd," the "people of the land") only through the imaginative faculties (not the "intellect" and "reason") are given an argument that leads to a loss of faith, it's nevertheless obvious that they've understood the argument. Such thinking (or "engineering") assumes "progress," so the custodians of order (take your pick) exert "caution" by creating hierarchies, withholding information, and mystifying terms of relation and description.

3. "Against Wisdom as Such"

The places that haunt, the moments that steal back into consciousness when you least expect them, make up a counterlife, like the earliest memories that are so much a part of the way we act we can no longer remember them. It takes so long to learn, not only with the head but with the head and the heart, just how false the models of sophistication and complexity we have been given are. In "Notes Towards an Oppositional Poetics," Erica Hunt writes:

> The languages used to preserve domination are complex and sometimes contradictory. Much of how they operate to anesthetize desire and resistance is invisible; they are wedded to our common sense; they are formulaic without being intrusive, entirely natural—"no marks on the body at all." These languages contain us, and we are simultaneously bearers of the codes of containment. Whatever damage or distortion the codes inflict on our subjectively elastic conception of ourselves, socially we act in an echo chamber of the features ascribed to us.[7]

It is in this echo chamber that so much "critical discourse" seems to reverberate, undaunted in its refusal to recognize the need for what the Palestinian poet Mahmoud Darwish has called a "memory for forgetfulness." While this kind of "memory" might only seem like an antidote to remembrance inscribed upon the body through a ritual wound, it also points to other intentions, closer to what the Egyptian Jewish writer Jacqueline Kahanoff suggested might be "the covenant of Sarah and Hagar":

> We need not be bound forever by the terms set by our ancient myths and holy scriptures. While recognizing the crucial role they play in shaping us, we might interpret

> them within the context in which we now live. By objectively prodding those areas where our myths clash, we may become more rational in appraising the passionately irrational element at the core of most human actions, where the feeling of identity is concerned.[8]

In thinking through the series of questions that this text is supposed to be a response to, I could not help but think that many myths are not even ancient and much of what has come to be considered scripture not holy at all. Rather, they are "prerequisites," in the literal sense of the term, "dis*courses*" that need to be "mastered" before "alternatives" can be proposed. Perhaps I am as guilty as anyone. We are operating, at this point, within systems. The question, it seems to me, is how much pressure, isolation, or uncertainty each and every one of us trying to address the issues at hand is prepared to bear in order to disrupt the stranglehold that even, and perhaps most insidiously, "adjusted" academic discourse exerts upon what is deemed legitimate work. We must be willing not only to insist but come to expect a multiplicity of idioms and a true democracy of both sources and "proofs" that inform our explorations out of the echo chamber. As the American poet Bernadette Mayer put it:

> This final page of my notes is about deception, a tree falls. There is the blank face of indifference in the afternoon of staring happily and thoughtlessly into your child, the ultimate learning, there is the face of hardheartedness, the adorned face of the confusion of having been taken by storm before thought could leap up, take you higher, and there is the face of wickedness, again the face of my eduction upon me which I walk backwards like a devil on a moral precipice to cast off.[9]

4. The Return

In the end, Brer Rabbit always outsmarts Brer Wolf. In one of my son's favorite bedtime stories, Brer Rabbit tricks Brer Wolf into thinking that houses talk. Once he rousts Brer Wolf from his hiding place and safely reinstalls his family in the house, Brer Rabbit triumphantly proclaims: "Houses don't talk, you know that."[10] But no matter how hard we try, our words stick to places and those places hold our words, our way of being in the world. By now I've almost lost the sound of colored vowels I overheard uttered by the women of Bukhara and Kurdistan while waiting for buses in the Katamonim. The qualities of those vowels, nurtured by time, the particular timbre of sky and clarity of air in which they were imbibed and transmitted, are fading too. People *can* be transformed, for better or worse, memories distorted and rechanneled. Nothing proves the spirit indomitable. Defeat is entirely possible. As Etel Adnan writes:

> They teach the children to obey: it is a castration. They teach the children the names of cities that have disappeared: they make them love death. There should only be one

school, the one where you learn the future . . . without even any students. Located in the guts of the species. Where you would say:

"If you could step out of your mind and walk in the fields, what would you do?"

"Nothing."

"What do you mean? If you could step out of your mind and walk in the fields, where would you go?"

"Nowhere."

"What do you mean?"

"I myself would like to know."[11]

I am in awe of journeys that stay their course, that breach no concession to roles that are so readily made to be filled, that resonate against the echo chamber. Like the *Mountainous Journey* taken by the Palestinian poet Fadwa Tuqan:

Enough for me to die on her earth
be buried in her
to melt and vanish into her soil
then sprout forth as a flower
played with by a child from my country
Enough for me to remain
in my country's embrace
to be in her close as a handful of dust
  a sprig of grass
      a flower.[12]

The layers such a poem traverses are almost unfathomable, given the simplicity of utterance and the use of a language that can be taken so many ways, once removed then reconnected to the context of the poet's life and the role prepared for her even before birth. Such a language is a shield against opportunism of all kinds, against the nationalism of hotel rooms or the intellectual production of conferences, where what the Algerian writer Assia Djebar has called "the rebuilding of ancestral barriers"[13] keeps taking place. Posing as absolute submission, the "enough" of this poem is a record of bitter determination to sow the seeds of a new resistance, one that embellishes the courage of perseverance with the raw material of the body, given over to the earth in final union, just as some terraced olive groves blend imperceptibly into the hills before slowly fading off into the desert, just as a house stands sentry against the outside world while re-creating a paradise that absorbs all the shocks of cruelty and tenderness exchanged between men and women, parents and children, brothers and sisters, within its very walls. Insisting on the logic of a language and poetry that "makes judgement on judgement itself" remains central to human existence and reason; it has to do with what waiting means and how we occupy time rather than space, what we do while we wait during the greater migration that is life itself in this world as we witness the effects of absence, the gaping wounds sutured over so readily by histories produced and consumed as governing realities. But houses still stand and even if we know they don't talk, we still try to speak to them, to speak for them, to speak for ourselves and those no longer with us, fixed steadfast in our memory of the future.

Notes

1. Fedwa Malti-Douglas, *Woman's Body, Woman's Word: Gender and Discourse in Arabo-Islamic Writing* (Princeton: Princeton University Press, 1991).

2. Yosef Ibn Chikitilla, *Shaare Or* (Gates of Light), ed. Yosef Ben Shlomo, 2 vols. (Jerusalem: Mossad Bialik, n.d.), 54; my translation.

3. In Ammiel Alcalay, ed., *Keys to the Garden: Israeli Writing in the Middle East,* trans. Yonina Borvick (Madison, NJ: Fairleigh Dickinson University Press, 1994), 335; special issue of the *Literary Review* 37.2 (1994).

4. Deut. 31:19; translation from *The Holy Scriptures* (Jerusalem: Koren, 1977), 250.

5. Alcalay, *Keys to the Garden,* 332–335; my translation. A revised and expanded version of *Keys to the Garden* will be published in May 1996 by City Lights Books in San Francisco.

6. Fanny Howe, "The Contemporary Logos," in *Code of Signals: Recent Writings in Poetics,* ed. Michael Palmer (Berkeley: North Atlantic Books, 1983), 54.

7. Erica Hunt, "Notes Towards an Oppositional Poetics," in *The Politics of Poetic Form,* ed. Charles Bernstein (New York: Roof Books, 1990), 199–200.

8. From unpublished manuscript by Jacqueline Kahanoff.

9. Bernadette Mayer, *Eruditia ex memoria* (Lenox: Angel Hair Books, 1977), unpaginated.

10. Linda Hayward, *Hello, House* (New York: Random House, 1988), 32.

11. Etel Adnan, "In the Heart of the Heart of Another Country," *Mundus Artium* 10.1 (1977): 31.

12. Fadwa Tuqan, *A Mountainous Journey: A Poet's Autobiography,* trans. Naomi Shihab Nye, from Arabic (St. Paul: Graywolf, 1990), 231.

13. Assia Djebar, "A Forbidden Glimpse, A Broken Sound," trans. J. M. McDougal, in *Women and Family in the Middle East: New Voices of Change,* ed. Elizabeth Warnock Fernea (Austin: University of Texas Press, 1985), 350. Originally in Assia Djebar, *Femmes d'Alger dans leur appartement* (Paris: des femmes, 1980), 167–89.

On Seams and Seamlessness

Rebecca Alpert

When Laura Levitt, my friend and colleague at Temple University, asked me to participate in this forum, my first response was a categorical no. Laura and I have talked about our different perspectives on postmodern approaches to Jewish feminism infrequently over the past several years. The conversations always end with our restating our differences, agreeing to disagree. Because my feelings are so strong about this subject, I was reluctant to have this conversation in public. Yet, Laura persuaded me to consider participating, in full knowledge that this would be an airing of our differences, and I have taken the risk of doing so. My contribution, a letter to Laura, is an effort to bring my love for her into the context of what is, for me, a passionate and acrimonious intellectual debate that has important implications for the future of Jewish feminism.

January 1995

Dear Laura,

I have read and reread your questions and Miriam's essay many times now, looking for a way to engage in honest conversation. It is not an easy task. I have strong and positive feelings about our friendship and admire the work you have done. But these questions and this essay perplex me deeply. I fear we do not speak the same language and as a result efforts at communication may not be fruitful. Yet I am compelled to respond to you, to articulate for you what I don't understand, what I think is not unique about this work, what I disagree with, and where our visions part.

I don't understand why you get so passionate about categories, definitions, and terms. Really, aren't there greater and more significant conflicts than those about what specific words mean? When you argue over words, you run the risk of engaging in debates about words only. How I translate my beliefs into action is more salient than the words I use to describe those actions and beliefs.

The words you use get in the way of my understanding as well. Why must you invent words like *tropes* and *signifiers*? Do you really expect people outside the academy to benefit from your work when they can't understand what you're talking about? The beauty of the feminist enterprise has been its ability to make connections between activists and academicians. Likewise, the Jewish feminist enterprise has enabled people who practice Judaism—in whatever way—to gain access to Jewish feminist ideas emanating from the academy. However do we justify speaking in a language that is at best self-referential and at worst elitist, as well as alienating to those we want to reach?

The other thing I don't understand is why you are so deeply disturbed by the Enlightenment. I believe, as I'm sure you do, that the Enlightenment served a useful purpose, opening up new ways of thinking about the world and about God. Without these major changes in the possibilities for Jewish life in Europe and North America, we could not be asking the questions we ask today. Yet you invariably look at the Enlightenment as the embodiment of all you disdain. I'm often troubled when I see you repeating the mistake that you assign to the Enlightenment, that of creating "binaries." In effect, you turn Enlightenment consciousness into an "Other" against which you can react. I just don't understand your need to do this.

Although I appreciate some of your insights, *I don't see what's so unique about them.* Hasn't feminism for years contended that knowledge is partial, and that what is wrong with traditional approaches is that they universalize Man? And didn't feminists come years ago to the realization that universalizing Woman was also problematic? Acceptance of difference among us is an important feature of Jewish feminism as we have struggled for years to accept one another's differences in religious perspectives, political orientation, sexuality, cultural background, class, and so on.

We certainly agree that you cannot "add women and stir" to bring questions about gender into the conversation. Miriam acknowledges this as a truism. Her solution of teaching Seltzer and Baskin side-by-side, and teaching historiography as well as history is a useful strategy, but she is not unique in her approach. Others have been finding ways to make gender a crucial factor in the teaching of Jewish history and other subjects for quite some time.

It is also not a new insight that students of Jewish history have glossed over the subversive and radical elements in the Jewish past, in the effort to make Judaism appear to be seamless. The feminist project of looking at the past means always searching out what is hidden. Miriam's analogy about the construction site is a good one. I would be surprised if any feminist scholar disagreed.

But I also disagree with much of what you say. Understanding complexity, looking at the building blocks is crucial to the production of knowledge. But messiness is not a virtue, it is merely a part of the process of rebuilding. My profound disagreement with your perspective is that you seem to think you're finished with a project when you have exposed all the wiring. What is important is to expose the structure and then to rebuild the building, retaining always the awareness of what it looked like inside. Living with the contradiction that a seemingly seamless garment is in fact made up of seams—that should be the goal.

I am also deeply troubled by Miriam's approach to the midrashic and historical methods of inquiry. In the first place, the historical method of Jewish scholarship is much more a product of modernity than is midrash. The *maskilim* were the first to value historical research, and the first postbiblical histories of the Jews, other than those of the first-century writer Josephus, were produced by *Wissenschaft* scholars. In contrast, midrash has received scant attention in nonfeminist modern Jewish thought. The work of Yerushalmi that so disturbs Miriam was not a move to discount history but to render another dimension to the historical enterprise.

Miriam contends that history is more accessible than midrash, "distributed orally throughout various levels and types of schools." But she is wrong about this. History is much less accessible and widely distributed than is the telling of stories. Hanukkah is the perfect example. To the person who knows little of Judaism, Hanukkah does not commemorate a historical event; it is more likely to be understood as the "miracle of the oil." Because of its hold on the popular imagination, midrash is a much more effective means of making the feminist project accessible to many people.

But accessibility doesn't seem to be a goal. Miriam disagrees with the idea that feminism should be providing the opportunity for all women to speak. Aware of the problem that not all women speak as feminists, she abandons the essential commitment to providing opportunities for all women's voices to be heard. This is the most objectionable dimension of her analysis. Surely, feminists want to give women an opportunity to say what we are thinking, even if we disagree, and even if much of what we say is bound up in a masculinist perspective. How else can we create change if not by our commitment to providing opportunities for everyone to have her voice heard, for dialogue to exist?

Midrash succeeds in presenting an alternative to historical research, and to the real "dominant discourse" in Judaism, halakhah. The creation of feminist midrash has been an amazing process of re-creating our people's history and questioning Jewish "norms." Jewish life is based much more on a collective memory and perception, on stories of how we came to be, than Miriam acknowledges. In Jewish communities all across North America, Jewish feminists have made women part of the Jewish landscape by telling stories about Sarah's role in the binding of Isaac, making Miriam comparable to Moses as a leader of the Jewish people, recognizing Vashti as a possible role model alongside Esther, and reexamining the significance of Ruth as ancestor to converts and paradigm of passionate friendship between women. These stories have done more to shape a feminist consciousness than a hundred archaeological digs. This is true because these stories rely on imaginative reconstruction. They can be written by anyone, of any age, including children. Again, accessibility is a crucial component for creating change.

My final problem with your approach is that *I don't see how you expect to bring about your vision for Jewish feminism.* Miriam says that your goal is to make the "marginalization of women and gender intellectually impossible." The goal sounds right, but how you will get there isn't clear. Miriam suggests at the end of her essay that her linguistic moves don't change things very much; an engendered Judaism still retains the separation of the categories gender and Judaism. She doesn't have an answer to her own question about what critical tools are really necessary to explain how genders are engendered.

But I wonder if those are the right questions. What does this perspective add that isn't already being discussed in progressive and feminist Jewish circles beyond inaccessible language and hypercritical arguments? An exciting vision for Jewish feminism is to continue to cast a critical eye and at the same time to create events and images that have and will make Judaism look different. We must learn to live with the contradictions within what will inevitably be an imperfect enterprise.

We must also be sure that we do not make gender the only category we discuss in Jewish contexts. Our differences are about geography and age, sexuality and race, physical ability and religious preferences. And they are also about approaches—orthodox, zionist, secular, reconstructionist, postmodern, feminist, progressive, and any combination of these and others. We need to learn to live with the contradiction that we can both disagree and live in harmony, and with the idea that there is room in the Jewish world for us all.

So I write in the spirit of dialogue and in the hope that the angry and hurt tones these conversations across generations have begun to take do not keep us from seeing the vision we share of living and changing Judaism. Those of us who have been engaged in this effort for a long time feel frustrated when we look around and see that not as much has changed in the Jewish community as we would have liked, given our efforts and struggles. And we also feel anger when our work is judged harshly by those in the next generation of Jewish feminists, who we hoped would find within our work the blueprint to continue the process of change. The only solution to the problem is to keep talking and working in concert. Although I began this effort feeling uncomfortable about arguing with you in public, I end the process seeing the advantage of keeping the channels of communication open.

In hope that this discussion can continue in peace and friendship,

Rebecca

Notes from the Second Generation

Beth S. Wenger

In 1987, while I was in my first year of graduate school, an article in the *New York Times Magazine* declared that feminist criticism, "once a sort of illicit half sister in the academic world," had "assumed a respectable place in the family order."[1] For me and for most of my colleagues in graduate school, such firm proclamations seemed plausible. I had studied women's history in college and participated in graduate seminars that usually included some discussion of gender. I belong to a generation of teachers and scholars who did not pioneer but rather have inherited a new arena of academic inquiry.

To be sure, we were legacies to an emerging, not a fully defined, intellectual discipline. In a span of only two decades, women's history has progressed through at least two distinct stages. What began as an effort to provide new information about women and reclaim women's experience for the historical record has evolved into a more complex consideration of the role of gender in shaping categories of knowledge, tradition, and power. This enormous conceptual growth in women's history informed the intellectual initiation of my generation of scholars. Yet, having arrived in the academy during the second stage in the development of women's studies, having benefited from female teachers as role models, and having had access to a growing body of scholarly literature about women, our generation has not yet fulfilled the optimistic predictions once announced so confidently in the *New York Times*. Feminist scholarship has indeed become part of academic discourse, but its relationship to other disciplines and its impact upon the master narratives of history remain inconsistent, often contested, and, in the worst cases, even nonexistent.

Few fields have been slower to integrate gender analysis than Jewish Studies. A traditionally text-based area of inquiry, centered on intellectual rather than social history, and lacking a rigorous theoretical approach, Jewish Studies has lagged noticeably behind other fields in acknowledging gender studies as a legitimate enterprise. Nevertheless, in my own discipline of Jewish history, there has recently been a remarkable increase in works about Jewish women. From studies of Jewish women in the ancient world through works that address the differing gendered experiences of Jewish modernity, the past ten years have witnessed an enormous production of Jewish feminist scholarship.[2] The literature of Jewish women's history has certainly increased at a rapid pace, but I am not convinced that Jewish historians have taken significant steps toward integrating gender as a category of analysis. How much have gender perspectives transformed our writing and teaching of Jewish history? Do our students leave our courses with an understanding of gender as integral or rather as marginal to Jewish experience? Although our knowledge of Jewish women's lives continues to grow, how much is that knowledge changing the ways we conceive and present Jewish history? In the following pages, I want to raise a few of my greatest concerns about the current status of gender studies within Jewish history.

Women as an Objectified Category

During the past year, I have attended two Jewish history conferences, both organized by leading male scholars, that made conscious attempts to include papers about women and gender. Without a doubt, the effort reflected the organizers' recognition of the progress of feminist scholarship and their commitment to support new work on gender. During the conferences, within selected panels, participants discussed topics ranging from Jewish women's religious experience to their social and political roles. However, when the panels "about women" concluded, the conversation turned back to an unexamined male-centered view of Jewish history, without any attention to gender issues. At both conferences, sessions about Jewish historiography, religious leadership, and social history proceeded without any consideration of female actors or gender analysis. This exemplifies the prevailing state of gender studies within Jewish history. The annual Association for Jewish Studies (AJS) conferences contain an increasing number of papers "about women" each year, but gender topics remain relatively rare on panels not devoted to women's issues. Our male colleagues have come to the point of recognizing the need to place women on the historical agenda, and, to be fair, some of them have truly incorporated gendered perspectives into their own work. However, the discourse within Jewish history remains premised on a model that addresses women as a separate and enclosed category rather than considering gender as a social construct signifying power and as an epistemological means of defining tradition and change. As long as Jewish women continue to remain an objectified "it" within Jewish history, we will continue to perpetuate the notion of women as an isolated class.

The boundaries separating gender study from "mainstream" Jewish history extend beyond the problematic organization of conference sessions. The traditional focus of Jewish scholarship and the consequences of choosing to work on gender topics remain serious obstacles. As graduate students in the late 1980s and early 1990s, those of us who chose to write dissertations about women and gender were often warned that we might be jeopardizing our success on the job market, particularly in Jewish Studies programs. Such biases may be weakening, but scholars who write "about women" continue to be regarded as part of an intellectual discourse isolated from the larger dialogue of Jewish Studies. After I had chosen to write a dissertation inclusive of but not exclusively devoted to women or gender, I can recall informing a former teacher of my dissertation topic and listening to him express his surprise that I had not chosen to work on a "women's topic." A few articles "about women" early in my graduate career had already placed me in a distinct class of Jewish scholars. Despite significant progress in the field within the past decade, gender scholarship remains an objectified "Other" within Jewish Studies. Gender analysis has not yet penetrated and certainly has not sufficiently challenged the ongoing legitimacy of the traditional core of Jewish Studies.

The boundaries keeping gender study from full integration within Jewish scholarship are not only methodological but also political. Although other professional academic organizations have made attempts to remedy gender inequity, the Association for Jewish Studies has been reluctant to initiate such steps. The Women's Caucus of the AJS has struggled for formal recognition within the organization, and the AJS has only just begun formulating guidelines for proper interviewing and hiring procedures. These examples reveal the serious political barriers to women within Jewish Studies that still exist in the 1990s. The professional standards and practices of Jewish Studies organizations cannot and should not be separated from the problems of scholarly inquiry. If feminist theory has taught us anything, it is that the political dimensions of scholarship are inextricably intertwined with the production of knowledge.[3] We should not allow the scholarly accomplishments of recent years to obscure the continuing resistance to gender equality and representation in Jewish professional organizations and its role in perpetuating indifference to gender within the field.

The Problem of Marginality

As Miriam Peskowitz persuasively describes in her essay, even those of us trained in and committed to gender analysis have struggled with integrating that approach in our teaching. During the past two years while I have been teaching at the University of Pennsylvania, one of my chief duties has been to teach the survey course in modern Jewish history. In a course that rapidly covers several centuries and considers Jewish life in many different national contexts, there is little opportunity for depth and detail in any area. The pace of a survey makes the challenge of presenting gender as an integral component of modern Jewish experience particularly daunting. Because the master narrative of Jewish modernity has been defined so decisively by *Wissenschaft des Judentums* (the Science of Judaism), traditional presentations of modern Jewish history generally privilege intellectual and religious developments along with the contributions of elites over the social consequences of modernization and the experience of non-elites, including women.[4] The difficulty of teaching an undergraduate course is that sufficient attention must be paid to the key turning points of Enlightenment, emancipation, and religious reform without obscuring the role of women and the importance of gender in shaping these broad movements.

Newer works of social history have helped to redress the traditional bias of modern Jewish history and have facilitated the inclusion of women and gender in the narrative of Jewish modernity. Because of the enormous production of literature about Jewish women, it is now possible to assign appropriate readings to students so that they can study the experience of women in conjunction with other facets of the modern Jewish experience. For example, Chava Weissler's work on Jewish women's private expressions of spirituality can be assigned alongside material about Kabbalah and Hasidism.[5] Marion Kaplan and Paula Hyman have both produced studies that discuss the distinct roles of women in the process of Jewish assimilation and highlight the ways that modernization varied according to gender.[6] These and other scholarly works have certainly enabled us to teach more sophisticated, gender-inclusive survey courses.

However, I have been concerned that despite my attempt to present women as integral to Jewish modernity, students too often leave the course continuing to consider women's experience as marginal. The problem arises in part from the nature of the literature about women and gender. More often than not, the contributions of gender scholarship have been in the realm of social history, examining private life, the home and family, and the domestic sphere as the central locus of women's life. Such scholarship has been invaluable and reflects the pioneering role that Jewish social historians have assumed in exploring gender issues, but it has allowed public processes such as political emancipation and religious reform to be relegated to accounts devoid of gender analysis. New research and conceptual reevaluations of public as well as private experiences may correct some of these difficulties, but there are greater issues at stake. Personally, I have tried to avoid the term *marginal* in my teaching. Once I tell students that women (or any other group) are marginal, I have noticed that they internalize the view that women are not a part of "mainstream" Jewish history. As much as I attempt to destroy the notion of a normative Jewish experience and to emphasize the limited scope of emancipation debates and the small number of Jews involved in the Haskalah and reform movements, undergraduates seem more drawn to these phenomena than to the social history of modern Jewry. I continue to stress the importance of the approach of social history, but I have consciously omitted the term *marginal*, so often applied only to women, because it seems to underscore the phenomenon of otherness and objectification that is in my view one of the most pressing issues in contemporary Jewish feminist scholarship. Similarly, I have tried to avoid the terms *public* and *private* without a lengthy explanation of the shifting boundaries of this dichotomy, for such conceptions also encourage a model of center and periphery that perpetuates the notion of women as outsiders in the essential processes of Jewish modernity.

The solution, of course, will lie not in the use of a few words but in the theoretical reevaluation of the field. The term *marginality* is only one way that we, as scholars, have encoded the isolation of women in our own teaching and research. The success of gender analysis will come in our ability to reconceptualize the framework of modern Jewish history, to redefine our understanding of such key movements as Enlightenment, emancipation, and reform in a manner inclusive of gender. In sum, we need more works that are not companion pieces "about women" to place on our reading lists but strategies for rethinking the categories of Jewish modernity. This scholarly process has already begun with the publication of a few pathbreaking works, but the process is far from complete and remains a future challenge for us as teachers and also as scholars.[7]

The Time Lag Within Jewish Scholarship

Most of my contemporaries who engage in work on gender have either been trained by the handful of senior feminist Jewish historians in the field or, more commonly, have studied with American or European women's historians. Conceptual creativity and advances in gender analysis still emerge most frequently outside the realm of Jewish Studies. Most of us continue to bring what we have learned in other disciplines to the arena of Jewish research. This may be the core of the problem in Jewish Studies. Although other fields have embraced a more nuanced and rigorous approach to gender study, Jewish Studies seems (with a few notable exceptions) to be stalled in an earlier stage of feminist scholarship that seeks only to insert women in the gaps of historical narratives. Many of my colleagues believe, or perhaps hope, that because Jewish history has consistently made slower progress in theory and methodology than other historical disciplines, our field will soon follow the lead of others and move beyond a conceptual framework that considers gender only in its narrowest sense as topics "about women." Such hopes follow a certain logic; women's history began later within Jewish Studies, so that we might expect that scholars will take longer to employ gender critiques in examining the foundations of Jewish knowledge. However, I am concerned about relying upon such expectations for improvement. Despite the remarkable progress of the last decade, resistance to gender analysis may be too formidable within Jewish Studies to be overcome only by the passage of time. What does this mean for the future of gender study within Jewish history? In the first place, it suggests that we must continue the process of research and writing, recovering and producing information about female experience. Yet, we cannot be satisfied simply with providing new work or conducting a conversation limited to a small group of feminist scholars. We must continue to challenge the fundamental categories of Jewish scholarship, work toward curricular integration, and claim the right to redefine the parameters of the field. The past ten years of Jewish feminist research have provided a legacy of both promise and peril for future generations, building a solid foundation of scholarly inquiry but also exposing the limitations, theoretical shortcomings, and ongoing obstacles that still await the gendered transformation of the Jewish past. It is time for Jewish scholarship to stop following the problematic logic of "catch up" and to embrace methodological tools that reconceptualize Jewish men and women, masculinity and femininity, Jewish community and culture, leadership and power, and tradition and change.

Notes

1. Elizabeth Kolbert, "Literary Feminism Comes of Age," *New York Times Magazine*, 6 December 1987, 110.

2. The list of such works would be far too lengthy to reproduce here. See, for example, the recent anthology in Jewish women's history that contains essays covering the biblical period through twentieth-century America. Judith Baskin, ed., *Jewish Women in Historical Perspective* (Detroit: Wayne State University Press, 1991).

3. For insights into the connections between professional politics and gender scholarship, see Joan Wallach Scott, "Women's History," in *American Feminist Thought at Century's End: A Reader*, ed. Linda S. Kauffman (Cambridge, MA: Blackwell, 1993), 234–57.

4. For a useful discussion of these issues in the context of teaching modern Jewish history, see Shulamit S. Magnus, "Modern Jewish Social History," in *The Modern Jewish Experience: A Reader's Guide*, ed. Jack Wertheimer (New York: New York University Press, 1993), 109–22.

5. Chava Weissler, "The Traditional Piety of Ashkenazic Women," in *Jewish Spirituality from the Sixteenth-Century Revival to the Present*, ed. Arthur Green (New York: Crossroad, 1987), 245–75; and "The Religion of Traditional Ashkenazic Women: Some Methodological Issues," *Association for Jewish Studies Review* 12.1 (1987): 73–94.

6. See the following works by Marion A. Kaplan: *The Making of the Jewish Middle Class: Women, Family, and Identity in Imperial Germany* (New York: Oxford University Press, 1991); "Tradition and Transition—The Acculturation, Assimilation, and Integration of Jews in Imperial Germany—A Gender Analysis," *Leo Baeck Institute Yearbook* 27 (1982): 3–35; and "Priestess and Hausfrau: Women and Tradition in the German-Jewish Family," in *The Jewish Family: Myths and Reality*, ed. Steven M. Cohen and Paula E. Hyman (New York: Holmes & Meier, 1986), 62–81. See also the following works by Paula Hyman: *Gender and Assimilation; Roles and Representations of Women in Modern Jewish History* (Seattle: University of Washington Press, 1995); "Gender and Jewish History," *Tikkun* 3 (January-February 1988): 35–38; and "Culture and Gender: Women in the Immigrant Jewish Community," in *The Legacy of Jewish Migration: 1881 and Its Impact*, ed. David Berger, Social

Science Monographs (Brooklyn: Social Science Monographs—Brooklyn University Press, 1983), 157–68.

7. Among these works are Magnus, "Modern Jewish Social History," and Deborah Hertz, *Jewish High Society in Old Regime Berlin* (New Haven: Yale University Press, 1988). American Jewish historians have recently outpaced their European counterparts in incorporating studies of women and gender within the larger discussion of immigrant adaptation and acculturation. For two examples, see Andrew R. Heinze, *Adapting to Abundance: Jewish Immigrants, Mass Consumption, and the Search for American Identity* (New York: Columbia University Press, 1990); and Susan A. Glenn, *Daughters of the Shtetl: Life and Labor in the Immigrant Generation* (Ithaca, NY: Cornell University Press, 1990).

Teaching Jewish Studies

Ellen M. Umansky

If one of the legacies of modernity has been the image of the self as unified and universal, the persistence of such images testifies to what Miriam Peskowitz has called the cultural persuasiveness of the Enlightenment. Many scholarly works written today still attempt to describe "*the* American Jewish experience," as if there were a set of experiences that all American Jews have shared; "*the* Jewish woman," as if the beliefs and concerns of all Jewish women were the same; and "*the* traditional Jewish family," as if all Jewish families traditionally conformed, or wished to conform, to a universally agreed-upon model.[1] Such universalizing minimizes or ignores the religious lives of most Jews, especially Jewish women. It also leads to the omission of questions necessary for a fuller, more complex, understanding of Jewish religious history. Among such questions are: What cultural, historical, and religious influences led to a particular understanding of Judaism? In what ways does gender shape, determine, or limit the religious roles assumed by men and women in a given Jewish community (and/or in a particular geographical location, or literary text)? And, finally, to what extent do these roles seem to be continuous or discontinuous with those assumed by women and men in the past?[2] Although I have reflected on the importance of gender as a critical tool of inquiry in my work on Jewish history,[3] I have never before written about my classroom attempts to portray Jewish history and thought as engendered. Nor have I written about the personal style and pedagogical methods that are central to how I see myself, and to my presentation of myself as feminist scholar and teacher.

I suspect that among feminist scholars I am not alone in finding it more difficult to incorporate the lived experiences of women (and non-elite and/or non-Western men) into teaching Jewish theology and history than it is to incorporate such experiences into my own writing. This is because, as Miriam Peskowitz's description of the difficulties encountered in teaching "Introduction to Judaism" so clearly shows, the texts we assign students often do not present Jewish history as the history of men and women. Nor do they present Judaism itself as encompassing a multiplicity of experiences and interpretations. To address this problem, Peskowitz suggests that assigned introductory textbooks that minimize or ignore women's experiences be "supplemented—or interrupted" by writings that focus on women, with the professor pointing out to students the necessity, and problems, of doing so. This is a short-term strategy, and is certainly a step in the right direction. Unfortunately, though, it does little to dislodge the perception of women as "other" than normative Jews with "other" than normative (i.e., male) experiences.

My approach to introductory-class book selection shares some elements in common with Peskowitz's. Given the scarcity of textbooks that incorporate the lives of women and men into their understanding of Jewish religious history, and because I believe that lengthy textbooks are often, if not inherently, boring, I assign a minimum of four books, usually more, in every semester-length course that I teach. I draw on both primary ("Jewish religious texts") and secondary ("scholarly") materials in an attempt to provide cohesion and coherence. And I make use of detailed syllabi, informal lectures (the length and frequency depends on the course), and handouts (e.g., historical time lines and extensive glossaries of key words, individuals, and concepts to be covered during the semester). Although I constantly try new books and add or delete topics, the sources selected, the topics covered, and my own presentation of the material are crucial factors in offering a view of Jewish religious history that includes the lived experiences of women and men.

For example, in the fall of 1994, I taught "Introduction to Judaism" to a class of more than thirty (predominately non-Jewish) undergraduates. I had not taught such a course in almost ten years, and I decided not to look at my old syllabi until after I had written the new one. This decision was a good one, because it led me to realize something earlier than I might have otherwise: that I could not teach Judaism as an ongoing, meaningful religious tradition while also presenting Jewish history as the lived experiences of Jewish women and men in different historical periods and geographic settings. To add complexity and diversity without narrowing the course's scope in unacceptable ways, I needed to create two separate courses. Out of this insight, I developed "Introduction to Judaism" and "History of the Jewish Experience."

Here is part of the difference: ten years ago, my "Introduction to Judaism" was largely historical in focus. It began with biblical religion and ended with a discussion of contemporary Judaism, particularly in the United States and Israel. It included sections on modern Jewish thought and the Holocaust. Although the course emphasized both continuity and diversity, its focus resembled that of graduate courses that I had taken. Like them, it concentrated on biblical and rabbinic texts, great thinkers of the past, the experiences of Ashkenazi Jewry, and elite formulations of modern Jewish identity. Although I regularly incorporated discussions of women into my lectures, the scope of the course was limited by the books I knew or could obtain. It was further limited by its unconscious privileging of public religious life and of prescriptive rather than descriptive texts. In contrast, the introductory course that I first taught in 1994 (and, with modifications, plan to teach each fall) examines Judaism as it has been defined and developed as a way of thought and a way of life. After an introductory lecture presenting an overview of Jewish history, the course focuses on central religious concepts, holidays, life-cycle ceremonies, and various forms of religious expression, including prayer and ritual, in an effort to help students understand what it means, and has meant, to be a Jew. This structure easily lends itself to an inclusion of women's (and non-elite men's) experiences, for it not only examines the theological and social implications of such religious concepts as covenant, *b'tzelem elohim* (creation "in the image of God"), and *tikkun olam* (repairing the world) for men and women but also views Judaism, after the destruction of the second Temple in 70 C.E., as focusing on two spiritual centers: the synagogue (a house of prayer, study, and assembly that rabbinic Judaism identified as men's natural domain) and the home—that center most closely identified with women by generations of rabbis and also, for much of Jewish history, by women themselves.

"History of the Jewish Experience," taught in the spring, explores the nature and content of the historical religious experiences of the Jewish people, from the biblical period through the present. The course title, which I did not create but inherited, suggests a uniformity of experience that, as my course description and syllabus make clear, does not exist and never has. Nonetheless, the title accurately reflects the course's historical focus and allows for great variation in terms of the religious communities and historical texts that we examine. Thus, new studies that explore Jewish communities or aspects of Jewish life previously receiving little if any scholarly attention (including those in which women are or were greatly involved) can easily be incorporated into the course's existing structure.[4] The framework of the course explicitly encourages students to recognize in Jewish religious history groups and individuals whose understandings of Judaism were diverse and, at times, antithetical to one another.

Throughout, I emphasize the importance of gender as a category for understanding what each group or community offered its real or potential members. I also stress the broader implications that can be derived from such an analysis. For example, a study of texts found at Qumran (near the Dead Sea) underscores the importance of maleness to the first-century Jewish community of (in all likelihood, priestly) elites that lived there, but it also reveals concepts of family, sexuality, divine election, and life after death that stand in sharp contrast to those simultaneously developed by the Pharisees and, later, by generations of rabbis. Similarly, in "Introduction to Judaism," our discussion of covenant and the significance of the ritual of male circumcision not only includes the question "Are women as fully covenanted as men?" but also asks, "What does it mean to view the covenant as one of descent rather than assent, that is, one in which membership is primarily understood, even in cases of conversion, within the context of family?"

As important as structure and content are to my courses, so too is pedagogical method. Although I have never studied pedagogy in any formal way, I have learned a great deal by watching others in the classroom and participating in weekend or weeklong institutes in which faculty have the opportunity to learn from one another. Because I believe that successful teaching begins with the building of relationships between student and teacher and among students themselves, I am particularly interested in discovering how others create relationships within a classroom setting, which includes learning students' (or classmates') names.[5] Of course, feminists were not the first to understand the importance of learning within the context of community. Indeed, the rabbinic model of study is also one of relationships. Pupils study in pairs (based on a model called *hevruta*, from the root *haver*, meaning friend and colleague); scholars identify themselves collectively as disciples of a particular teacher. Like the rabbis, I think it possible to create teacher-student relationships, but I recognize that in a hierarchical setting power largely rests in the hands of the teacher, who gives grades, writes recommendations, and so on. In the classroom, then, my goal as a feminist scholar is not to encourage discipleship but rather to create an atmosphere of openness and comfort that encourages students to offer questions and answers of their own.

I further attempt to create such an atmosphere through my own willingness to share with students *who* I am, not only as scholar and teacher but also as mother, wife, daughter, political liberal, and Jew. Frequently, I add relevant personal anecdotes to our discussions. I bring ritual objects of my own into the classroom, particularly those used on the Sabbath and holidays. And I try to provide informal opportunities for my students to meet members of my family, both on and off campus. Finally, when I teach I wear clothing and accessories (especially earrings, for which I have a great fondness) that visibly remind students that I am not a disembodied scholar but rather both a scholar and a woman. In so doing, I attempt to underscore the pedagogical point that we can see ourselves and one another as embodied persons, with gendered voices and bodies, and that this helps us to understand the importance of teaching and learning about the lived experiences of women and men.

The Jewish "tradition" that modern scholars have viewed as a seamless unity was never experienced as such either by previous generations of Jews or their biblical ancestors. Neither did they see themselves as either genderless or unified, as the biblical narratives, rabbinic arguments, liturgical prayers, private devotions, communal regulations, and ethical wills so clearly demonstrate. With a few notable exceptions, Judaism has sustained a conviction that the body, and therefore also sex and gender, is central to who we are. Rarely has this conviction been overshadowed by a Hellenistic spirit-body dualism, or by a preference for "the world to come" over "this world." Teaching and writing about Jewish religious history as engendered may be new to us, but insisting on the significance of gender and sexual difference is at least as old as Judaism itself.

Notes

1. Rather than single out a few books that are guilty of such universalizations, I invite the reader to peruse recent Judaica acquisitions in libraries, visit bookstores that have Judaica sections, examine publishing catalogs, and look at the titles or indices of books they themselves own. The recently published books that I own include titles, subtitles, or chapter subheadings such as *The German Jew*, "The American Experience of German Jews," "The Jew as [Medieval] Townsman," and "Reflections on the World of the Jewish Woman" (the last being the subtitle of a book published in 1993).

2. In my study of Lily Montagu, founder and later leader of the Liberal Jewish Movement in England, for example, I explicitly asked (and attempted to answer), "What was it about the late nineteenth- and early twentieth-century Anglo-Jewish community that, *unlike emancipated Jewish communities elsewhere,* enabled an exceptional Jewish woman like Lily Montagu to assume a religious leadership position? . . . What, then, made the Anglo-Jewish community different and more specifically, which [economic, social, cultural, religious, and gendered related] factors best explain Lily Montagu's rise to prominence?" Ellen M. Umansky, *Lily Montagu and the Advancement of Liberal Judaism: From Vision to Vocation* (Lewiston, NY: Edwin Mellen Press, 1983), 2. See too my edited *Lily Montagu: Sermons, Addresses, Letters and Prayers* (Lewiston, NY: Edwin Mellen Press, 1985).

3. See, for example, my *Lily Montagu and the Advancement of Liberal Judaism*, and my essay "Piety, Persuasion, and Friendship: Female Jewish Leadership in Modern Times," in *Embodied Love: Sensuality and Relationship as Feminist Values*, ed. Paula M. Cooey et al. (San Francisco: Harper & Row, 1987), 190–206.

4. Some recent, varied examples include Jenna Weissman Joselit, *The Wonders of America: Reinventing Jewish Culture, 1880–1950* (New York: Hill and Wang, 1994); Victor Pereira, *The Cross and the Pear Tree: A Sephardic Journey* (New York: Knopf, 1995); and Ruby Daniel and Barbara Johnson, *Ruby of Cochin: An Indian Jewish Woman Remembers* (Philadelphia: Jewish Publication Society, 1995).

5. One method that I have regularly used with classes ranging in size from ten to one hundred I learned from Carol Christ almost twenty years ago. An assistant professor at Columbia University, Carol began her "Women and Religion" class by asking each student to say, in turn, his or her name and then repeat all of the names already mentioned (I can't remember whether Carol asked for first and last names; I ask for only the first). Thus, in a class of students named A, B, C, and D; A simply says "A." "B" says "A" then "B;" "C" says "A," "B," "C," and so on. By the time we've gone around the room and heard each name several times (and in a large class, this might take several class sessions to accomplish), we find that we've begun to learn one another's names while also beginning to feel, among ourselves, a sense of community.

Rabbinic Judaism and the Creation of Woman

Judith R. Baskin

Feminist Jewish studies scholars have frequently focused on images of women in rabbinic literature. Miriam Peskowitz's essay raises provocative questions about this approach. Although I appreciate efforts to render the "marginalization and/or invisibilization of women and gender intellectually impossible" in Jewish studies scholarship, I believe that such efforts cannot fully overcome literary constructions of gender embedded within ancient Jewish texts. It is sometimes possible to read canonical Jewish texts in new ways and "against the grain" to tease out evidence of women "struggling within and against patriarchal culture." However, finding evidence of struggle should not obscure the evidence of patriarchy. I will argue that scholarship that explores "images of" women in classical Jewish texts also tells us important things about the marginalization of women in much of rabbinic thinking.

Rabbinic discourse is far from monolithic in the views and attitudes it expresses. It includes a variety of competing interpretations and opinions. Given this multivocality, it is not surprising that rabbinic literature expresses a diversity of attitudes toward women. What unites these views, however, is the conviction that "women are a separate people" (B. Shabbat 62a),[1] different from men in innate qualities as well as in social and legal status. In some of my previous writings I have asked why it was so vital for the male framers and subsequent adherents of rabbinic Judaism to place women in this marginal position despite evidence to the contrary, including women's vital place in family life, their ongoing participation in economic activities, and their various roles in Jewish ritual observance. Given the social centrality of women, why have they been constructed as essentially others, and even as potentially harmful to men? Why are women of concern only when they have an impact on male affairs?[2] Miriam Peskowitz observes that in scholarship such as mine, "the study of 'women' may be removed from the study of rabbinic Judaism, and made marginal to this enterprise." I suggest, however, that androcentrism is an inherent feature of the classical texts of rabbinic Judaism; this literature overwhelmingly constitutes women as objects of male agency, rather than as subjects of their own lives. An examination of some aggadic (nonlegal) biblical interpretations or midrash concerned with the creation of the first woman confirms these observations.

The Hebrew Bible contains two separate accounts of the creation of human beings. The first passage, Genesis 1:1–2:4, and the second passage, which begins at Genesis 2:5, were traditionally read as one continuous text. In Genesis 1, male and female entities are created equally in the divine image. To rabbinic readers, these same entities were also the husband Adam and wife Eve, formed from her husband's rib, of Genesis 2:5ff. These two accounts presented problems to rabbinic exegetes, for whom revelation could not be contradictory. In *Genesis Rabbah*, a rabbinic midrash anthology, we find the rabbis attempting to respond to the contrast of the two creation stories: the apparently equal and simultaneous creation of male and female (Gen. 1), in which both parties are created in the divine image and jointly charged with the imperatives to fertility and propagation, and the secondary creation of Eve from Adam's rib (Gen. 2:22).

Thus, *Genesis Rabbah* 8:1 presents the notion of an androgynous primordial being, sharing male and female physical characteristics, which was only later split into male and female entities:

> R. Jeremiah b. Leazar said: "When the Holy One, blessed be He, created the first adam,[3] He created it with both male and female sexual organs, as it is written, '*Male and female He created them, and He called their name adam*' " (Gen. 5:2). R. Shmuel bar Nachman said, "When the Holy One, blessed be He, created the first adam, He created him with two faces, then split him and made him two backs—a back for each side."[4]

These two complementary traditions were based on Psalm 139:5, "*You have formed me before and behind.*" In both traditions, male and female human beings, literally married in the flesh, are the result of one simultaneous creation; their differentiation into a separate Adam and Eve is a subsequent development. But, more important, the text of *Genesis Rabbah* 8:1 immediately counters this midrash with an unattributed objection, based on a prooftext from Genesis 2:21: "*And He took one of his ribs*" to show that woman was not created by God in the divine image but was formed later from the body of the already-created man. The notion of the simultaneous creation of man and woman becomes a minority position, supported by no other passages in *Genesis Rabbah*.[5]

The view of woman as a secondary and subordinate conception is upheld throughout rabbinic literature. In an extended midrashic excursus on the second version of creation, *Genesis Rabbah* 18:2 asks why Eve was formed from Adam's rib. The text answers that the rib, which is always covered, was chosen to ensure female modesty. Despite divine intentions, the text continues, women are swelled-headed and flirtatious eavesdroppers, light-fingered gadabouts prone to jealousy. Comments in *Genesis Rabbah* 17:8 also assert that women are both other and lesser than men, as a result of the secondary nature of their creation:

> R. Joshua was asked: "Why does a man come forth [at birth] with his face downward, while a woman comes forth with her face turned upwards?" "The man looks towards the place of his creation [the earth], while the woman looks towards the place of her creation [the rib]," he replied. "And why must a woman use perfume, while a man does not need perfume?" "Man was created from earth," he answered, "and earth never putrefies, but Eve was created from a bone. For example: if you leave meat three days unsalted, it immediately goes putrid."

Continuing in this vein, the midrash also attributes shrill voices and an importunate manner to female creation from a bone. The tenor of this discussion becomes increasingly caustic:

> "And why does the man make [sexual] demands upon the woman, whereas the woman does not make demands upon the man?" "This may be compared to a man who loses something," he replied; "he seeks what he lost, but the lost article does not seek him," "And why does a man deposit sperm within a woman while a woman does not deposit sperm within a man?" "It is like a man who has an article in his hand and seeks a trustworthy person with whom he may deposit it" [a woman can be assumed to be sexually trustworthy since she is limited to one husband at a time, but not a man since he may be polygynous]. "Why does a man go out bareheaded while a woman goes out with her head covered?" "She is like one who has done wrong and is ashamed of people; therefore she goes out with her head covered." "Why do [women] walk in front of the corpse [at a funeral]?" "Because they brought death into the world, they therefore walk in front of the corpse. . . ." "And why was the precept of menstruation given to her?" "Because she shed the blood of Adam [by causing death], therefore was the precept of menstruation given to her." "And why was the precept of dough (*hallah*) given to her?" "Because she corrupted Adam, who was the dough of the world, therefore was the precept of dough given to her." "And why was the precept of the Sabbath lights given to her?" "Because she extinguished the soul of Adam, therefore was the precept of the Sabbath lights given to her."

Although this complex passage requires far lengthier explication than is possible here, I cite it because it so clearly articulates a conviction of woman's essential difference from and inferiority to man. This results from the secondary nature of her creation and from her inherent moral failings, as demonstrated by Eve's actions in leading Adam into disobedience and mortality in Genesis 3. These fundamental female flaws explain why women are subject to so many perceived disabilities in comparison to the far more desirable lives of men. They also justify the subordination of wives to their husbands.[6]

The possibility that man and woman were created simultaneously is considered in three places in the Babylonian Talmud: Berakot 61a, Erubin 18a, and Ketubot 8a. The discussions in Berakot and Erubin begin with R. Jeremiah ben Eleazar's declaration that the first man had two full faces, based, as in *Genesis Rabbah* 8:1, on "*You have formed me behind and before*" (Psalm 139:5), apparent confirmation of the view that the first human being was androgynous. However, as in the midrashic text I have already cited, opposing views are immediately offered when other sages assert that the verse refers to the order in which Adam was created: "R. Ammi said: [Adam was] behind [last] in the work of the creation and before [other created entities] for retribution."

By contrast, B. Ketubot 8a raises the issue of the creation of woman in the context of a discussion of whether the appropriate number of benedictions to be recited at a wedding feast is five or six. The debate turns on whether or not the blessing "*Blessed art thou O Lord, Creator of adam*"[7] is redundant because a previous blessing already refers to the creation of man and of woman from his rib:

> Do they differ in this: that one side [which favors five benedictions] holds that there was one creation [of man, and that woman was subsequently formed from him] and therefore the third benediction: "*Blessed are thou . . . who has created man in his image, in the image of the likeness of his form, and has prepared unto him out of himself a building forever*" (i.e., Eve) [is sufficiently inclusive], while the other holds that there were two simultaneous creations [of man and woman, and therefore one much recite both benedictions]? No. The whole world agrees that there was only one creation [and it was of man alone], [but they differ in this] one holds that we go according to the [divine] intention [which had been to simultaneously create two human beings, man and woman] and the other holds that we go according to the fact [only man was created and woman was later created out of him]. [This is the import] of that statement of Rab Judah [who] asked: It is written, "*And God created adam in his own image*" (Gen. 1:27), and it is written "*Male and female He created them*" (Gen. 5:2). How is this [to be understood?] [In this way]: In the beginning it was the intention [of God] to create two [human beings], and in the end [only] one was created.

This ingenious resolution of the conflicting creation stories reflects a majority view among the rabbinic sages: the original human being was male, created in the divine image; only later was a female formed from his body. The view that only men are created in God's likeness, with all the implications of male potency, dominance, and generativity that follow from it, is an essential component of the rabbinic construction of gender relations. And yet, rabbinic literature preserves the minority view of an androgynous being, created in the divine image and split by God into separate male and female entities. Perhaps this midrash was valued for its homiletical benefits. It seems to teach that only when male and female are united are they truly adam, that is, truly human; in so teaching it provides a strong endorsement and encouragement of marriage.

Genesis Rabbah 8:1 and its talmudic echoes are reminders that rabbinic literature is complicated, multivocal, and occasionally surprising. Yet the preponderance of rabbinic voices that support a vision of female creation as subsequent and secondary to the creation of man makes clear that most rabbinic writers were concerned to construct a social policy in which women were separate from and subservient to men in a number of ways.[8] By rereading these rabbinic texts I have tried to demonstrate that explorations into the "images of" women in classical Jewish texts continue to tell us important things about how Jewish knowledges are engendered.

Notes

1. "B." indicates a citation from a tractate of the Babylonian Talmud. Italics in cited passages indicate verses from the Hebrew Bible. Underlining indicates either a non-English word, or emphasis by the author. Square brackets provide words absent but implied in the original texts.

2. See, for example, works by Judith R. Baskin: "Rabbinic Reflections on the Barren Wife," *Harvard Theological Review* 82 (1989): 1–14; "From Separation to Displacement: The Problem of Women in *Sefer Hasidim*," *Association for Jewish Studies Review* 19.1 (1994): 1–18; and "Silent Partners: Women as Wives in Rabbinic Literature," in *Women in Jewish Culture*, ed. Maurie Sacks (University of Illinois Press, 1995), 19–37.

3. The Hebrew '*adam* in Genesis 1:26 is most often translated as "man," but it seems to me that "humanity" or "human beings" is more accurate in this context of a simultaneous creation of woman and man.

4. The idea that the first human being was androgynous is not unique to Jewish literature. In the *Symposium* 189d, 190d, Plato makes a similar suggestion, and it is found, as well, in other ancient Near Eastern traditions.

5. Rabbinic literature does offer an alternative view to the contradictory creation traditions: that a different woman is referred to in each creation story. This legend of the "first Eve" appears in several rabbinic sources and in the Middle Ages was combined with long-standing legends about Lilith, a major figure in Jewish demonology with roots in ancient Near Eastern folklore. According to the *Encyclopedia Judaica* 11:246–7, it is the *Alphabet of Ben Sira*, a midrashic work of the Geonic period (probably eleventh century), that first identifies Lilith with the "first Eve," who rebelled against Adam's authority.

6. For an alternate reading of *Genesis Rabbah* 8.1, see Daniel Boyarin, *Carnal Israel: Reading Sex in Talmudic Culture* (Berkeley: University of California Press, 1993), 88–94.

7. See note 3, above.

8. It is important to remember that rabbinic texts tell us very little about the actualities of women's lives in any particular time or place. The rabbinic Judaism we derive from rabbinic texts, never a monolithic entity in any case, was doubtless frequently at odds with the Jewish cultures that existed in the different times and places during which the literature of rabbinic Judaism was produced.

Justify My Love

Daniel Boyarin

From almost the first sentence in my first preparatory course in reading the Talmud, I was charmed—in the full antique sense of the word. Here was a world so strange and rich, so colorful and exciting, with myths and legends, challenges to the intellect, and most of all, personalities rendered so vital that they seemed living men, men, moreover, who devoted their lives to the elaboration of what it means to live correctly as a Jew. And all this was "mine." I became Orthodox for love of the Talmud. I admit freely, if ruefully, that it was all so absorbing that I hardly noticed at all that they *were* all men, or that the texts were primarily addressed to me just because I was a Jewish *man.* I failed to see the exclusions and oppressions that those facts encode and mystify.

There is no textual product of human culture, I believe, quite like the jumbled, carnivalesque, raucous, vulgar, vital, exciting Talmud, nor any practice quite like the practices of study that characterize it and the way of life it subtends. And just as the Talmud entranced me, so much that I decided to devote my life to it, others have been drawn to it, including women and lesbigay people. I feel a deep love for and connection to rabbinic texts and culture, and more so, to the Rabbis themselves. But there is much that I find deeply disturbing as well, and much of that has to do with the oppression of women.

Awareness of these oppressions also came from other significant encounters. In the late 1980s I attended the School for Criticism and Theory, and for reasons that I cannot now remember or reconstruct, I joined a feminist reading group, as one of two men among approximately twenty women. This little community provided me with my first direct experience of feminism as theory, and of the experiences that had produced it as practice. Although very different from the affect that had compelled me to devote my life to the study and practice of Talmud, this experience was no less compelling. By the end of the summer I could no longer describe myself as an Orthodox Jew. I now had to say (and for a long time only to myself), that being a male feminist constituted and defined my experience of myself. For a number of years, the contradictions seemed so ungappable that I just endeavored to live with them, until I could no longer do so. Unable, however, to let go or even diminish either of these components of my self, I discovered that I had to find ways to theorize a rapprochement (or at least to make the contradictions creative).

My endeavor is to justify my love, that is, both to explain it and to make it just. I explain my devotion in part by showing that Judaism provides exempla and ideals for an Other kind of masculinity, one in which men do not manifest "a deeply rooted concern about the possible meanings of dependence on other males,"[1] and thus one within which "feminization" is not experienced as a threat or a danger. I cannot, however, paper over, ignore, or explain away the oppressions of women and lesbigay people that this culture has practiced, and therefore I endeavor as well to render my love just by presenting a way of reading the tradition that may help it surmount or expunge—in time—that which I, and many others, can no longer live with. In this respect, my project is homologous to other political and cultural acts of resistance in the face of colonialisms.

For some three hundred years now, Jews have been the target of western and central Europe's civilizing mission. Laura Levitt makes palpably clear the homologies between the "liberal" colonizing impulse directed locally toward those Others within Europe, and outward toward those colonized outside Europe's geographic borders, insofar as both were made to "reform" their sexual practices in order to conform to the liberal bourgeois regime.[2] One of the most common of liberal justifications for the extension of colonial control over a given people and for the maintenance of the civilizing mission is the imputed barbarity of the treatment of women within the culture under attack. The fact that Jewish women behaved in ways that European bourgeois society considered masculine was simply monstrous to the civilizing mission and its Jewish collaborators—the "Enlighteners." This civilizing mission, in turn, led to the development of modern Jewish culture, with its liberal, bourgeois aspirations and its preferred patterns of gendered life. As Paula Hyman has recently demonstrated, the very religiosity of the modern bourgeois Jewish family is an assimilating mimicry of Protestant middle-class piety, not least in its portrayal of proper womanhood.[3] The richness of Jewish life and difference has largely been lost. I think the gains that the European Enlightenment held for Jewish women have been largely illusory. So, the Jewish anticolonial project (perhaps like many others) may seek to protect traditional culture from destruction from without. But such a project must also engage a trenchant, unflinching, and unapologetic internal critique of the harsh oppressions within that very culture.

I repeat that I deeply love and feel connected to rabbinic texts and culture, but there is much within them that disturbs me. Jewish culture may have been a place of safety for the sissy, the effeminate Jewish man. But it has hardly—to understate—provided such felicitous conditions for Jewish women. My project is a feminist one, to the extent that it owes its life to feminism and the work of feminist critics. The tasks of male self-fashioning have consequences for women. Male critique of masculinity can be feminist, as Tania Modleski states, when "it analyzes male power, male hegemony, with a concern for the effects of this power *on the female subject* and with an awareness of how frequently male subjectivity works to appropriate 'femininity' while oppressing women."[4] I try to meet Modleski's challenge, in the process of reclaiming Judaic culture from the depredations of the civilizing, colonizing onslaught to which it has been subject(ed). I want to keep from interfering with—and perhaps even contribute to—the ongoing project of feminist critique of that same traditional culture that I seek to uphold. Whether or not my work is part of the solution, I do not want it to be part of the problem. Thus the duality of my political project: to resist the delegitimization of Judaic culture from without, and to support the feminist critique from within.

* * *

In some sense I have always been more of a "girl" than a "boy." I was a sissy who did not like sports. I want to find in the Talmud a genealogy for the sissy, the Jewish male femme, and to use this genealogy as a positive site for a critical practice. As I came of age in New Jersey, my mother used to holler at me to stop reading and go out and play. And, in fifth grade I went out for ballet, which I explained to the guys as a kind of sophisticated bodybuilding. In itself, this is a rather familiar story, a story of inexplicable gender dysphoria. It had for me, even then, a rather happy end: I didn't think of myself so much as girlish but, rather, as Jewish.

I start with what I think is a widespread sensibility in our culture, that being Jewish renders a boy effeminate. Recognition of this sensibility could have led me to try to "pass," to become a "man." But in my case, it reinforced the desire to remain a Jew, where being a sissy was all right. To be sure, this has meant accepting a marginal status, and it has left me with a persistent sense of standing outside something and looking in, with my nose pressed to the glass. Still, my understanding of the cultural and communal place that a sissy occupied in my social world was not one that enforced rage and self-contempt.

There is critical force left in the idea of a culture and a cultural memory within which "real men" were sissies. Rather than denying the image of the effeminate Jewish man as an antisemitic fantasy, my theoretical-political work attempts to reclaim it. I find in the nineteenth-century Austrian notion of the feminized Jewish male only one example of a Jewish ideal that goes back to the Babylonian Talmud. In this ideal I hope to locate a model for a gentle, nurturing masculinity (no matter how often it was, or was not, realized); a man who could be so comfortable with his little, fleshy penis that he would not have to grow it into "The Phallus," a sort of velvet John. The feminized Jewish male, colonized and considered contemptible in the past—both by the dominant culture and by those Jews who internalized its values—may be useful today. "He" may help us in the attempt to construct an alternative masculine subjectivity that does not rely on such cultural archetypes as Iron Johns, knights, hairy men, and warriors within.

Thinking about the sissy body of the "Jewish man," I think simultaneously about another discourse and practice—one that is possibly but not necessarily liberatory—that constructs the male body in a very different way. The "gay male gym body" is another body constructed as an alternative to that of the heterosexual male. David Halperin (following in part D. A. Miller) has recently given us a brilliant and moving account: "What distinguishes the gay male gym body, then, in addition to its spectacular beauty, is the way it advertises itself as an object of desire. Gay muscles do not signify power." He makes the impeccable point that the (ideal) gay male body does not look at all like the straight macho body:

> [Gym bodies] are explicitly designed to be an erotic turn-on, and in their very solicitation of desire they deliberately flaunt the visual norms of straight masculinity, which impose discretion on masculine self-display and require that straight male beauty exhibit itself only casually or inadvertently, that it refuse to acknowledge its own strategies. If, as Foucault hypothesized in *Discipline and Punish*, those whom modern disciplinary society would destroy it first makes visible, then gay male body-builders, in visibly inscribing their erotic desires on the surfaces of their bodies, have not only exposed themselves to considerable social risks in the course of pursuing their ethical projects but have also performed a valuable political service on behalf of everyone, insofar as they have issued a challenge of defiance to the very mechanisms of modern discipline.[5]

All this is inarguable, but it nevertheless maintains a standard for male beauty whose form of muscular development emphasizes the dimorphism of the gendered body and thus participates in, rather than resists, the general cultural standard of masculinity.

The pale, limp, and semiotically unaggressive "nelly" or sissy male body is not seen as beautiful or as erotic at all—but, it can be. Lori Lefkowitz makes the point that in midrash, Joseph's body is explicitly designed to be an erotic turn-on, but not on the model of the muscle-Jew. He pencils his eyes, curls his hair, lifts his heels. Moreover, his beauty is like that of his mother, Rachel, and it was this beauty that so attracted Potiphar's wife and indeed all of the noblewomen of Egypt![6] Thus, on the one hand, I think that Halperin is clearly right that

> the hypermasculine look of gay clones is deceiving. What the new styles of gay virility represent, paradoxically, is a strategy for valorizing various practices of devirilization under the sign of masculinity, thereby forging a new association between masculinity and sexual receptivity or penetrability, while detaching male homosexuality from its phobic association with "femininity" (conceived in phallic terms as "passivity" or as an absence of phallic aggressivity). (90)

On the other hand, I fear this strategy backfires, insofar as it continues to register only one kind of male body—"clonedom"—as attractive (I do not claim, of course, that this is true for all gay male culture). But just as the gay male gym body dislodges the negatively coded sense of passivity and separates it from a stereotyped "femininity," so must a new view demystify the ideology that interprets the penis that enters another body—male or female—as naturally signifying "penetration" and thus phallic domination. In this same way, the valorization of masculinity as "topness" can give way to a better valuation of receptivity, or "bottomness," in all sectors of our sexual culture.[7]

One place to find the eroticized sissy is in a reading of the rabbinic textual tradition. This tradition clearly privileges sexual connections between men and women (to understate the case).[8] It also clearly prescribes some forms of social domination of men over women. At the same time, sexually, it does not privilege "masculine" "tops" over "feminine" "bottoms." Nor does it stigmatize "femininity" in anything like the ways that hegemonic European culture has come to, particularly since the nineteenth century. In part, Jewish culture demystifies European gender ideologies by reversing their terms. This is not, I hasten to emphasize, an essentially liberatory process. But it can be mobilized—strategically—for liberation.

As a tool for liberation, my project of reclaiming the eroticized Jewish male sissy faces a conflicted legacy, in that the traditional valorization of "effeminacy" for Jewish men hardly secured good news for Jewish women. There is no question that women were disenfranchised in many ways in traditional Jewish culture. The culture authorized, even if it did not mandate, efflorescences of misogyny. If the ideal Jewish male femme has some critical force vis-à-vis general European models of manliness, at the same time a critique must be mounted against "him" for his oppression of Jewish women—and indeed, frequently enough, for his class-based oppression of other Jewish men as well, namely, the "ignorant" who were sometimes characterized as being "like women."[9] Any attempt at a male feminist rereading of Jewish tradition must come to terms with this material fact and with the legacies of pain that it has left behind. My goal is not to preserve rabbinic Judaism "as we know it" but to reconstruct a rabbinic Judaism that will be quite different in some ways from the one we know and yet will be and feel authentically grounded in the tradition of the Rabbis. My work is one of changing ethos and culture, and I hope it joins with a stream of feminist work on rabbinic Judaism that includes the researches of Judith Baskin, Judith Hauptman, Miriam Peskowitz, Laura Levitt, Susan Shapiro, and others.

Certain apologies for Judaism have used the fact of Jewish women's economic activity in traditional culture as an alibi for the entire system of oppression of women. This economic activity, however real, was a double-edged sword. Iris Parush has captured something of this paradoxical double charge of Jewish gender culture in modern Europe:

> Over the years, the lifestyle which crystallized in Jewish society caused the men to cluster under the sacred tent of Torah study, and the women to stand at the front line of the daily confrontation with the outside world. . . . An interesting combination of weakness and power—of inferiority in terms of the traditional Jewish perspective, and superiority in terms of the trends of Europeanization—opened the "door of opportunity," so to speak, for certain circles of the female population.[10]

The "fact," then, that Jewish women (of certain classes) had opportunities in the secular world and access to education and economic power and autonomy beyond those of their husbands must not be permitted to erase the fact that within Jewish culture these roles were genuinely less valued than those of men. The time for the apologetic strategy of pointing to "positive" structures or ideals and allowing them to excuse whole systems of repression has passed. I have no desire to return to it, for it is fundamentally reactionary. I do not want to discount, excuse, or pretend that there was not powerful oppression of women but, rather, to displace that oppression by arguing that such abuse is the product of a particular reading of the past and its canonical texts, a reading that is not ineluctable. I hope, then, to make a very different move: to maintain the passion of critique of what has been, and simultaneously, to mobilize that same past for a different future by consciously reinterpreting it.

To participate in this work is the calling of the scholar. My role model for this kind of scholarship is Bertha Pappenheim, contemporary of such giants of Jewish scholarship as Shmuel Krauss, and, among her accomplishments, teacher in Rosenzweig and Buber's *Lehrhaus.* I want to claim Bertha Pappenheim as a model for an alternative to the pseudo-objectivity of the *Wissenschaft des Judentums.* Although I can barely stake out my claim here, I suggest that it was her first-wave feminism that fueled her achievements in Judaic scholarship, just as it is second-wave feminism that has empowered engaged, politically frank scholarship and critique in our generation. Pappenheim remained an Orthodox Jew all her life and thus is the prototype for me of a radical critic of the oppression of women within traditional Judaism, who yet remains within the traditional culture. She also criticized bourgeois European culture and its effect on the female subject, by identifying with historically Jewish alternatives and models for women's lives, notably the life of Glikl of Hameln. Pappenheim empowered herself by remaining "deviant" from the bourgeois heterosexual ideal; a strand of the gendering of traditional Jewish women became her own, to be used as a tool in the struggle for women within Judaism and outside it. I seek to do the same, to save myself and also contribute something to others, through a parallel (but not identical) reclamation of the Jewish sissy. Pappenheim teaches us that the struggle against oppression within Jewish culture need not lose sight of the critical force that Jewish culture can bring to bear on models of gender that were developed within romantic European culture. I hope to be continuing her work.

Notes

Many warm thanks to Laura Levitt and Miriam Peskowitz—colleagues in the richest sense of the word. Their help here has gone far beyond the work of editors.

1. Lee Edelman, "Redeeming the Phallus: Wallace Stevens, Frank Lentricchia, and the Politics of (Hetero)sexuality," in *Engendering Men*, ed. Joseph A. Boone and Michael Cadden (New York: Routledge, 1990), 50.

2. Laura Levitt, *Reconfiguring Home: Jewish Feminist Identity/ies* (Ph.D. diss., Emory University, 1993), 152–173, forthcoming as *Ambivalent Embraces: Jews, Feminists, and Home* (New York: Routledge)

3. Paula E. Hyman, *Gender and Assimilation in Modern Jewish History: The Roles and Representation of Women* (Seattle: University of Washington Press, 1995), 26–27.

4. Tania Modleski, *Feminism Without Women: Culture and Criticism in a "Postfeminist" Age* (New York: Routledge, 1991), 7.

5. David M. Halperin, *Saint Foucault: Towards a Gay Hagiography* (Oxford: Oxford University Press, 1995), 117.

6. Lori Lefkowitz, "Coats and Tales: Joseph Stories and Myths of Jewish Masculinity," in *A Mensch Among Men: Explorations in Jewish Masculinity*, ed. Harry Brod (Freedom, CA: Crossing Press, 1988), 21.

7. Lawrence D. Kritzman, ed., *Michel Foucault: Politics, Philosophy, Culture, Interviews and Other Writings, 1977–1984* (New York: Routledge, 1988), 300.

8. But see Daniel Boyarin, "Are There Any Jews in the 'History of Sexuality'?" *Journal of the History of Sexuality* 5 (1995): 333–355.

9. Chava Weissler, "For Women and for Men Who Are Like Women," *Journal of Feminist Studies in Religion* 5 (1989): 7–24.

10. Iris Parush, "Women Readers as Agents for Social Change: The Case of East European Jewish Society in the Nineteenth Century," *Gender and History* (forthcoming).

Medievals Are Not Us

Kalman P. Bland

Miriam Peskowitz seeks to amend Jewish historiography, and perhaps Jewish history, by engendering it.[1] Her project evoked in my memory W. H. Auden's "*Dichtung und Wahrheit* (An Unwritten Poem)."[2] The poem ironically explores a predicament shared by thoughtful lovers and compassionate scholars: "Expecting your arrival tomorrow, I find myself thinking *I love you*: then comes the thought—*I should like to write a poem which would express exactly what I mean when I think these words.*" Knowing that such precision is elusive and that silence begs the question, Auden reverts to paradoxical eloquence. Stanza *XXV*, for example: "this poem I should like to write is not concerned with the proposition 'He loves Her' (where He and She could be fictitious persons whose characters and history the poet is free to idealize as much as he choose), but with my proposition *I love You* (where *I* and *You* are persons whose existence and histories could be verified by a private detective)." Traveling in the company of Auden's lover, scholars also commute on the shuttle connecting freedom to constraint, universals to particulars, theories to evidence, abstract ideas to specific bodies, and political loyalties to scientific disinterest. Scholars, however, do not resolve their predicaments by writing ironic "unwritten poems."

Working toward precision, Peskowitz resembles Auden's poetic lover and "private detective": they demand actually embodied and situated "persons whose existence and histories could be verified." She is not deceived by "fictitious persons whose characters and history the [scholar] is free to idealize," patronize, demean, or make invisible. She prefers the reconstruction of a specific ancient Jewish society authenticated by archaeological research to the flattering and ageless self-portraits contrived by Judaism's patriarchs. She also resembles Foucault. Explaining what motivated him to write the history of sexuality, Foucault named "curiosity . . . not the curiosity that seeks to assimilate what it is proper for one to know, but that which enables one to get free from oneself. . . . The object [is] to learn to what extent the effort to think one's own history can free thought from what it silently thinks, and so enable it to think differently."[3] With Miriam Peskowitz's exemplary essay in mind, "think differently," act differently, and for the better, one might add.

"Engendering Jewish Religious History" also reminded me that on our way to becoming professional colleagues at Duke, Miriam Peskowitz and I used some of the same texts in teaching that same intractable introductory course in Judaic civilization. I still do, aiming for similar goals with the same cross-listing in Women's Studies. We also share a "late twentieth-century" perplexity regarding "the proliferation of theoretical electives and scholarly performances . . . none of which are essentially or necessarily liberatory." Her invitation to consider "the terms and categories of our feminist conversations" spoke to the philosopher in me. I therefore welcomed the chance to examine which of those terms and categories "have served well, but which need not always organize our inquiries." I became fascinated by the implications of the essay's technological metaphors: tailor-made "seamless garments" and "threads"; architectural "constructs," "construction sites," "tools," and "excavation"; and their hybrid, "dismantling." Finally, being a bookish historian of medieval Jewish thought with a penchant for abstract metaphysics and an acquired taste for arcane epistemologies, I was unable to hide from the troubling questions raised by the essay's final sentence: As a scholar "engaged in the production of an always-already-politicized knowledge," what politics do I perpetrate? Although I too refuse the tokenism "add women and stir" and want to accomplish more than making medieval Jewish women conspicuous by their absence among the literate intelligentsia,[4] am I nevertheless an accomplice to oppression? Is my scholarship a wrongdoing?

"*Tun wir ihnen immer Unrecht*—we constantly do them wrong. Sometimes they are overvalued, at other times undervalued." So wrote Wittgenstein in 1931, referring explicitly to the "Jew" who in "western civilization . . . is always measured on scales which are inappropriate to him."[5] Presumably, Wittgenstein was exploiting the scientific and political ambiguities of "right" and "correct" to observe that Western civilization fails to understand Jews correctly and fails to treat Jews justly. The same is true for so many Others. Women, for example: Western civilization constantly does them wrong. Sometimes women are unrealistically overvalued and idealized, at other times undervalued and demonized. Misogyny and antisemitism, being pernicious social practices and mistaken scholarly opinions, therefore resemble racial prejudice. They show two faces: inappropriate glorification and vilification.

Thinking with Wittgenstein and pondering Miriam Peskowitz's arguments for engendering Jewish religious history, the cynic in me grumbles: "Why fall short and draw the line at engendering? Feminism itself is a many-splendored hyphenated-thing, and are not sex and sexuality the more fundamental and problematic social categories?[6] Therefore, if antisemitism, androcentric misogyny, and racism, then why not heterocentric homophobia; and if antisemitism, sexism, racism, and homophobia, then why not Eurocentric Orientalism;[7] and if antisemitism, sexism, racism, homophobia, and Orientalism, then why not religious Fundamentalism; and if antisemitism, sexism, racism, homophobia, Orientalism, and Fundamentalism, then why not nationalism and its offspring, imperialism and colonialism? And if to unmask and eliminate antisemitism, sexism, racism, homophobia, Orientalism, Fundamentalism, and nationalism, then why not capitalism?"

My cynic is an idiot savant, a well-read, sanctimonious, perverse egalitarian, too. His litany unfolds with paralyzing logic: "If to unearth and dislodge antisemitism, sexism, racism, homophobia, Orientalism, Fundamentalism, nationalism, and capitalism, then surely essentialism and foundationalism deserve the same. And since essentialism and foundationalism, then surely Idealism's metanarratives and reifications. And, logocentrism. Speaking of which, there is manly Cartesian dualism with its escapist flights into objectivity and its abject failure to 'think through the body.'[8] Hence, as Zeno's paradox teaches, there is no point in even beginning a course in Jewish Studies. No matter how long the syllabus, it will never reach Adam, to say nothing of Zionism. So why bother?"

Then comes the cynic's clincher: "Naive utopians are all the same. We forget that Revolution's wake is the Reign of Terror. Well intentioned, we want ego where there was id, equality where there was subordination, but we ignore Freud's warning: 'prejudices . . . are powerful things. . . . They are kept in existence by emotional forces and the struggle against them is hard . . . society makes what is disagreeable into what is untrue.'[9] Deluded by self-aggrandizement and wishful thinking, some academicians mistake theory for pragmatic behavior, they confuse the classroom with Main Street: they assume that academic rites are effective political actions, that scholarship is somehow capable of fixing a broken society because academic knowledge is produced and therefore 'politicized.' Why bother delivering learned lectures when there are social wounds to be healed, patriarchies to be smashed, battered wives and abused children to be defended, workplace discriminations to be abolished, impersonal bureaucracies to be humanized, economic boycotts to be coordinated, voters to be mobilized, corrupt officials to be unseated, politicians to be lobbied? Why not leave real politics to the partisan activists? Why not just teach Jewish Studies? Why not stick to Maimonides, Averroan Neo-Aristotelians, hypothetical disjunctive syllogisms, and the possibility of conjunction with the Active Intellect?"

Like any housebroken dog, my cynic annoys by barking too much. But the curmudgeon never bites. Animal that he is, the cynic is also constitutionally incapable of telling lies. Neither does he favor books over people, which is why I prefer his needling company to the wizened harangues of an Alan Bloom. Bloom's unexpected 1987 potboiler, *The Closing of the American Mind,* was subtitled *How Higher Education Has Failed Democracy and Impoverished the Souls of Today's Students.*[10]

Bloom's canonic diatribe against feminism proves that a more accurate subtitle would have been "How Democracy Has Failed Higher Education and Impoverished the Souls of Today's Students." Arguing that the "latest enemy of the vitality of classic texts is feminism" and that feminists are more blameworthy than the intrusive political activists of the sixties and the seventies, Bloom condemned all those "radicals" for ruining academia: "The democratization of the university helped dismantle its structure" (65).

The escapist motif of "classic texts" is sounded throughout Bloom's book, but nowhere more defiantly than in its final three pages. The "Conclusion" assures us that "men may live more truly and fully in reading Plato and Shakespeare . . . because then they are participating in essential being and forgetting their accidental lives" (380). By "accidental lives," I presume Bloom makes negligible the factors of race, gender, class, sexuality, and culture. No wonder he disdains so-called popular culture and objects to anthropologically or historically minded intellectuals who insist on placing those particularizing variables on the scholarly agenda. Unlike Auden's lover, who craves embodied specificity, and Foucault and Peskowitz, who are devoted to social and intellectual reform, Bloom wants to forget accidental life because it is "an imperfect humanity, which we can no longer bear." He proclaims that we suffer from "culture despair" because we have lost touch with what is "best in man, independent of accidents, of circumstance" and because "we feel ourselves too dependent on history and culture" (381). Bloom's prescription for emancipation and a tolerable life is philosophy. Sounding like an apologist for the nineteenth century's genteel version of bourgeois Jewish Studies,[11] Bloom monastically proclaims that thinking about certain books "might be what it is all for" and that "books in their objective beauty are still there." Bloom tells the anecdote of a "serious student . . . with deep melancholy" who was comforted by being told that he "did not have Socrates, but he had Plato's book about him, which might even be better," because bookish philosophizing with a few friends is the "only real friendship" where "the contact people so desperately seek is to be found. The other kinds of relatedness are only imperfect reflections of this one" (381).

Downwind of Bloom's obtuse scholasticism, my cynic senses that Bloom's politics are as contemptible as his scholarship is suspect. No longer chasing his tail futilely, the cynic quips: "Starving, the Bloomians would rather read menus than raid the 'fridge. Hearing the 'binding of Isaac,' they improbably imagine leather covers protecting the Great Book of Books. What are they, salesmen working on hefty commissions for some Buy-the-Book-of-the-Week Club? I take it all back. Far better the indispensable first step of engendering Jewish religious history than the pernicious stagnation of Bloom's upwardly displaced anxiety over philosophy's survival. Better a noisy postmodernist course in Jewish Studies that shuttles between anti-semitism, racism, misogyny, homophobia, nationalism, and capitalism without ever arriving at Jewish Studies than yet another course that inevitably gets its history wrong by turning deaf ears to the quotidian clamor of actual people and egalitarian politics.[12] Better the potential embarrassment, libidinal excitement, and realistic anxiety of touching the body politic than the fetish of books and the refuge of syllabi designed to teach that we do not have Moses, but we have Maimonides' 'book about him, which might even be better,' and so-and-so's supercommentary to Maimonides' book and so-and-so's glosses to that supercommentary and so-and-so's marginal interpolations to those glosses, which prove that one so-and-so, was influenced by another so-and-so who in turn borrowed this from that. (See CAVIL: An Imaginary Journal of Texts and Studies in Texts and Studies Devoted to Pusillanimadiversion)."

The intemperate cynic must be reading Alice Miller, again. She is a Swiss psychotherapist, the champion of all victims, especially abused children. In her essay "When Isaac Arises from the Sacrificial Altar,"[13] Miller wonders about ideologically inspired violence and oppression, the prevention of war, and everything else that Miriam Peskowitz includes among the "things that need our best thinking." Like Foucault, Miller asks, "How, then, can a condition that has endured for millennia be changed?" (143). Being a psychotherapist rather than an archaeologist of knowledge, Miller's response differs from Foucault's:

> What would happen if Isaac, instead of reaching for the knife, were to use every ounce of his strength to free his hands so that he could remove Abraham's hand from his face? . . . He would no longer lie there like a sacrificial lamb but would stand up; he would dare to use his eyes and see his father as he really is: uncertain and hesitant yet intent on carrying out a command he does not comprehend. Now Isaac's nose and mouth would be free too, and he could finally draw a deep breath and make use of his voice. He would be able to speak and ask questions. . . . The new Isaac—with his questions, with his awareness, with his refusal to let himself be killed—not only saves his own life but also saves his father from the fate of becoming the unthinking murderer of his child. (143–145)

These are precisely the intellectual goals and humane methods of "Engendering Jewish Religious History," even though the metaphors differ. Miller does not unmask and undo oppressive institutions and practices by impersonal "dismantling." Her humanitarian and liberatory metaphors are relentlessly embodied in living flesh and blood. "Instead of reaching for the knife," she asks us to "free" our hands, "remove" the paternalistic oppressor's "hand" from our "faces," "stand up," "see" things as they really are, "draw a deep breath," "speak" in our own voice, and "ask questions." The cynic in me looks at the Bloom in me and knows that there but for the grace of Alice Miller go I, a mendacious and trivializing antiquarian. There but for the grace of Alice Miller, W. H. Auden's poetic lover, Foucault, Miriam Peskowitz, and all the other feminists, postmodernists, epistemologists of the closet,[14] and social historians who complicate everything by insisting on body, gender, sexuality, race, class, artifactual evidence, and popular culture go I, an errant historian who never "sees things as they really are,"[15] squandering the chance to become or encourage others to be the "new Isaac."

As I have slowly come to understand the overlapping moral implications and academic imperatives of social history and cultural studies as inflected by feminism and the "new Isaac," I have been compelled to reconsider my professional life.[16] By temperament, training, and field of interdisciplinary medieval endeavor, I am always tempted to stick to Maimonides and arcane arguments over the possibility of conjunction with the Active Intellect. I delight in mapping how the Kabbalists and philosophers struggled to come to terms with one another's conceptual and experiential schemes. I am fascinated by the ways in which the Jewish intelligentsia domesticated Islamic theology and philosophy. I am enchanted by the ingenuity of biblical exegetes whose semiotic legerdemain tricked classical rabbinic midrash into speaking medieval Platonism and Aristotelianism. I am transfixed by the stories of how premodern Jewish philosophy and Semitic philology were conscripted in the struggle against Christianity, and I am astonished by the twists and turns of Jewish thought as Europe transformed itself into a "persecuting society" and its Jews into an "alienated minority,"[17] especially in hostile fifteenth-century Spain.

In the very beginning, it seemed as though the medieval thinkers replicated me. Enjoying the prerogatives of patriarchy, I therefore thought that my research topics were intrinsically interesting, that my infatuations justified my teaching and research. Perhaps, too, they contained hermeneutically decipherable, edifying messages for contemporary Jews. Such naive confidence and parochialism were eroded by any number of things, chief among them living with a significant Other, an art historian, a Byzantinist, and ingesting Marxist and feminist critiques that argue that philosophy, like politics, is warfare by other means. Teaching medieval Jewish philosophy as if business were usual became an embarrassment.

Then came Lucien Febvre's face-saving maneuver: "We instinctively bring to bear on [our] texts our ideas, our feelings, the fruit of our scientific inquiries, our political experiences, and our social achievements. . . . Just because the sequence of ideas in these texts confers on them a kind of eternal verity, to our eyes at least, can we conclude that all intellectual attitudes are possible in all periods? Equally possible?"[18] Febvre's answer was no. His thoroughgoing academic historicism seemed to dovetail with Miller's humanitarian and liberatory call to see things as they really are: contingent, and therefore subject to change, perhaps for the better.

Teaching medieval Jewish intellectual history became less of an embarrassment. With the help of Febvre and the Marxists, it became obvious that the medieval philosophers and mystics could be made meaningful by re-attaching them to the specifically urban, political, and economic circumstances that made their ideas possible and necessary. Challenged by feminism's intense engagement with the body and provoked by the debates swirling around Orientalism, I found myself tracing the historiographic myth of Jewish ("Semitic") aniconism and discovering the neglected field of medieval Jewish aesthetics. Freed by Febvre from the burden of reading the medieval intelligentsia apologetically, of sifting their words to find some timeless and edifying truths, I began to see the medieval philosophers for the pugnacious, belligerent, and feisty intellectuals they were. No one was more scornful of obscurantist spirituality, mindless hedonism, and ethnic chauvinism than they. Freed by Febvre and Miller from the burden of impersonating me, the medieval Jewish intelligentsia retroactively became less my anachronistic, fictitious idealizations and more the embodied and situated aliens they truly are: Ashkenazic or Sephardic, pre-State of Israel, pre-Holocaust, pre-Gutenbergian, pre-Newtonian, pre-Darwinian, pre-Freudian, non-coffee-drinking, non-potato-eating, non-wristwatch-wearing, non-fax-using, medieval Jewish men who were shaped by and reproduced medieval misogyny.

To emulate Auden's poetic lover and honor Miriam Peskowitz's project of amending Jewish historiography, books like Genevieve Lloyd's feminist critique, *The Man of Reason: "Male" and "Female" in Western Philosophy*,[19] would therefore have to be assigned their rightful place in my teaching and research. How else would the multiple, diverse voices within our selves, originating in the elusive past and amplified by the cantankerous present, be given a fair hearing? How else might the factual be winnowed from the fictitious, and my students encouraged to get their strangers right, becoming the "new Isaac?"

Notes

1. See Seyla Benhabib, "Feminism and Postmodernism: An Uneasy Alliance," reprinted in *Feminist Contentions,* ed. Linda Nicholson et al. (New York: Routledge, 1995), 16. (The feminist counterpoint to the "Death of History" would be the "Engendering of Historical Narrative.")

2. See *W. H. Auden: Collected Poems,* ed. Edward Mendelson (New York: Random House, 1976), 489–499.

3. See Michel Foucault, *The Use of Pleasure: The History of Sexuality,* trans. Robert Hurley, vol. 2 (New York: Vintage Books, 1990), 8–9.

4. See Gershom Scholem, *Major Trends in Jewish Mysticism* (New York: Schocken Books, 1961), 37–38.

5. See Ludwig Wittgenstein, *Culture and Value,* trans. Peter Winch (Chicago: University of Chicago Press, 1984), 16.

6. For the hyphens, see Sandra Harding, *The Science Question in Feminism* (Ithaca, NY: Cornell University Press, 1986), 163ff. For the categorical priority of sex and sexuality, see, for example, Donna J. Haraway, *Simians, Cyborgs, and Women: The Reinvention of Nature* (New York: Routledge, 1991), esp. 127–181; and Eve Kosofsky Sedgwick, *Tendencies* (Durham, NC: Duke University Press, 1993).

7. See Vassilis Lambropoulos, *The Rise of Eurocentrism: Anatomy of Interpretation* (Princeton: Princeton University Press, 1993).

8. See Susan Bordo, *The Flight to Objectivity: Essays on Cartesianism and Culture* (Albany: SUNY Press, 1987); Jane Gallop, *Thinking Through the Body* (New York: Columbia University Press, 1988); and Maxine Sheets-Johnstone, ed., *Giving the Body Its Due* (Albany: SUNY Press, 1992).

9. See Sigmund Freud, *Introductory Lectures on Psychoanalysis,* ed. and trans. James Strachey (New York: Norton, 1977), 21, 23.

10. See Alan Bloom, *The Closing of the American Mind: How Higher Education Has Failed Democracy and Impoverished the Souls of Today's Students* (New York: Simon & Schuster, 1987).

11. See Gershom Scholem, "The Science of Judaism—Then and Now," in *The Messianic Idea in Judaism* (New York: Schocken Books, 1971), 304–313; and the fuller, more pungently critical Hebrew version reprinted in G. Scholem *Devarim Be–Go* (Explications and Implications) (Tel Aviv: Am Oved, 1982), 2: 385–403.

12. See Aaron Gurevich, *Historical Anthropology of the Middle Ages,* ed. Jana Howlett (Chicago: University of Chicago Press, 1992), 3–20. ("So that the sources, the creations of people from the epoch studied, may speak, they must be asked the questions posed to the historian by the pressing needs of his own time" [p. 5].)

13. See Alice Miller, *The Untouched Key: Tracing Childhood Trauma in Creativity and Destructiveness,* trans. Hildegarde and Hunter Hannum (New York: Doubleday, 1990), 137–165.

14. See Eve Kosofsky Sedgwick, *Epistemology of the Closet* (Berkeley: University of California Press, 1990); and Daniel Boyarin, *Carnal Israel: Readings in Talmudic Literature* (Berkeley: University of California Press, 1993).

15. The irony of resonance with Ranke's discredited "*wie es eigentlich gewesen*" does not escape me. See Peter Novick, *That Noble Dream: The "Objectivity Question" and the American Historical Profession* (Cambridge: Cambridge University Press, 1988), esp. 26–31. Although I live where postmodern thoughts are insistent, I myself am not postmodernist if postmodernism necessarily entails the end of efforts to get history right. Because the search is not for a monomythic essentialist Real in History but for multiple, realistic histories, perhaps "*wie es wirklich gewesen,*" ought to decorate my t-shirts. For more discussion on the alliance between feminism and historiography, see *Feminist Contentions* cited above in note 1. Also on behalf of academic history, I defer to the eloquence and pragmatic confidence of Yosef Hayim Yerushalmi, *Zakhor: Jewish History and Jewish Memory* (New York: Schocken Books, 1989 [orig. 1982]), 116 ("Against the agents of oblivion . . . the assassins of memory . . . only the historian, with the austere passion for fact, proof, evidence . . . can effectively stand guard").

16. For a sample of what happens when Jewish Studies meets cultural studies, see *Poetics Today* 15.1 (1994), a special issue edited by Daniel Boyarin entitled "Purim and the Cultural Poetics of Judaism." For the meeting with "Body Studies," see Howard Eilberg–Schwartz,

People of the Body: Jews and Judaism from an Embodied Perspective (Albany: SUNY Press, 1992).

17. See Kenneth R. Stow, *Alienated Minority: The Jews of Medieval Latin Europe* (Cambridge: Harvard University Press, 1992); R. I. Moore, *The Formation of a Persecuting Society: Power and Deviance in Western Europe, 950–1250* (Oxford: Blackwell, 1990); and Mark R. Cohen, *Under Crescent and Cross: The Jews in the Middle Ages* (Princeton: Princeton University Press, 1994).

18. See Lucien Febvre, *The Problem of Unbelief in the Sixteenth Century: The Religion of Rabelais,* trans. Beatrice Gottlieb (Cambridge: Harvard University Press, 1982), 5–6.

19. See Genevieve Lloyd, *The Man of Reason,* 2d ed. (Minneapolis: University of Minnesota Press, 1993).

Part Two:

Studies

A Jewess, More and/or Less

Amy-Jill Levine

The eminent scholar of Christian origins welcomed his Duke University graduate students to his seminar on Paul with detailed bibliographies, extensive references to Pirke Aboth 1.1, and personal greetings to all participants. At one point during such introductory matters, he interrupted his greetings with ". . . and, ah, a Jewess." I looked around quickly: there's a Jewess in the room! Get a fly swatter, a butterfly net, an archivist. An etymologist or an entomologist . . .

It took a moment before I realized he was talking about me.

The Sign

Merriam-Webster's Collegiate Dictionary reads, "Jewess/*n* (14c): a Jewish girl or woman—sometimes taken to be offensive."[1] Who considers it offensive—the speaker, the hearer, Jews, gentiles, the "culture"—remains unstated. Nor is it clear why the term would offend, although it likely carries both taxonomic and taxidermic transgression. It is on the one hand a generic classification of a particular group of women with anthropological if not zoological implications, and, on the other, it is both a derivative of and a supplement to *Jew.*

Jewess perpetuates the almost abandoned practice of gendering people according to ethnic, religious, and racial categories. Americans do not linguistically gender Italians, Republicans, the rich, Caucasians, Presbyterians, and others. We do not speak of a Hindess or an Eskimess. Nor is it simply a vestige of inflected European designations, such as *la Juive* or *die Jüdin.* As with all other translations of European models, the English could have been "a Jewish woman." Rather, gendered corporate or ontological categories[2] in American English are primarily references to the animal kingdom, which themselves are then reapplied to women: *tigress, lioness, bitch.* The similarly antiquated term *Negress*[3] supports the observation: the feminized designation applies to anthropological categories that are perceived by the dominant culture to be other, less desirable than, and potentially dangerous to, the norm.

The Jewess is not distinguished by religious affiliation but, rather, by ethnic or racial markers, which are often sexually charged; thus she is not be a convert (Kate Capshaw is not a "Jewess"). She is located more easily than her male counterparts at the borders of Jewish and gentile society, perhaps because she does not bear the mark of circumcision, perhaps because she is by her very ethnic foreignness yet proximate location more desirable to the (male) gentile subject. As Jonathan Z. Smith succinctly states: "The 'other' has appeared as an object of desire as well as an object of repulsion; the 'other' has rarely been an object of indifference."[4] The Jewess's position as proximate other to gentile men increases her threat to their identity and produces the attendant cultural need that she be either removed or domesticated.

Examples in the *Oxford English Dictionary* confirm the Jewess's transgressive possibilities. The first appearance of the term in English is apparently Wyclif's 1388 rendition of Acts 16:1 as "Timothe, the sone of a Jewesse cristien" (the Greek is "son of a Jewish woman believer": *huios gynaikos Ioudaias pistis*). The next biblical translation cited, Tyndale's 1526 version, mentions "Felix and his wyfe Drusilla which was a jewes" (Acts 24:24: *Ioudaia*). That these initial references occur not in "Jewish" texts but in the New Testament already demonstrates the Jewess's location on group boundaries. Moreover, both women are precisely indicated to be Jewesses in the context of the boundary-breaking event of intermarriage. Timothy is the son of a Jewish (Christian) woman and a gentile (non-Christian) father; his ethnic identity is therefore placed in dispute, and Paul resorts only two verses later to having him circumcised "out of consideration for the Jews in that region, for they knew that his father was a gentile" (Acts 16:3).[5] Drusilla, known also from Josephus's *Antiquities* 18–20 (cf. *War* 2), is more than a second example of intermarriage. This beautiful daughter of Agrippa I had been betrothed by her father to Epiphanes of Commangene; following Agrippa's death Epiphanes recanted his promise to be circumcised, and the marriage was called off. Drusilla was then betrothed by her brother, Agrippa II, to Azizus of Emesa, who gained a wife but lost a foreskin. (The Syrian king later lost Drusilla also; she dissolved her marriage and wed the Roman procurator Antonius Felix, who had been pursuing her.) The *OED* includes as well a reference to *Ivanhoe*'s beautiful Rebecca, and to this group could be added such figures as the brilliant salonière Rachel Varnhagen,[6] the neurotic Whore of Mensa (de)constructed by Woody Allen,[7] the castrating viragos Judith and Salome, even the lovely Queen Esther.[8]

Noted for her sexual desirability and so her sexual threat, the Jewess is tied to the exotic, the primitive, and the atavistic. She is therefore distinguished from the categories "Jewish woman" and "Jewish mother." Like the "Christian woman" and the "German woman," the "Jewish woman" is safely circumscribed within linguistically conventional, socially secure borders. The Jewish woman is signified by the *ēshet hayyil* of Proverbs, who works at home while her (Jewish) husband sings her praises at the city gates. There is the Jewish mother who dispenses chicken soup, love, and guilt. That is to say, Mrs. Portnoy is not a "Jewess." Should the Jewess marry a gentile, her threat remains, and it is enhanced by the potential problems her children will pose for group identity. Thus Timothy must be circumcised (although the mother "naturally" embodies her Jewish identity, the son requires a "cultural" operation to enter). The undomesticated, the threatening Jewess must either be removed (Rebecca is sent off, single, to Jerusalem), be replaced (the Whore of Mensa is replaced by an archetypal shiksa[9]), or die.[10]

Yet these "natural" properties belie another tradition that sees the Jewess not as "more than a woman" in the gendered sense of sexual but as "less." Beyond her sexuality, she is also noted for her intellect, sophistication, and attempts at self-determination, which in turn contribute to her desirability even as they add to her threat. Drusilla and Salome manipulate court politics, Judith proves the only competent leader in Bethulia, Sir Walter Scott's Rebecca was famous for her healing arts. The salonières titillated their gentile guests with their ability and desire to engage in public discourse, something "Christian women" did not do. The Whore of Mensa "was barely nineteen years old, but already she had developed the hardened facility of the pseudo-intellectual."[11]

More than, and less than, "woman," the Jewess is also both more and less than "Jew." The term is itself derived from the normative category "Jew" (cf. Genesis 2:23 on *ish* and *ishah*, or the etymologically false derivative "woman" from "man"). *Webster's* definition of *Jew* once again establishes the norm: "A member of the tribe of Judah . . . Israelite . . . a person belonging to a continuation through descent or conversion of the ancient Jewish people . . . one whose religion is Judaism." It does not say "Male Jew." It does not say that *Jew* has derogatory connotations (the verb *to jew* as in "to jew the price down" does not appear in this volume, although it does appear in the *OED*).

As secondary and derivative to Jew, the Jewess is something less. However, in supplementing the Jew and so containing the potential to complete or replace the categorization, the Jewess is something more. Her femaleness, her *ess-ence*, makes her more assimilable. Therein lies her threat, for she penetrates the dominant group easily, without its realization. Hence her "Jew"ness becomes yet again ambiguous, and ambiguity is a threat. Brandishing her dangerous supplemental "ess," the Jewess is an ideal sign for conveying cultural anxieties. Further, as cultural icon and as anomaly, the Jewess is more than simply a cipher for gender roles, be they literary, historical, or both. She outstrips this category of analysis even as she reinforces it.

The Significance

By recognizing what is expected of me by those who would see me as "Jewess," I can both anticipate any potential offense (even if the initial contact is *intended* in a fully complimentary way) and address the gaps where the other's perspective does not match my own. Moreover, the dynamics of the threat posed by the signifier *Jewess* enable me to rethink both the history and the historiography of its purported referent, Jewish women.

In June 1995 I completed an essay for a collection on the gospel of Matthew. The original introduction, after summarizing the process by which papers were selected, noted that my contribution "was especially commissioned by the editors for this volume in order to fill what would otherwise be a significant void." Unstated was the void: Jewish exegesis? Feminist exegesis? Jewish-feminist exegesis (not [yet] regarded as a significant void in essay collections on the gospels)? Exegesis with a sense of humor? Exegesis by a Jewish woman (with here a focus on the person rather than the method)? We are back to the "Jewess" problem: the product is expected to be other than the norm, if not sexually charged, intellectual, and likely both threatening and titillating.

To some extent, this classification comes from the anomaly of my working in Christian origins. The traditional expectation is that women study women, and Jews study Jews. Crossover investigation is suspect whether it is generated "from above" or "from below": the Christian who studies Judaism or a man who studies women now risks accusations of co-optation; Jews who study Christianity, or women who study men risk accusations ranging from disloyalty against their own group to polemic against the object of investigation. Moreover, although Jewish studies and women's studies are increasingly welcomed to the academic banquet, they do not yet have seats of honor. There is literature, and then there is Jewish literature; there is history, and then there is women's history. Comparably rare are majors in Judaica and women's studies, which are interdisciplinary and therefore anomalous. Worse, women's studies/studies by women are often dismissed as mushy-minded, unimportant, and only for women; Jewish studies are viewed as parochial, ancillary, and only for Jews.

Conventional expectations, in like manner but even more insidiously, posit that a member of a group can only, and only can, speak for that group, which is itself implicitly regarded as monolithic. The professor of that graduate class on occasion directed to me questions beginning "What do the Jews think about . . . ?" Since the object of such questions tended to be "Galatians" or "Acts," I had an excellent excuse for my inability to answer. And several fellow students took the *Frauenfrage* approach: "What do women think about . . . ?" Each time the topics of Jews or women arose, eyes turned to see my reaction (this was not the case in discussions of apostolic authority or justification by faith). Ironically, the "Jews" and "women" addressed in that class were all Christians (those to whom Gal. 3:28 was addressed, the pillars in Jerusalem, etc.), and, obviously, I was not actually part of the unfortunately titled "circumcision party." But I became nevertheless the incarnation of those Christians of antiquity who did not prevail: women who heard that "in Christ Jesus there is not male and not female"; men who insisted that their brothers in the church be circumcised. Thus I became domesticated as the house heretic or class Jew.

What I needed was to appropriate and transform the model of the Jewess: attuned to matters of both Jews and women, cognizant of conventions, conversant with the discourses and interests of the dominant (male, gentile) culture, willing to transgress disciplinary boundaries and gender roles, unafraid to name patriarchal practices and supersessionist readings. The paradigm would be the Apocryphal original, Judith (*Ioudith*, lit.: Jewess) of Bethulia. Both by acknowledging my own interests and by responding to those imposed upon me, I found in the Jewess both a method and a subject matter. Not unexpectedly, I then faced the task of contextualizing my interests and theories such that they could become part of the wider academic and cultural conversation.

Specifically, I am interested in the representations of women and Jews in the narratives of Hellenistic Judaism and early Christianity. These two foci are mutually implicated, even as they are both other to the regnant concerns of the synagogue and church. That is to say, classifications of Jews and women by gentiles and men tend to utilize similar language. The Jews share the associations discussed above in relation to the Jewess: they are primitive, atavistic, overly concerned or identified with the body. One does not need to evoke explicit psychoanalytic connections among circumcision, castration, demasculinization, and feminization in order to support this conclusion. From antiquity comes Chrysostom's polemical feminization of Judaism and Jews;[12] from the Middle Ages comes the well-known legend that Jewish men menstruated; from fin-de-siècle Vienna comes the slang term *Jew* (*Jud*) for the clitoris. More subtle is the association between women and (male) Jews in Jewish literature;[13] the model ranges from the figurations of the covenant community as divine beloved, lamenting widow, adulterous wife, and so forth in the Prophetic literature to the more fully developed metonymous women of the Hellenistic novellae: Judith, Susanna, Esther, Sarah.

Such concerns for gender roles and folk traditions, for vicious polemic and comparably benign metonymic representation, remain yet on the margins of what the academy, the synagogue, and the church regard as important. Simultaneously, these subject areas threaten and offend the self-definition of the very disciplinary categories and traditions that would dismiss them. The Apocrypha, a term connoting something "hidden" and "spurious," is thus aptly named.

Studies of the Apocryphal novellae, that is, studies of narrative fiction, have been seen in the university and the seminary as less "important" than studies of history and theology, as if there is a great intrinsic distinction among the three genres. First Maccabees and the Wisdom of Solomon have received more attention in the secondary literature than have Judith, Susanna, and Tobit. Similarly, the depictions of women in the gospels (as characters, as figures in parables) and the use of feminine imagery (for example, of Sophia) are only now receiving more than a brief notice in the major textual resources of New Testament exegesis. The women in question have been much more welcomed in the world of art than in the world of text: the Apocrypha and the gospels provide ample models of naked women (Susanna), phallic women (Judith, Salome), virgin women (Mary), and fallen women (the Magdalene).[14] No-longer-active characters who manifest their religiosity through prayer and acts of piety, who manifest their intellect by argument and self-determination, they become frozen objects coded primarily on a sexual register rather than on religious or intellectual ones. To bring these figures prominently into scholarly discussion necessarily involves examining the subjects of sexuality and the body and so the attendant reactions of embarrassment, anxiety, and offense.

Material about men, or at least material that does not appear to concern women, has, moreover, been seen as having greater importance than texts with prominent female characters.[15] But neither genre nor subject matter explains fully the comparative lack of attention both Christians and Jews have paid to these Apocryphal women. To a great extent, these narratives have been ignored for confessional reasons. Preserved by the church, the Apocryphal documents became increasingly removed from both Jewish interest and Jewish linguistic expertise. Jews have traditionally ignored the Greek products of Hellenistic Judaism in favor of the Hebrew and Aramaic Torah, Targum, Tosefta, and Talmud. Considered "Deuterocanonical" by Roman Catholic and Eastern Orthodox traditions, and merely "worthy of reading," if that, by most Protestants, the Apocrypha is within church contexts the poor stepsister to the "Old Testament" and the "New." Although the majority of the women of the gospels are technically "Jewish," Jews have ignored them even as they have ignored Jesus and Paul in reconstructing their own history. Nor have these women received great attention from the church. To see them as representative of women's prominence in the early Jesus movement, as some feminist exegetes have been arguing for more than two decades, continues to offend and to threaten those who see themselves as guardians of the faith. To see them instead as rejecting Judaism (in this case characterized as oppressively patriarchal, misogynistic, repressive, spiritually dead, and so on) in favor of Jesus' (here not-"Jewish") movement is an offense both to scholarly rigor and to Judaism.[16]

These various offenses, to church and synagogue, to disciplinary structures and conventional wisdom, indicate the threats posed by these Jewesses to contemporary constructs and institutions. The women of the Apocrypha and, to a lesser extent, those of the gospels transgress the implicit boundaries of Judaism and Christianity: ethnically in one group but preserved by the other, they find a home in neither. These figures have a similar effect for the cultures that produced them. Metonymies for the covenant people, the Hellenistic novellae's representations of women and the church's reception of the Virgin and the Magdalene embody both the threats to and the survival of their respective communities. They provide the stage upon which the anxieties of the communities that display them can be expressed, mapped, and alleviated.

The Hellenistic age witnessed an increasing affiliation of gentiles within the borders of Judaism—through intermarriage and proselytism—and a correlate shift of Judaism from a biologically determined ethnic group to a multicultural *ethnos* with prominent communities located in a diaspora. Appropriately, the narratives then depict the Jewess as negotiating those borders: between enemy camp and virgin town (Judith); between young Judean morality and elderly Babylonian sin (Susanna); between diasporic demons and virtuous angels (Sarah of Tobit); between genocidal silence and pietistic salvation (Esther). The church, similarly, came to recognize the two Marys as models for the community: as virgin and pure, and as fallen but redeemed (the Magdalene receives no direct sexual reference in the gospel texts; only later is she transformed from the politically prominent position of the resurrection's first witness to the safe confines of sexual categorization).

For these Jewesses of antiquity, neither the gender constructs nor the portrayal of Judaism are equivalent. Although each embodies the covenant community, not all emphasize the same concerns. Nor should they. Gender constructions and representations of Jews are not universal, natural, or transhistorical; they are, rather, contingent and culture-specific.[17] Judith is not to be equated with the Whore of Mensa, any more than Mary Magdalene serves as a typology for *Ivanhoe*'s Rebecca. The Jewess, then, is a sign that signifies different cultural and gendered constructs for different times and different places. A heuristic model, the Jewess cannot be fully controlled or domesticated. Therein ultimately lies her threat, her offense, and her perpetual ability to reveal the fault lines in cultural, disciplinary, and religious borders.

Notes

With many thanks to Jay Geller, a significant other with significant insights, corrections, and references.

1. 9th ed. (Springfield, MA: Merriam-Webster, 1990). Laura Levitt pointed out to me that the *American Heritage Dictionary*, 3d ed. (Boston: Houghton Mifflin, 1992), defines *Jewess* as "n., *Offensive.* A Jewish woman or girl." The usage note reads, "Like the feminine form of other ethnic terms, such as *Negress*, the word *Jewess* has come to be widely regarded as offensive, since it seems to imply that the conjunction of Jewish and female sex is sufficient to establish a distinct racial or social category. Where reference to gender is relevant, the phrase *Jewish woman* can be used: "*As a Jewish woman. Rosa Luxemburg was doubly sensitive to the discrimination that underlay social attitudes in late nineteenth-century Europe. See usage note at Negress.*"

My observations hold primarily for North American audiences. The professor described above is from the British Commonwealth; there was clearly no insult—quite the contrary—intended by his terminology (there are in fact many positive uses of the term in Western discourse). The impetus for these reflections is not his intent but rather my reaction.

2. I distinguish between ontological categories such as race and ethnicity, where gendered terminology is lacking in American English, and vocational categories (actress, waitress, hostess), where it remains. Although this second group is not stigmatized by the uniqueness that accompanies *Negress* and *Jewess* in relation to all other ethnic and religious designations, it nevertheless retains the derivative and therefore dismissive implications that the two terms connote. "White-collar" positions, such as judge, lawyer, and doctor, lack feminized forms.

3. The Algonquin term *squaw* remains in the English language; *Merriam Webster's* classifies it as a "jocular usage." The model is not the same as *Negress* or *Jewess* in that the term both is indigenous and is not derivative. A better comparison is *giantess*, which is the example *Merriam Webster's* provides for the definition of the suffix "-ess."

4. Jonathan Z. Smith, "What a Difference a Difference Makes," in *"To See Ourselves as Others See Us": Christians, Jews, Others in Late Antiquity*, ed. J. Neusner and E. Frerichs (Chico, CA: Scholars Press, 1985), 3–48 (citation on p. 16).

5. The transgressive nature of the entire incident is exacerbated by Paul's own insistence, in his epistles, that circumcision is for (gentile) Christians unnecessary, foolish, and a denial of both divine grace and the sacrifice of the Christ (cf. Gal. 2:3, 5:11, and 6:15). Increasingly ironic, the two New Testament "pastoral epistles" addressed to Timothy (1 and 2 Tim.) along with that to Titus present the most restrictive exhortations concerning women's roles in the church. There will be no "Jewess" in the congregation that follows the injunctions in 1 Tim. 2:9–15.

6. See the essay in this volume by Jay Geller. The first English edition (London: East & West Library, 1958) of Hannah Arendt's biography of Rachel Varnhagen was subtitled *The Life of a Jewess*. When the American, slightly revised edition appeared sixteen years later (New York: Harcourt Brace Jovanovich, 1974), the subtitle changed to *The Life of a Jewish Woman*.

7. Woody Allen, *Without Feathers* (New York: Random House, 1975), 32–38, cf. 37: "For three bills, you got the works: a thin Jewish brunette would pretend to pick you up at the Museum of Modern Art, let you read her master's, get you involved in a screaming quarrel at Elaine's over Freud's conception of women, and then fake a suicide of your choosing." The term *mistress*, with its underlying ambivalence, shares much in common with *Jewess*.

8. Indeed, every bordello had its handsome Jewess, the *belle juive*. See J. K. Huysmans, *Against the Grain* (1884; New York: Random House, 1956), 75.

9. Allen, *Without Feathers*, 38. "Later that night, I looked up an old account of mine named Gloria. She was blond. She had graduated cum laude. The difference was she majored in physical education. It felt good."

10. Cf. Judith Wachs, "The Heart of Her People," in *The Tribe of Dina: A Jewish Women's Anthology*, ed. Melanie Kaye/Kantrowitz and Irena Klepfisz (Boston: Beacon Press, 1986), 30, on the nineteenth-century Moroccan ballad of Sol Hatchuel (*sol la saddika*, Sol the Righteous). This young girl who chooses martyrdom rather than convert to Islam and enter the Sultan's harem speaks in the poem, "*Aunque jure y perfecte otra ley / hebrea tengo que morir*"; "But although I may swear allegiance to another law / I will die a Jewess." Appropriately, "hebrea" is rendered "Jewess" rather than "Hebrew" or "Hebrew woman." Wachs also cites a *ro-*

mança sung at Passover concerning the midwives of Exodus 1: "*Las comadres eran judías / Del Dío eran queridas / Arrecivían y fuivan / Emperó nació Moxé*"; "The midwives were Jewesses / Beloved of God / They disobeyed, and by their resistance / Moses was born" (31). Again, the Jewess is connected with ethnic borders and transgressive acts, although here the references are not at all derogatory.

11. Allen, *Without Feathers*, 35. Thus "Jewish American Princess" is not synonymous with "Jewess" although it shares the offending connotation; *Merriam-Webster's* offers "Jewish princess" ("a daughter of a well-to-do American Jewish family—called also Jewish American princess; usually used disparagingly").

12. See the discussion by Ross S. Kraemer, "The Other as Woman: An Aspect of Polemic among Pagans, Jews, and Christians in the Greco-Roman World," in *The Other in Jewish Thought and History: Constructions of Jewish Cultural Identity*, ed. Lawrence Silberstein and Robert Cohn (New York and London: New York University Press, 1994), 121–144.

13. On the implications presented by the representation of the (male-defined) covenant community as female, see Howard Eilberg-Schwartz, *God's Phallus and Other Problems for Men and Monotheism* (Boston: Beacon Press, 1994).

14. The implications of these works for studies of the representation of/cultural meaning accorded to Jewish women is an underexplored subject. Also relevant for this discussion are matters such as the feminized conception of *art* history (versus the more "masculine" task of history), the ambivalent relationship between Jewish tradition and iconic representation, the Christian reclamation of these "Jewish" figures, and the relationship between the artistic representation of Jewish women versus that of Jewish men according to contemporary stereotypes.

15. The question of what a text is "about" is problematic. For example, the account of Susanna need not be seen as concerned primarily with a woman falsely accused of adultery. Rather, it may be "about" the introduction of Daniel as a wisdom figure or the breakdown of leadership in the Babylonian diaspora.

16. This concern for Christian-feminist anti-Judaism itself has a decades-long history. See the discussion in Amy-Jill Levine, "Yeast of Eden: Second Temple Judaism, Jesus, and Women," *Biblical Interpretation* 2.1 (1994): 8–33.

17. Eloquently discussed in the summary chapter of Daniel Boyarin's *Carnal Israel: Reading Sex in Talmudic Culture* (Berkeley: University of California Press, 1993).

A Matter of Discipline: Reading for Gender in Jewish Philosophy

Susan E. Shapiro

Methodological Prelude

Reading for gender in Jewish philosophical texts is an uncommon critical practice. Yet, for both philosophical and feminist reasons, such a hermeneutic is importantly engaged. In this essay, I will first clarify what I mean by "reading for gender" and why I think such a practice should be undertaken. I will then, given the constraints of space, demonstrate what I am talking about by gesturing toward a reading of Maimonides' *Guide of the Perplexed* in these terms.[1]

Reading for gender requires attending to the rhetoricity and textuality of a work, that is to its patterning of metaphors and other figures and tropes, and not only to its logic. This already represents a shift in certain, but not all, traditional philosophical practices. Rhetoric and poetics may be marginalized in Anglo-American philosophical styles of analysis and argument, but Jewish philosophy has long paid close attention to the role of stories and metaphors in its texts. However, even those who have noticed these metaphors and stories as part of their critical practice have, ultimately, made these aspects of the texts serve merely pedagogical, secondary functions in their interpretations. By contrast, the reading for rhetorics and poetics of gender in Jewish philosophical texts that I propose treats the relation between rhetoric and logic in the reverse; the logical arguments of a text are understood to be prefigured and, thus, made possible by its central rhetorical tropes. These tropes are, thus, considered constitutive and not secondary formations of the logic of philosophical texts.

Reading for gender, however, does not mean reading either for women or as a woman. To read for metaphors of "woman," "body," "gender relations," or "sexuality" is not to read for some actual woman or women that the text, somehow, represents. Nor does reading for gender mean reading as an "essentialized" woman reader who, as a woman, can (supposedly) locate the "feminine" stratum of the text. Rather, to read for gender is to read for constructions and performances of gender in these texts with an interest in the intellectual and cultural labor these tropes enact. It is to read, as well, with an interest in their consequences, both within these texts and for readers today. That is, the work performed by these gendered tropes will be found to be philosophical, requiring a rethinking of what we understand philosophical texts to be and how they, therefore, may best be read.

A genealogy of key tropes for gender and gender relations in Greek, Jewish, and Arabic philosophy will provide a context for the reading of Maimonides' *Guide of the Perplexed* undertaken here. In this essay, I will be able to indicate only the outlines and basic shape of this interpretive context. This reading, part of a larger work-in-process, makes clear, however, how such a genealogical reading works and why it is important. Finally, let me note that in making this turn to rhetoric I am not seeking to reduce other forms of discourse, such as logic, to "mere rhetoric." Rather, I am attempting to demonstrate rhetoric's constitutive relation to logic without, thereby, collapsing logic into rhetoric. To do so would simply reverse the ususal effacement of rhetoric by logic, a reversal that would betray the critical purposes and potential of the rhetorical turn I propose to undertake.

A Genealogical Introduction

Attaching the unruly aspects of textuality and interpretation to women and the feminine is an ancient topos and philosophical practice. Indeed—as I have argued elsewhere—the very disciplinarity of philosophy is in many respects constructed through a marginalization and governance of such putatively disruptive and unreliable functions as rhetoric and poetics.[2] Plato, for example, distinguishes philosophy—rhetoric made just through dialectic—and its other, unethical rhetoric: the cosmetic knack of mere appearance and deception. This originary disciplinary moment, thus, required a splitting within rhetoric. Through a dialectic of identity and difference, philosophy was built in opposition to rhetoric as its primary other. Philosophy thereby effaced its own rhetorical origins and character even as it relied on rhetoric to construct its own identity in opposition to her. The *locus classicus* for the constituting of philosophy over against mere rhetoric is Plato's *Gorgias*:[3]

> Socrates: Well then Gorgias, the activity [rhetoric] as a whole, it seems to me, is not an art, but the occupation of a shrewd and enterprising spirit, and of one naturally skilled in its dealings with men, and in sum and substance I call it "flattery." . . . There are then these four arts which always minister to what is best, one pair for the body, the other for the soul. But flattery perceiving this—I do not say by knowledge but by conjecture—has divided herself also into four branches, and insinuating herself into the guise of each of these parts, pretends to be that which she impersonates. And having no thought for what is best, she regularly uses pleasure as a bait to catch folly and

> deceives it into believing that she is of supreme worth. . . . [T]his then I call a form of flattery, and I claim that this kind of thing is bad . . . because it aims at what is pleasant, ignoring the good, and I insist that it is not an art but a routine, because it can produce no principle in virtue of which it offers what it does, nor explain the nature thereof, and consequently is unable to point to the cause of each thing it offers. And I refuse the name of art to anything irrational. (*Gorgias* 245–247)

This feminine figuration of rhetoric, and its required masculine governance by dialectic to be made just, is a gender division and hierarchy built into the very emergence of philosophy as a discipline. Indeed, philosophy as such is constituted through this splitting of rational and irrational, and constituted further by the gendered splits upon which it is based (soul and body, the good and pleasure, truth and illusion) in which the former term both characterizes and governs (that is, disciplines) the latter term. It is a disciplinary practice repeated throughout the history of both philosophy and the art of rhetoric. Yet, in this Greek context, the association of deception with the nature of the feminine may find its genealogy in the story of Zeus's creation of Pandora as a punishment to mankind. Hesiod wrote of Pandora's fabrication in two places, the *Theogony* and *Works and Days.* I will quote here from the briefer account, *Theogony*:

> The famous Lame God plastered up some clay / To look like a shy virgin just like Zeus wanted, And Athena, the Owl-eyed Goddess, / Got her all dressed up in silvery clothes and with her hands draped a veil from her head, / An intricate thing, wonderful to look at. . . . He made this lovely evil to balance the good, / Then led her off to the other gods and men Gorgeous in the finery of the owl-eyed daughter / Sired in power. And they were stunned, Immortal gods and mortal men, when they saw / The sheer deception, irresistible to men. From her is the race of female women, / The deadly race and population of women, A great infestation among mortal men. . . . / That's just how Zeus, the high lord of thunder, Made women as a curse to mortal men, / Evil conspirators. And he added another evil To offset the good. Whoever escapes marriage / And women's harm, comes to deadly old age Without any son to support him. . . . / Then again, whoever marries. As fated, and gets a good wife, compatible, / Has a life that is balanced between evil and good, A constant struggle. But if he marries the abusive kind, / He lives with pain in his heart all down the line, / Pain in spirit and mind, incurable evil. / There's no way to get around the mind of Zeus.[4]

Pandora is a cosmetic creature, made to deceive and ensnare man through that which is pleasing, not good. Pandora is impersonation herself, a "shrewd and enterprising spirit, naturally skilled in dealing with men."[5] It is not at all difficult to hear and see this "female woman," Pandora, in Plato's characterization of rhetoric as a mere deceptive knack of appearing to be that which she is not. Plato's trope of deceptive femininity and its connection to lies and rhetoric, thus, seems to find its root, its genealogy, in the figure of Pandora.[6] Mastering Pandora's deceptive and dangerous powers is part of the work of philosophy. It is no surprise, therefore, to find dialectic governing rhetoric in masculine terms, reasserting the power of men over Pandora.[7] The disciplining of rhetoric in Plato's—and, certainly not only Plato's—thought, thus, is accomplished by the mutual configuration of body and discourse through a gender system in which maleness is considered superior to, and more trustworthy than, femaleness and in which, as a rule, men should govern women.

Jewish Philosophy: Intersecting Genealogies

The practice of marginalizing the body and the feminine is evident in Jewish philosophy as well, with important consequences both for the gendering of the Jewish philosophical subject and for the lives of Jewish women and men. Through an examination of selected aspects of the writings of Moses Maimonides, I will demonstrate how this practice of engendering philosophy works in Jewish thought and with what cultural and social consequences. (I am not, however, thereby claiming to characterize all of Jewish philosophy. Rather, here, I separate out a genealogy of one of its most important strands.) I will pay close attention, especially, to how this practice of marginalizing the body and the feminine is instituted and naturalized through figures and tropes of gender difference and hierarchy. I will do this with an eye to the repetition of the earlier disciplining of rhetoric in these terms in Greek thought, now overlaid by the intersection of these tropes with the imagination of idolatry as the dangerous other.

In turning to the works of Maimonides, I will focus on his use of the "married harlot" as a metaphor for matter in the *Guide of the Perplexed.* In so doing, I am purposely selecting one metaphor—a gendered one—through which to represent the relation between body and soul. I am not interested here in the other ways in which Maimonides represents this relationship. Likewise, I am not asserting that this metaphor represents all that Maimonides has to say (even implicitly) about women and female sexuality.[8] I am interested, rather, in tracing the genealogy of a specific trope of female character and sexuality and its various disciplinary roles. Thus, the metaphor of the "married harlot," while of interest in itself, is important, I will argue, in ways that go beyond the literary scope of the *Guide of the Perplexed.* I am interested not only in how this metaphor resonates with Plato's figuration of rhetoric or with Aristotle's understandings of desire but in how it serves other functions within specifically Jewish thought.

For Maimonides, "matter" is considered the source of all corruption (at least, in the sublunar realm). "Form" is considered permanent and, in and of itself, free of all corruption. Because reason and soul must be embodied, form is necessarily tied to matter. Maimonides' asceticism does not go to the extreme of separating body and soul, matter and reason, in this world. The Jewish man must not be celibate but, rather, must marry and have children. The relation between body and reason, matter and form, is itself figured as a marriage, a marriage in which form rules matter, reason rules body, and "husband" rules "wife." Consider in this regard the following key text from the *Guide of the Perplexed*:

> How extraordinary is what Solomon said in his wisdom when likening matter to a married harlot [Prov. 6:26], for matter is in no way found without form and is consequently always like a married woman who is never separated from a man and is never free. However, notwithstanding her being a married woman, she never ceases to seek another man to substitute for her husband, and she deceives and draws him on in every way until he obtains from her what her husband used to obtain. This is the state of matter. For whatever form is found in it, does but prepare it to receive another form. And it does not cease to move with a view to putting off that form that actually is in it and to obtaining another form; and the selfsame state obtains after that other form has been obtained in actu. It has then become clear that all passing-away and corruption or deficiency are due solely to matter. (*Guide* BK III:8)

This metaphor of matter as a married harlot is a bit distracting.[9] What are the implications and genealogy of Maimonides' development of the trope in this way? One strand of its genealogy may be located in a metaphoric development of Aristotle's distinguishing of the respective cosmological roles of matter and particularized privation, in which the latter is figured as a kind of "evil agent." Aristotle sets up an analogy between the relationship of form and matter to male and female as follows: "The truth is that what desires the form is matter, as the female desires the male and the ugly the beautiful—only the ugly or the female not per se but per accidens" (*Physics* BK I, ch. 9, 192a22–23). Matter's desire for form is, according to Aristotle, for "something divine, good, desirable." The cosmological building blocks or elements are the same in Aristotle's and Maimonides' thought and both figure their relation through the desire of matter for form. But Aristotle's version is a milder analogy whereas Maimonides' metaphor of matter as a "married harlot" is both more specific and more extreme. Maimonides develops this trope of female matter desiring male form not only into a tropics of monogamous marriage but into an asymetrical marriage between matter as the unfaithful, indeed, nymphomaniacal harlot wife and form as the faithful, always cuckolded husband. Thus, of the three existents subject to generation and corruption in the sublunar realm (matter, form, and particularized privation), it is matter that Maimonides figures most negatively. Matter is the sole cause of corruption (Maimonides follows Plato more than Aristotle in this regard), and its figuration as the harlot wife of form further feminizes and sexualizes this corruption.[10]

The problem, for Maimonides, is how to make matter as good (that is, as obedient to form or reason) as possible. In this way, form will be less corrupted in its relations with matter. It is here that we see the masculine governance of reason reappear, to discipline the married harlot, that is, the male philosopher's body. As Maimonides notes, "he [God] granted . . . the human form . . . power, dominion, rule, and control over matter, in order that it subjugate it, quell its impulses, and bring it back to the best and most harmonious state that is possible."[11]

That the subject of this disciplining is not literally a wife but, as it were, "only" a figurative one—the feminized body of the male philosopher subjugated in its "marriage" to his reason—does not mean that this marriage metaphor is either neutral or benign. In a brief glance at the genealogy of this trope, we find that the rule of the master's masculine reason over the defective or nonauthoritative reason of the females in his household is to be found first, of course, in Aristotle's *Politics* (1254b13–14, Jowett trans.: "Further the male is by nature superior and the female inferior; and the one rules and other is ruled"). This gender hierarchy resonates as well with Plato's mastering of rhetoric as dialectic's feminized other in the *Gorgias.* Should there be a question of what Maimonides' interpretation of woman's nonauthoritative deliberative or practical reason might be—as there is in Aristotle scholarship on this issue—the implications of the metaphor of the "married harlot" seems clear. It is not that woman does not have reason. Nor that it does not function. Rather, woman's reason is weak and fails to have authority over her more powerful, especially sexual, passions.[12] What this trope makes evident, in any case, is that matter's inconstancy and moral corruption is due to its, as it were, "female sexuality," here imagined as promiscuous to the point of nymphomania. Again, we must recall that in the context of the *Guide of the Perplexed*, the matter referred to is that of the male philosopher whose body is thus feminized and in need of masculine disciplining by reason and the commandments. Perhaps the most extreme example of this disciplining is to be found in the *Guide of the Perplexed* Part III:49:

> If a man becomes sexually excited without having intended it, he is obliged to direct his mind to some other thought and to reflect on something else until this sexual excitement passes away. The *Sages, may their memory be blessed*, say in their precepts, which perfect the virtuous: *My son, if this abominable one affects you, drag him to the house of study. If he is of iron, he will melt. If he is of stone, he will break into pieces. For it is said: Is not my word like as fire? saith the Lord; and like a hammer that breaketh the rock in pieces?* [The Sage] says to his son with a view to giving him a rule of conduct: If you feel sexual excitement and suffer because of it, *go to the house of study*, read, take part in discussions, put questions, and be asked in your turn, for then this suffering will indubitably pass away. Marvel at this expression, *this abominable one*, and what an *abomination* this is! . . . Similarly with regard to *circumcision*, one of the reasons for it is, in my opinion, the wish to bring about a decrease in sexual intercourse and a weakening of the organ in question, so that this activity be diminished and the organ be in as quiet a state as possible. . . . In fact this *commandment* has not been prescribed with a view to perfecting what is defective congenitally, but to perfecting what is defective morally. The bodily pain caused to that member is the real purpose of circumcision. . . . The fact that circumcision weakens the faculty of sexual excitement and sometimes perhaps diminishes the pleasure is indubitable. . . . The *Sages, may their memory be blessed*, have explicitly stated: *It is hard for a woman with whom an uncir-*

> *cumcised man has had sexual intercourse to separate from him.* In my opinion this is the strongest of the reasons for *circumcision.* Who first began to perform this act, if not *Abraham* who was celebrated for his chastity . . . , with reference to his dictum: *Behold now, I know that thou art a fair woman to look upon.*[13]

While Maimonides is clearly concerned in this passage with disciplining the male body, he accomplishes this through reference to two kinds of "women." Undisciplined male desire is exemplified by the uncircumcised man, but it is the difficulty of "a woman . . . to separate from him" that represents the very excess of this desire. In this way, the male body is feminized. Like an overly passionate woman, the male body requires disciplining. And Abraham's chastity, exemplified through his circumcision, his properly governed body, is portrayed as a "fair woman to look upon." The excessively passionate woman and the fair woman represent two opposed states of the male body: undisciplined passion versus properly governed passion. The passionate woman is the uncircumcised male and is like the "married harlot," whereas the "fair woman" is the circumcised male and is like the "woman of virtue." In the "marriage" of the male philosopher's reason and body, the commandments—especially circumcision—play an integral role.

Although the consequences of this "marriage" trope, thus, may not be benign for men, it is, as I have already suggested, not thereby without negative consequences for women. There are social and cultural consequences for the tropes philosophers—and others—use to prefigure and make possible their more "properly" logical arguments. As is evident in the text about circumcision (quoted directly above), the disciplining of the male body is itself feminized. As the text and argument continue, Maimonides further intensifies the related metaphor of the "husband's" rule over his "wife":

> As for [Solomon's] dictum, "A woman of virtue who can find" [Prov. 31:10], . . . if it so happens that the matter of a man is excellent, and suitable, neither dominating him nor corrupting his constitution, that matter is an excellent gift. To sum up: it is easy . . . to control suitable matter. If it is unsuitable, it is not impossible for someone trained to quell it. For this reason, Solomon . . . inculcated all these exhortations. Also the commandments and prohibitions of the Law are only intended to quell all the impulses of matter.

In Hesiod's view of marriage, the quality of life for the husband depends on the kind of wife to whom he is married. Hesiod speaks of the "good wife" and an "abusive kind" of wife. In Maimonides' marriage metaphor, matter is figured as a "woman of virtue" or as a "married harlot." While Maimonides portrays "marriage" to suitable matter as a gift, the "husband's" fate depends on more than just the kind and quality of his "wife." Maimonides' "husband" has at his disposal all the commandments and prohibitions of the Law, with which he may quell, discipline, and control unsuitable matter. Even a "woman of virtue" will also always already be a "married harlot" (except, perhaps, for the prophetic virtue finally achieved by Moses). Therefore, the "husband" is enabled to rule his "wife" one way or the other.

So, what difference does it make? One might suggest at this point that this is all much ado about metaphor—metaphors, furthermore, that apparently refer not to actual women but to the body of the male philosopher! And what do metaphors have to do with disciplined philosophical argument, anyway?

To address this question about the role of metaphor in philosophical argument, I will first shift the genre of discourse a bit and consider a text from Maimonides' legal writings. In Chapter 21 of his *Treatise on Marriage* from the *Mishneh Torah*,[14] Maimonides describes the various kinds of work that a wife, and only a wife, must perform for her husband. These include spinning wool; washing his face, hands, and feet; pouring his cup for him; spreading his couch; and waiting on him. If they are poor, she has additional obligations to bake bread, cook food, wash clothes, nurse her child, put fodder before her husband's mount, and attend to the grinding of corn. "A wife who refuses to perform any kind of work that she is obligated to do," Maimonides tells us, "may be compelled to perform it, even by scourging her with a rod." A husband may legally batter his wife with a rod to discipline her, to "quell" her unruliness. However, when a man is to be compelled by the rod, it can be administered only by the court and never, under any circumstances, at the behest of his wife or, indeed, by any woman.

The asymmetry of the marriage metaphor in which husband rules over wife in Maimonides' philosophical work, the *Guide of the Perplexed*, is shown to be no "mere metaphor." As his ruling in the *Mishneh Torah* demonstrates, this asymmetry is violent in its consequences for actual wives and women. I am not suggesting that Maimonides required the metaphor of the "married harlot" to hold this position on wife beating. Nor do I argue that he held this position on the permissibility, even desirability, of wife beating simply because of his metaphoric disciplining of matter as a "married harlot" in the *Guide of the Perplexed*. The metaphor didn't make him do it. Rather, I am suggesting that this trope of marriage in his philosophical work fails to offer corrective resistance to his understandings of marriage in the *Mishneh Torah* and that it further reinforces, rationalizes, and justifies such violence against wives and women. Metaphors matter. They have consequences.

How, then, are we to read the metaphors, figures, and tropes that prefigure and configure philosophical texts? Are we to read them as secondary ornamentation, as elaborations or affectations added to a logical ediface of an already built and free-standing argument? Certainly, that is how these philosophical texts, from Plato's on, would have us read—or, rather, not read—them. But, we have already noted that philosophical discourse instituted a disciplinary opposition between rhetoric and philosophy that was accomplished through figures of gender hierarchy in which the masculine rules over and governs the feminine. Minimally, the very circularity of these claims should suggest the importance of adjudicating between these opposing positions—either that metaphors are marginal and secondary to logic or that metaphors prefigure, make possible, and are, thus, constitutive of philosophical argument. A choice between these two alternatives must be made through examining, among other matters, their respective social consequences and, at a minimum, by undertaking a hermeneutic of suspicion of what political, social, and cultural interests are being served through these discursive arrangements.

I have already indicated the negative consequences of these metaphors for women's lives. I will further suggest that the unarticulated values that undergird, make possible, and shore up philosophical argument are to be found precisely in the seemingly peripheral metaphors, figures, and tropes of philosophical texts. These figures and tropes perform intellectual and cultural labor that is necessary if the so-called properly philosophical work of these texts is to be done. It is labor, furthermore, that only these figures and tropes can perform. The labor of these tropes, however, must be effaced if philosophy is to fulfill its disciplinary telos or dream of self-sufficiency and mastery.[15] Reading for metaphors, for figures and tropes, and for the effaced intellectual and cultural labor they perform in philosophical texts is a way of reading these texts "otherwise," through a redemptive critique. It is to read them for the sake of a transformation of their very subject, their disciplinarity, and their effects.[16]

One of the ways of getting at these figures and tropes by reading otherwise is through their genealogy. That is, one may ask, as I have here: What economies of thought and practice are being established, institutionalized, and maintained through the workings of particular figures or tropes in a given text, say that of the metaphor in the *Guide of the Perplexed* of matter as a "married harlot" who must be disciplined to approximate the "woman of virtue"? I have already traced these tropes within both Greek and Jewish texts. To address this question more fully, it is necessary to turn now to a genealogy of the trope of the "married harlot" at the intersection of Greek and Jewish texts. While in this limited space I cannot adequately focus on the cultural location of this meeting, it is important to note that this intersection occurs in the context of Arabic philosophy.

Jews writing in Arabic or Judeo-Arabic were subjects in a dramatic cultural dynamic and exchange.[17] Admiring much in Arabic culture and thought, Jewish writers were both accomodating and appropriative. Yet, these adaptations were also driven by competition and the need for self-justification. This was, certainly, the case for a Jewish philosopher such as Maimonides. Idolatry was a central issue in Muslim thought; indeed, Judaism was seen as not sufficiently iconoclastic by comparison. It was in this cultural and religious context that Maimonides wrote the *Guide of the Perplexed*, a text whose project as a whole may fairly be described as a critique of idolatrous worship, interpretation, and belief.

In Part I of the *Guide of the Perplexed*, Maimonides systematically reinterprets scriptural references to God that are corporeal, either apparently or implicitly so. In this way, he forestalls possible idolatrous consequences; these bodily references could result in worshipping, as it were, the "wrong" God or wrongly conceiving of the "right" God. The critique of idolatry is the necessary precondition of true discourse about or addressed to God, inasmuch as this "true" discourse entails an iconoclastic understanding of the limits of discourse to represent—or to refer at all—to God. Maimonides' asceticism about bodily terms in scripture that appear to refer or relate to God has, therefore, to do (at least in part) with his concern that they not be misinterpreted through a literal reading, improperly to impute that God is corporeal. This linguistic asceticism is related to Maimonides' suspicions of the imaginative faculty (except in its productive and reliable use in prophecy). His critique of idolatry is further instituted by the insistence that these bodily terms be read figuratively and that these figures, in turn, be arranged and ruled by logic. This discursive hierarchy, certainly, is related to the general denegration of rhetoric in favor of logic by the Arabic philosophers of his milieu who mediated (and altogether made posssible) Maimonides' knowledge of Greek philosophical texts and traditions.[18] Especially for the philosopher, a proper suspicion and reading of these bodily terms as figurative is emphasized in which, as I have already noted, logic rules over poetic and rhetorical forms of speech. Logic so disciplines in order to guard against idolatrous misinterpretations wherein God has a body (and thus, is not one but many). In Jewish philosophy, this is the theological scandal *par excellence.* It is a scandal, however, that is risked in the very contact of Jewish and Greek thought that the *Guide of the Perplexed* marks.

It is at this intersection that the genealogy of the metaphor of the "married harlot" becomes both evident and significant. For it is precisely idolatry that has been figured (in the biblical books of Ezekiel, Hosea, and Jeremiah) through the metaphor of Israel as the unfaithful wife of God, who goes a-whoring after other, foreign gods and thereby breaks the Covenant, with catastrophic consequences. Ezekiel 16:15–26, 28–34 resonates with the *Guide of the Perplexed*'s characterization of matter as a nymphomaniacal, "married harlot" in Part III: 8:[19]

> But confident in your beauty and fame, you played the harlot: you lavished your favors, [Israel], on every passerby; they were his. . . . You played the whore with your neighbors, the lustful Egyptians—you multiplied your harlotries to anger Me. . . . In your insatiable lust you also played the whore with the Assyrians; you played the whore with them, but were still unsated. You multiplied your harlotries with Chaldea, that land of traders; yet even with this you were not satisfied. . . . [You were like] the adulterous wife who welcomes strangers instead of her husband.

Aristotle employed a more subtle and less specific metaphor of matter as a woman desiring a man (that is, form) in the *Physics.* This metaphoric usage, however, would not work in the *Guide of the Perplexed,* because if the problematic of idolatry is to be introduced into the constitution of matter and its relation to form, matter must be married, even if unfaithfully. Without, as it were, the regulative ideal of Israel's monogamous marriage to God, all one would have is a radical, because unlimited, polytheism. And because God is incorporeal, body and matter become associated with the other of God, with the idolatrous. The connection between idolatry and sexuality (especially, female sexuality) goes back to Exodus 34:15–16: "You must not make a covenant with the inhabitants of the land, for they will lust after their gods and invite you, and you will eat of their sacrifices. And when you take wives from among their daughters for your sons, their daughters will lust after their gods and will cause your sons to lust after their gods." It is interesting to note that the problem of idolatry in Exodus is figured in terms of "foreign women" and their seductive importation of other gods. Even in the incident of the Golden Calf, the Midrash insists that the Hebrew women refused to yield their jewelry for the purposes of molding this idol. It is most striking, therefore, that by the time of the prophets, the problem of idolatry was figured in the endogamous terms of Hebrew women's disloyalty, faithlessness, and adultery.

If Aristotle's metaphor of desiring matter is to be made to work at all in the context of a Jewish argument against idolatry such as Maimonides', matter will have to be married to form the way Israel is married to God. The problem is that idolatry—as the desire for other gods or "husbands"—seems to be the state of matter (and of Israel?) as such. As matter (and as Israel), she is married, even if a harlot. And just as disciplining by her "husband" is required to keep or make matter obedient to form, so are God's commandments and laws necessary to keep Israel faithful, to make her a more virtuous "wife" of God. The metaphor of matter as a "married harlot" thereby unites Greek and Jewish thought, tying together in one figure the sins of Israel, the imagination, idolatry, and undisciplined, unethical matter.[20] Like the disciplining of feminized rhetoric as the other of philosophy in Plato's *Gorgias*, and the rule of the male's reason over his wife (and her nonauthoritative reason) in the household of Aristotle's *Politics*, the disciplining of matter—the wayward wife of form—and of Israel—the unfaithful wife of God—through the commandments of the Law so as to make each one more a "woman of virtue" is performed in Maimonides' *Guide of the Perplexed* through a hierarchy of gender relations, in which male rules female and the masculine supplements and corrects the feminine.[21]

A significant part of the intellectual, indeed philosophical, labor that the trope of the "married harlot" performs in the *Guide of the Perplexed*, then, is to connect Greek and Jewish thinking about matter in an anti-idolatrous text. Different cosmological views, biblical and Greek, are thus made to inhabit the same text—however uncomfortably. The seams of their contradictions are, as it were, sewn together by metaphors (of the "married harlot" and the "woman of virtue"), giving the texture of the *Guide of the Perplexed*'s arguments a conservative and normative appearance. By reproducing a gender hierarchy in which men rule over women in Greek and Jewish, as well as Muslim, cultures, a sense of order and stability is given to an otherwise innovative and, possibly, disruptive philosophical enterprise. Further, in its attempts to appropriate as well as to surpass Muslim and Arabic culture, the *Guide of the Perplexed* trades on these gendered tropes in order to enact this double cultural exchange. The *Guide of the Perplexed*, apparently conserving both Jewish and Greek traditions and (cosmological) positions, radically transforms them through their juxtaposition in that hybrid genre written, in this case, in Judeo-Arabic: "Jewish philosophy."

Notes

I thank Laura Levitt and Miriam Peskowitz for providing this essay such a welcome home. I am fortunate in both their friendship and intellectual companionship, traces of which are, happily, to be found throughout this essay.

1. Moses Maimonides, *The Guide of the Perplexed*, trans. Shlomo Pines (Chicago: University of Chicago Press, 1963).

2. See my "Rhetoric as Ideology Critique: The Gadamer-Habermas Debate Reinvented," *Journal of the American Academy of Religion* 62.1:123–150.

3. Plato, *Gorgias* 463–466, trans. W. D. Woodhead, in *Plato: The Collected Dialogues*, ed. Edith Hamilton and Huntington Cairns (Princeton: Princeton University Press, 1961), 245–248.

4. Hesiod, *The Theogony*, trans. Stanley Lombardo in Contemporary Civilization Reader (New York: American Heritage, 1994), 23–24.

5. As Nicole Loraux notes, "The shimmering veil that Athena uses to cover her protegee, and the chiseled diadem that Hephaistos makes for her, add up to equivalents of woman herself. . . . Her veil does not conceal anything other than a woman: not a god, a demon, or a man. It hides nothing, because the woman has no interior to conceal. In short, in the *Theogony*, the first woman *is* her adornments—she has no body." Nicole Loraux, *The Children of Athena: Athenian Ideas About Citizenship and the Division Between the Sexes* (Princeton: Princeton University Press, 1993), 80–81. Froma Zeitlin puts the matter differently: "Bodiliness is what most defines her in the cultural system that associates her with the physical processes of birth and death and stresses the material dimensions of her experience, as exemplified, above all, in Hesiod's canonical myth of how the first woman, Pandora, was created. Men have bodies, to be sure, but in the gender system the role of representing the corporeal side of life in its helplessness and submission to constraints is primarily assigned to women." Froma Zeitlin, "Playing the Other: Theatre, Theatricality, and the Feminine in Greek Drama," in *Nothing to Do with Dionysos*, ed. Froma Zeitlin (Princeton: Princeton University Press, 1990), 74.

6. As Froma Zeitlin notes, "Fashioned at the orders of Zeus as punishment for Prometheus's deceptive theft of celestial fire for men, the female is the first imitation and the living counterpart to that original deception. . . . Artifact and artifice herself, Pandora installs the woman as *eidolon* in the frame of human culture, equipped by her 'unnatural' nature to seduce and enchant, to delight and deceive." Zeitlin continues with a—for us—relevant quotation from Pietro Pucci: "Pandora emblematizes the beginning of rhetoric; but at the same time she also

stands for the rhetoric of the beginning. . . . The text [Hesiod's *Theogony*] implies both the human dawn unmarked by imitation and rhetoric and a turning point that initiates the beautiful, imitative rhetorical process." Zeitlin properly reminds us, however, that in Hesiod's time (c. 700 B.C.E.), rhetoric had not yet been invented. "But his [Hesiod's] negative view of Pandora," she continues, ". . . can still serve as a preview of the later philosophical thought, which in testing the world of physical appearances, finds it deceptive precisely in the two spheres of carnal eros and artistic mimesis, specifically in the art of rhetoric itself." Froma Zeitlin, "Travesties of Gender and Genre in Aristophanes' *Themorphoriazousae*," in Froma I. Zeitlin, *Playing the Other: Gender and Society in Classical Greek Literature* (Chicago: University of Chicago Press, 1996), 412–413. See also her "Signifying Difference: The Case of Hesiod's Pandora," in *Playing the Other*, 53–86.

7. That such a reassertion of power is fated to fail is integral to Hesiod's account of Pandora's creation and nature.

8. For an informative discussion of some of these issues, see W. Zev Harvey, "Sex and Health in Maimonides," in *Moses Maimonides: Physician, Scientist, and Philosopher*, ed. Fred Rosner and Samuel S. Kottek (Northvale, NJ: Jason Aronson, 1993), 33–39.

9. I use the term "distracting" here to denote that the reader's attention is distracted by this metaphor away from certain philosophical problems implicit is this discussion—e.g., the question of whether the world is created or eternal in "both directions." Attention is redirected, instead, to matters of sexuality, gender, and marriage. Some readers of this metaphor may have found, as I will suggest below, its implications comforting, giving a sense of familiarity precisely where Jewish and Greek views would seem profoundly to conflict. (And, of course, the *Guide of the Perplexed* was written for various kinds and levels of readers. One might certainly argue—as has been suggested by those of a Straussian persuasion, as well as others—that these metaphors are directed to the many who can't understand the philosophical argument and claims of the *Guide of the Perplexed* and for whom such knowledge would have dangerous consequences. In this brief essay, I cannot address these issues of the varieties of audience response more fully, separating out between different kinds of reception of the metaphors of the *Guide of the Perplexed*.) However, for feminist readers, such metaphors are, certainly, not comforting. Rather, they raise questions for reading that precisely reveal the seams in the argument and the text that these metaphors were meant to conceal.

10. See Isaak Heinemann, "Scientific Allegorization During the Jewish Middle Ages," in *Studies in Jewish Thought: An Anthology of German Jewish Scholarship*, ed. Alfred Jospe (Detroit: Wayne State University Press, 1981), esp. 255–256: "The words of the prophets, even if taken literally, contain very useful things, but in their deeper meaning they contain the complete scientific truth. Thus 'the strange woman' in Prov. 7:5 ff. designates matter (according to III, 8, bad, unreceptive matter in contrast to good matter, the symbol of which is the good woman in Prov. 31:10ff.). The literal meaning is in no way meant to be disdainful. Indeed, Solomon wrote the book 'as a warning against unchastity and gluttony' (III, 8). But there is a good connection between this literal and the deeper significance, for it is matter which degrades the spirit. The interpretation is based on Plato's comparison of matter with a woman." But, as Shlomo Pines notes, "I 17 refers to Matter having been called a female by Plato and the philosophers who preceded him. With respect to Plato this is not quite accu-

rate, as the Receptacle—a term that was sometimes interpreted as signifying Matter—is designated in the *Timaeus* (51A) as Mother. However, Maimonides may have followed some later Platonistic interpretation." Shlomo Pines, "Translator's Introduction: The Philosophic Sources of *The Guide of the Perplexed*," in Moses Maimonides, *The Guide of the Perplexed* (Chicago: University of Chicago Press, 1963), lxxvi. Alfred Ivry follows up this insight further in his essay "Maimonides and Neoplatonism: Challenge and Response," in N*eoplatonism and Jewish Thought*, ed. Lenn G. Goodman (Albany: SUNY Press, 1992), 137–156. As Ivry notes on pages 152–153, "The indeterminate, 'free' status of matter, then, is not a positive value in Avicenna's scheme, and it is not surprising that the evil in the world is linked by him directly to matter: Unlicensed, uncontrolled, unmodified (by form), matter is seen as a cause of evil in the world. Yet beyond this, the very presence of matter, as the symbol of potentiality and change, is antagonistic to all that God represents."

11. Maimonides, *Guide of the Perplexed*, Part III:8, p. 432.

12. If this were, in fact, not already the more reasonable reading of Aristotle on this question of woman's nonauthoritative reason, I would hesitate more in reading this position into such a figurative treatment of matter as woman—specifically, as "married harlot"—in Maimonides' thought. See, e.g., Deborah K. W. Modrak, "Aristotle: Women, Deliberation, and Nature" in *Engendering Origins: Critical Feminist Readings in Plato and Aristotle*, ed. Bat-Ami Bar On (Albany: SUNY Press, 1994), 207–222; and Christine M. Senack, "Aristotle on the Woman's Soul," in ibid., 223–236. See also Nancy Tuana, "Mutilated Men: Aristotle" in her *Woman and the History of Philosophy* (New York: Paragon House, 1992), esp. 28–29.

13. Maimonides, *Guide of the Perplexed*, p. 608. (Italics in the Pines translation.)

14. Moses Maimonides, chap. XXI of *Laws Concerning Marriage* Treatise I in *The Book of Women, Code of Maimonides* (*Mishneh Torah*), Book IV. Ed. Leon Nemoy and trans. Isaac Klein. Yale Judaica Series, vol. 19 (New Haven: Yale University Press, 1972), 130–135, esp. Item 10 on 131–133. I would like to thank Ruth Sandberg, Leonard and Ethel Assistant Professor of Rabbinics, Graetz College, for bringing this passage to my attention.

15. As Michele le Doeuff suggests, "Philosophical discourse is inscribed and declared its status as philosophy through a break with myth, fable, the poetic, the domain of the image. . . . Philosophy has always arrogated to itself the right or task of speaking about itself, of having a discourse about its own discourse and its (legitimate or other) modes, writing a commentary on its own texts. This metadiscourse regularly affirms the non-philosophical character of thought in images. But this attempted exclusion always fails, for 'in fact, Socrates talks about laden asses, blacksmiths, cobblers, tanners'. Various strategies have been pursued to exorcize this inner scandal. One of them consists in projecting the shameful side of philosophy on to an Other. . . . [W]hether the image is seen as radically heterogeneous to, or completely isomorphous with, the corpus of concepts it translates into the Other's language, the status of an element within philosophical work is denied it. It is not part of the enterprise. In either case it falls within what Foucault calls the teratology of a knowledge—and the good reader, who has passed through the philosophical discipline, will know he should pass it by." Michele le Doeuff, *The Philosophical Imaginary*, trans. Colin Gordon (Stanford: Stanford University Press, 1989), esp. 1–6.

16. See my "Rhetoric as Ideology Critique" for a discussion of the role of rhetoric in redemptive critique.

17. Ross Brann, *The Compunctious Poet: Cultural Ambiguity and Hebrew Poetry in Muslim Spain* (Baltimore: Johns Hopkins University Press, 1991).

18. As Brann notes in *The Compunctious Poet,* 72–73: "Attitudes toward poetry, such as we find expressed in Judeo-Arabic poetic theory, were deeply influenced by the Arabic glosses on Aristotle's epistemology. The implications of the relationship between poetry and philosophy in literary theory were profound. Medieval speculative philosophers living in Islamic domains read Aristotle in such a way as to relegate the rhetorical arts, including poetry, to the bottom of the scale in the hierarchy of the intellect. According to the influential thinker al-Farabi (d. circa 950), for example, the use of persuasion (rhetoric) and imaginative representation (poetry) in shaping the theological opinions of the masses (who are incapable of grasping dialectical proofs) is an indication of the inferior logic and lowly status of rhetoric. Furthermore, . . . al-Farabi defines a wholly false statement as poetic and imitative. Since poetry lacks logical rigor, deals only with imitations (mimesis), and does not contribute to cognitive knowledge, philosophy defined it as an artistic enterprise (*sina a*) that bordered on meaningless activity. Jewish thinkers followed al-Farabi in dismissing poetry to an intellectual exile remote from philosophical truth. Moses Maimonides (1135–1204) . . . describes poetry in his treatise on logic as an art 'that praise[s] and blame[s] things in no ways other than by means of imitations." The fact that Maimonides' views of rhetoric and logic were derived from Arabic thought and that his knowledge of Greek philosophy was, of course, utterly dependent on its Arabic mediation, is a very important and, alas, in this brief essay, an underexplored site and link at the intersection of the two genealogies I am tracing here, that is, Greek philosophical and the Jewish scriptural texts and traditions. See also Arthur M. Lesley, "A Survey of Medieval Hebrew Rhetoric" in *Approaches to Judaism in Medieval Times,* ed. David R. Blumenthal, Brown Judaic Studies, no. 54 (Chico, CA: Scholars Press, 1984), 107–133; and Deborah L. Black, *Logic and Aristotle's* Rhetoric *and* Poetics *in Medieval Arabic Philosophy* (Leiden, The Netherlands: E. J. Brill, 1990), as well as *Essays in Medieval Jewish and Islamic Philosophy,* ed. Arthur Hyman (New York: KTAV Publishing House, 1977).

19. The relevant text from Maimonides is "How extraordinary is what *Solomon* said in his wisdom when likening matter to *a married harlot,* for matter is in no way found without form and is consequently always like *a married woman* who is never separated from *a man* and is never *free.* However, notwithstanding her being *a married woman,* she never ceases to seek for another man to substitute for her husband, and she deceives and draws him on in every way until he obtains from her what her husband used to obtain. This is the state of matter. For whatever form is found in it, does but prepare it to receive another form. And it does not cease to move with a view to putting off that form that actually is in it and to obtaining another form; and the selfsame state obtains after that other form has been obtained in actu." Maimonides, *Guide of the Perplexed,* 431. (Italics in the Pines translation.)

20. This disciplining of matter and of Israel does not finally resolve their inherent tendency to idolatry and promiscuity but, rather, merely holds it temporarily in check (except in the case of Moses). I thank Natalie Kampen for raising this question and for her most helpful close reading of this essay.

21. Again, as I have already noted, it is important to recognize the Arabic context for this intersection. I must, alas, defer treatment of this subject to another occasion.

While I don't enter here into the question of which texts of Greek philosophy Maimonides had access to and when, I will note that I am not suggesting that he had direct access to Aristotle's *Politics*, but that he probably had it in part through the mediation of Arabic philosophy. I have benefited from the comments and suggestions of Peter Awn and Elizabeth Castelli, for which I thank them both.

Circumcision and Jewish Women's Identity: Rahel Levin Varnhagen's Failed Assimilation

Jay Geller

From Rahel to Levin Varnhagen

Rahel Levin Varnhagen was born in Berlin in 1771, the eldest daughter of the wealthy jewel dealer Levin Markus and his wife Chaie. Her father was among the select group of Jewish men who possessed the *Generalprivileg*, which allowed his entire family to live and work in Berlin. Soon after her father's death (c. 1790), Levin Varnhagen opened her attic (*Dachstube*) salon. It eventually became the leading gathering place for writers, intellectuals, and young aristocrats, and remained so until Napoleon's 1806 occupation. In 1808 she met the literary dilettante Karl August Varnhagen (later, von Ense), a man fourteen years her junior, whom she would marry in 1814, following her baptism and renaming as Antonie Friedericke. When together with her husband she reopened her salon in 1821, the character of Berlin's intellectual life had long since changed. Fostered by the exclusively male Christlich-deutsch Tischgesellschaft (Christian-German Eating Club; 1811–1813) led by Achim von Arnim and Clemens Brentano, echoes remained of the nationalist and antisemitic tones that had emerged during the Napoleonic Wars. Nonetheless, Levin Varnhagen's intellect and insights still brought members of the liberal intelligentsia like Heinrich Heine, Ludwig Börne, and Karl Gutzkow to her home. After her death, her perceptions about contemporary social life attracted an even greater audience through Varnhagen von Ense's publication of her letters and diary entries in *Rahel. Ein Buch des Andenkens für ihre Freunde* (A memento book for her friends).

Rahel, the name by which she was known to her friends and to the reading public, is how the literature on this *salonnière,* in particular, and on Berlin Jewry in general, usually has addressed her. In this essay, however, I will refer to her as Levin Varnhagen, a name she never bore, in place of her other names: Rahel Levin, Rahel

Robert, Antonie Friedericke Robert, Antonie Friedericke Varnhagen, Antonie Friedericke Varnhagen von Ense, Rahel Varnhagen. The practice of calling a writer by his—or more often her—first name is a variant on the sort of familiarity that breeds contempt. First-name calling suggests that the person concerned is not worthy of the respect, the distance, accorded the (primarily male) Olympian greats.[1] Since at that time "Rahel" was almost exclusively a Jewish woman's name, it indeed embodies a significant part of her character, the Jewess. However, "Levin Varnhagen"—the artificial hybrid of Jewish patronym and Christian husband's name—signals other factors that are crucial to understanding how she constructed her identity: the normative Jewish identity figured by the male Jew; social integration through marriage; and the impossibility of Jewish acculturation[2] into Berlin (read German) society.

Salon women such as Levin Varnhagen were engaged, proleptically, with the conflicts and contradictions of Jewish identity that would mark the relationship between European Jewry and modernity. These women sought to mediate the paradox of Jewish emancipation: the European societies into which many Jews sought admission demanded assimilation, even to the point of obliterating any traces of jewishness or Judaism. Yet, often accompanying this demand was the assumption that Jews were constitutionally incapable of eliminating their difference. Previous studies have viewed Rahel Levin Varnhagen as a Jew and also as a woman,[3] but doing so reproduces the assumption that "Jew" was a gender-neutral category. Her writings indicate that she marked her empirical Jewish existence, her "unfortunate birth,"[4] as gendered: she is born a Jewess (*eine Jüdin*) and not born Jewish (*jüdisch*). Her writings also show that she marked the gendered nature of the generic Jewish destiny that she was attempting to identify and to identify with. This essay examines how, in her attempt to resolve this paradox and to answer the question of Jewish identity, Rahel Levin Varnhagen articulated her natal Jewish identity in figures of circumcision and the circumcised Jewish man.

The Rags of the Richest

If we adopt the common characterization of premodern Judaism "as a seamless garment . . . an identity cut from a whole cloth woven of tradition, intellection, and social ties [with an] unambiguous distinction . . . between being Jewish or Christian or Muslim"[5]—then the Judaism of Berlin's very wealthy Jewish community during the last quarter of the eighteenth century was in tatters.[6] Unlike other German cities Berlin had no ghetto. Jewish residences mingled with non-Jewish. Jews readily intermingled with non-Jews, both commercially and socially; the rules of Kashrut and Shabbat were honored more in the breach.[7] Further, the leaders of the community were not the rabbis but the rich. Within this elite both women and men acquired secular education (*Bildung*), and neither women nor, to a large extent, men had a traditional Jewish religious education. They adopted the Enlightenment thinking that ruled Berlin intellectual circles. Universal moral truths were posited as underlying both Judaism and Christianity, and the progressive convergence of Jews and Gentiles was optimistically portended. Members of this privileged group of Jews considered themselves different from their poorer, more traditional brothers and sisters in the rest of central Europe, and they sought to distinguish themselves from these other Jews.[8] Hence, the immediate goal of the Berlin Jewish elite was less civil equality (the usual understanding of emancipation) than social integration into and acceptance by high society and culture.

Despite much intermingling, such integration was not yet the reality. Clear legal and social differences remained. Besides levying special taxes, the state imposed strict limitations on how many and which Jews could reside or marry in Berlin, and there was no allowance for marriages between Jews and Christians. The Berlin Jewish elite thus formed a community in between.[9] Although the traditional fabric of Jewish corporate identity was shredded, it had not yet been replaced, as it would be, by the combination of religious reform and that Enlightenment-Romantic hybrid, the individual subject. In 1793 Levin Varnhagen could still write to her friend David Veit that "one can however do nothing other than wrap oneself with seemliness (*Anstand*) in one's own cloak (*Mantel*) and remain a Jew."[10]

Gentile Berlin of the 1790s too was an exceptional city. It had undergone a period of remarkable demographic and commercial growth, and amid the contradictions of the old regime it flourished rather than floundered. The capital-short aristocracy began to build residences in the city in order to attend the Prussian court and fill the state administration. Berlin was the center of the German Enlightenment, even though it lacked a university. Consequently, the second and third sons of the primogenitary Junker nobility flocked to Berlin, along with the underemployed university-trained sons of the bourgeoisie.

Once in Berlin, this collection of aristocrats and intellectuals socialized at the open houses, or, as they later became known, the salons of wealthy Jews. The Jewish women who presided over these gatherings, in which members of different religions, classes, and genders mixed, appeared to satisfy the conditions for achieving social integration. Most salonnières had wealth, acquired education (*Bildung*), and claimed the cultural ideal of the individual or unique personality. And these Jewish women lacked the bodily inscription—circumcision—that distinguished male Jews from their gentile *confrères*. In these salons, Jewish difference—that is, the identification of the individual as a Jew—enhanced the women's role as muse and object of exotic desire. But outside these gatherings, the index of social status and acceptance was marriage. Since civil marriage was nonexistent and mixed marriage legally impossible, the Jewish difference that the gentile community persisted in and insisted on ascribing to the *salonnières* remained the obstacle to their social inclusion.

The "nature" of this Jewish difference posed a problem for the salon women. Identity had been self-evident for those who had worn the seamless garment of premodern Jewry. Jewishness may have varied along community, class, and gender lines, but there was no question as to whether one was a Jew. By contrast, these Jewish Berliners were not sure where or upon whom to hang their frayed—not fringed—cloak. Meanwhile, as Jewish corporate identity collapsed under modernizing and emancipatory pressures, Jewish corporeal difference became prominent. For the gentiles who frequented the Jewish salons, circumcision distinguished Jew from non-Jew. Thus Wilhelm von Humboldt asked his fellow salon regular Gustav von Brinkmann to "extend his greetings to the Levy [that is, Levin Varnhagen] and to remember him to whomever else, circumcised or uncircumcised." In a later letter to Brinkmann, Humboldt commented that Levin Varnhagen's friend, the recently converted (1796) David Veit—a man who regularly and publicly repudiated his Judaism—still revealed "his circumcision in every fingertip."[11]

No less than their male counterparts, the Jewish salon women were identified as Jews despite their identification with the culture and values of Berlin high society. They found it continuously necessary to deny and/or represent this ascribed difference. The letters of Rahel Levin Varnhagen exemplify such self-fashioning. Modeling her epistolary self after the Rousseau of the *Confessions*, she sought to reveal her individuality—her "unique personality"—to the world,[12] while at the same time hiding her Jewish particularity. Through literary acts of self-revelation she attempted to transform her life into a work of art for the acknowledgment, approval, and ultimate acceptance by the legitimizing dominant society. But her *Bildung*—understood both as the acquisition of culture and as self-cultivation—failed as a means of social assimilation. Instead, her gentile peers viewed her as a parvenu, a bad copy, thus confirming all the more her pariah jewishness.[13] Levin Varnhagen desired to be accepted as an individual. Ironically, the jewishness that to a large extent distinguished her from other members of high society also defined her as a member of a group. Thus she found herself confronted by what she called "a little system of preconceived opinions which [people like Count Egloffstein] made about me before . . . ever hear[ing] a single word from me." Worse, after Egloffstein finally met her in public, she writes, "he does not perceive me: and therefore knows less of me than before because [able to claim personal acquaintance] he can now say to himself: 'I really know her!' "[14] For Levin Varnhagen, jewishness mediated the disjunction between the self-revelation of her inner truth and the "I really know her" of a Count Egloffstein.

Inscribed Inscriptions

In Levin Varnhagen's letters, her jewishness is corporeal. Because she was unable to find her Jewish particularity in a communal identity—"In Berlin, people deal with Jews as individuals, although not as a group"[15]—and because she assumed that the mind was both universal in form and individual in substance, Levin Varnhagen located jewishness on the body, the male Jewish body. Levin Varnhagen depicts her Jewish difference with allusions to circumcision and fantasies of circumcision-like inscriptions in her flesh. Her imagined defective body itself is marked with specific Jewish associations.[16] Rahel Levin Varnhagen identified her indelible Jewish difference through figures of her own phantasmally circumcised body. Dedication to *Bildung* was supposed to overcome the accident of birth, but for Levin Varnhagen, her imagined scar of circumcision could not be removed.

In a 1793 letter to David Veit, then studying at the university in Göttingen, Levin Varnhagen denies that she perceives herself as Jewish: "I shall never be convinced that I am a Schlemiel and a Jewess; since in all these years and after so much thinking about it [that is, thinking about her Jewish identity], it has not dawned upon me, I shall never grasp it."[17] She stresses her point by adapting a line from Goethe's *Egmont* (act 5, scene 2): "That is why 'the sound (*Klang*) of the executioner's ax *does not gnaw* (*naschen*) upon my roots'; that is why I am still living" (emphasis added). This act of citation affirms her identification with German culture as well as testifies to her *Bildung*.[18] But Levin Varnhagen altered the original text, which reads: "it is the sound (*Klang*) of the executioner's ax, *which is gnawing* upon my roots" (emphasis added). Varnhagen thereby implicates her own sense of identity and alludes to how German-Jewish difference is marked.

In *Egmont*, Goethe's Dutch Protestant hero utters the above line as he awaits beheading by his Spanish Catholic jailers. The death sentence that condemns him for his religious and national difference both confirms that difference and, upon execution, extinguishes it. By grafting a negation (the "ax does not gnaw") onto the original passage (the "ax which is gnawing"), Varnhagen grafts herself upon German roots and denies her own difference from her gentile peers. She is not Egmont. This appended negation also asserts that her nonrecognition of her own jewishness is self-willed. It is not the consequence of the violent extinction of her Jewish particularity by Prussian society. Furthermore, by refusing the figure of the executioner's ax, Levin Varnhagen undercuts the evocation of castration through decapitation, and she undercuts its symbolic substitute, the circumcision that identifies (male) Jews. This association of decapitation with the overcoming of Jewish difference (and hence the association of decapitation with the mark of that difference, circumcision) circulated in the recommendation that same year (1793) by the philosopher Fichte: "To give [the Jews] civil rights I see no other means than one night to cut off all of their heads (*die Köpfe abzuschneiden*) and replace them with ones in which there is not a single Jewish idea."[19] During the following two decades, decapitation (*Kopfabschneiden*) and the extirpation of Jewish identity would be correlated repeatedly with circumcision (*beschneiden*) in anti-Jewish discourse.[20]

Despite the protests of the twenty-one-year-old Levin Varnhagen, something was nibbling at her roots. It resounded in her denial and in her repeated return to the question of her jewishness. Almost two years later in another letter to David Veit, the thoughts that disowned a Jewish identity were replaced by a "fantasy" in which she acknowledged her desire to forget her Jewish origin. The refusal of martyrdom has been exchanged for an inevitable slow dying. First, Levin Varnhagen again alludes to Egmont's prison monologue where he describes how "like the earth-born (*erdgebornen*) giant, we [that is, humanity] spring higher aloft from every contact with our mother (*Mutter*)."[21] In contrast to the model of acquired *Bildung*, this passage connects natural origins with the development of greatness. Contact with the "roots" of the self infuses the individual with power. Levin Varnhagen's variant condenses the subject clause with a simple reiteration of *Earth* "nearer to the Earth (*der Erde näher*), like the earth-born (*erdgebornen*) giant." Her emphasis upon Earth as birthplace, and upon Earth's revivifying and empowering effects, is then immediately inverted by an image of a supermundane (*ausserirdisch*) origin with quite different effects. She recounts her fantasy of the extraterrestrial who, at her birth, used a dagger to etch into her heart the words: "Yes, have feeling (*Empfindung*), see the world, as only few see it, be great and noble, an eternal thinking I also cannot deprive you." This fantastic testament bears a codicil that ties her unique individuality to a collective destiny. She adds that she forgot to mention a last inscribed command: "Be a Jewess!" (*sei eine Jüdin*).[22] Levin Varnhagen's genius and her Jewessness are coeval and mutually implicated.

The consequences of this intrapartum impression are fateful. She continues: "And now my whole life is a bleeding to death; keeping myself still can prolong my life; each movement to still the bleeding is a new death; and immobility is only possible for me in death itself."[23] It is unclear whether the death sentence is due to the entire bloody inscription, or just the all-but-forgotten supplement: "Be a Jewess!" But the corporeal marking generates the double bind that tragically rules her life. Because she is a Jewess, she is also a *Kulturmensch*, a cultivated, universal individual. Because she is a Jewess, she can never be accepted fully as such an individual. Being a Jewess is not just a birth defect. Rather, the birth defect recalls the biblical circumcision of the heart (cf. Deut. 10:16; 30:6; Jer. 4:4; 9:26; Ezek. 44:7, 9). Paul had appropriated this biblical figure in Romans 2:29: "He is a Jew who is one inwardly, and real circumcision is a matter of the heart." By asserting its Jewish content—"Be a Jewess"—Levin Varnhagen's image substitutes an inner sign of male-defined jewishness for the outer sign that, as a woman, she lacks.

Her fantasy enacts a circumcision: the act of cutting that inscribes a (male) Jewish identity. Levin Varnhagen's Jewessness is written into her body. It maims her and names her—just as a Jewish male receives his Hebrew name at his circumcision. Whereas she had endeavored to forget the inscription of Jewessness and to deny her fate, now she seeks to render this hidden birth defect visible to her correspondent. Like Rousseau in the *Confessions*, Levin Varnhagen seeks to mediate before the court of public judgment the discrepancy between inner disposition and outer appearance (a discordance symbolized by the circumcised heart). Thus, she "translates" (*übersetzen*) for Veit the fantasy of her birthmark—her circumcised heart—into a "parable" (*Gleichnis*) about a man born lame, the effects of lameness upon his life, and the world's response to his handicap. In the analogy of jewessness with lameness, Levin Varnhagen is not merely substituting an exotic defect for a more familiar one, she is also carrying over the associations with male Jewish identity and its formation.[24] First, by embodying her "special misfortune" (*besonder Unglück*), Varnhagen adopts the persona of a man. She transforms the circumcised heart that determines her identity into a man's congenitally lame foot that names him (he is known as "the lame person," *der Lahme*). In fact, in narrating this parable about Jewish identity, she assumes the name of her male Jewish correspondent: "I will answer myself in your name (*in Ihren Name*)."[25]

Second, this conjunction of supermundane beings, wounds, lameness, names, and Jewish identity has a biblical precedent: it is already found in Jacob's wrestling with the angel (Gen. 32). When Jacob limps away from his nightlong struggle he bears a new name as well as a wound in the hollow of his thigh where the angel has touched him. With its implication of powerlessness before one's own fate—as well as its location—Jacob's wound evokes castration. Conjoined with the bestowal of a name, the permanent wounding recalls circumcision. Levin Varnhagen's account of her own origin retells the birth of Israel. Ironically, this (auto)biography of a lame Jew hides its origin. In telling this parable such that its form recapitulates its content, Levin Varnhagen masks her identity: the narrative "limps (*hinkt*) so much, that one would not be able to recognize my misfortune in it in the least, unless one would know it." Like her confessional letters, this parable seeks to expose the universal individual; simultaneously, it hides her particularity. Nevertheless, the parable betrays its writer's Jewish identity.

The Jew in the Little Red Hood

Several months earlier, Levin Varnhagen had already explored this relationship among a fateful commingling of contrarieties: her public persona, jewishness, identity, and cutting. The exploration occurs in response to a long missive by Veit in which he addresses the question of her identity, as revealed in her letters.[26] In her response, she rearranges Veit's language and appends glosses in order to unveil how his rambling mix of anecdote and idealistic meditation on truth and honesty attempts to hide his (and her) real concerns about being Jewish.

Veit reports that he had shown her critique of Jacobi's *Woldemar* to Alexander von Humboldt, and that Humboldt had responded by dismissing it as "an insignificant letter written by an ignorant young woman."[27] To validate his judgment of Levin Varnhagen's true worth and her worthiness as a speaker of truth, Veit proffers in his letter a "parody" of *Egmont* on the heights she has attained and will attain (cf. act 2, scene 2).[28] He then laments the "harmful mixture (*schädliche Mischung*) of forthrightness and reticence" in people's public utterances; their statements both belie what Veit believes to be their private—and true—feelings and vary depending upon the audience. He cannot understand why people do not fulfill the Enlightenment ideal and always tell the truth. Next, he provides an apparent commentary on such duplicitous encounters: "We [that is, Veit and Levin Varnhagen] suffer from a sickness," the nature of which he does not explicitly state. His meditation on truthfulness at an apparent end, Veit recounts his visit to a club in which normally separate groups—professors, women, and students like himself—intermix. He had previously avoided the club because of the expense (*Kosten*). Now, he describes how he successfully outwitted a "professor [who] wanted to embarrass him."[29]

Levin Varnhagen answers Veit's parody with a citation from another Goethe drama, *Torquato Tasso*:[30] "What if you came upon a friend whom you / Thought rich and found him to be a beggar? / You are quite right, I am myself no longer, / And yet I am such just as much as ever." Her deconstructive parody of Veit attempts both to understand Humboldt's response and to ignore the role of his (and her) Jewish difference in all interaction with gentiles. She identifies with Tasso, who "in his awareness of his poetic gifts had made the perilous assumption that, as an aristocrat by merit, he is the equal of these aristocrats by birth."[31] She, too, assumes that her *Bildung* can overcome the bias against her (Jewish) birth defect. But like Tasso—and unlike Veit—she too recognizes the gap between her own perception of herself and how others view her. Where Veit is concerned with her undervaluation, she addresses what she considers his overvaluation of her: she views herself as a nothing (*nichts*) because she does "absolutely nothing" except write the truth.

And then she proceeds to relate that truth. Unlike Veit, she recognizes the stakes of their situation, the expense of their "sickness." Their problem is not one of being truthful in a duplicitous world. Rather, they suffer from being Jews who want to join a club in which previously separate groups will socialize. They suffer from being Jews who consist of the "harmful mix" of *Bildung* and Jewish birth. Consequently, she may assume the position expressed by the statement "Why should I lie, when the truth costs (*kostet*) nothing." But, she apposes, this attitude makes her "the Jew in the little red cap" (*Der Jude im rothen Käppchen*).[32]

This apposition shifts Humboldt's denigration of Levin Varnhagen from a matter of misogyny—"ignorant young woman"—to one of ethno-religious identity defined as male: "the [male] Jew" (*der Jude*). Her identification with the male Jew is, however, part of another harmful mixture formed by the male Jew and the ignorant young woman, Little Red Riding Hood. The hybrid formulation implies that if she, here figured by the male Jew, acts like Little Red Riding Hood, always tells the truth, holds nothing back, without awareness of the consequences, then she risks betraying herself and being eaten by the wolves. Levin Varnhagen reminds Veit of the costs of his also acting like Little Red Riding Hood. She places Veit's experience at the club into the context of Jewish identity: "So the professors still want to embarrass you! indeed, one cannot escape jewishness."

Consequently, when she finally explicitly discusses the "harmful mixture" of honesty and discretion, she realizes that as much as she despises this (self-)damaging mode of being, she "cannot live without it"; several months later, she would have a similar recognition about that odd pairing of *Bildung*-based originality and

Jewish particularity. The Jew cannot afford to tell the truth all the time. There are indeed painful costs (*Kosten*) for a Jew to intermix. As a consequence of this double bind between the will to truth and the necessity to hide her inescapable jewishness, Levin Varnhagen describes herself as "lame" (*gelähmt*). This image anticipates her parable in the letter about the circumcised heart.[33]

Uprooting the *Rute* of Identity

Embodying this harmful mixture of honesty and reticence, of Jew and Berliner, still did not keep the wolves at bay. The problems of German-Jewish life and identity, of assimilation, conversion, and gentile anti-Jewish attitudes, in general as well as for them, were also a regular topic in the correspondence between Levin Varnhagen and her brother, the author Ludwig Robert, born Lipman Levin. In an 1806 letter she again employed circumcision-inflected rhetoric by voicing her desire to "extirpate" or "root out" her jewishness. As anti-Jewish chauvinism grew in Berlin during the losing war against Napoleon, Levin Varnhagen wrote to her brother:

> I shall not forget the humiliation [of being increasingly insulted and ignored by society because of her jewishness] for not one second. I drink it in the water, I drink it in the wine, I drink it with the air: therefore with every breath and I call out hail, and hail! that you are far away. That I do not see you really bent from being cast down, because what else was it [that is, the humiliation]!—although I find it hard to be alone. I remain in order to get away better. But no détail! The Jew within us, must be extirpated [*ausgerottet*]; this is the holy truth, and should life go with it.[34]

Once again, Levin Varnhagen defines their individual fates by using rhetoric that betrays associations with circumcision. To express the desire to cut off her jewishness, even at the cost of her own life, she choses the term *ausgerottet*—the sign of uncircumcision. In the biblical passage in which God first makes his covenant with Abraham and sets circumcision as its sign, "Every uncircumcised male, everyone who has not had the flesh of his foreskin circumcised, will be cut off [*ausgerottet*] from the kin of his father" (Gen. 17:14)—both Luther's *Bibel* and Mendelssohn's translation of Genesis counterpose *ausrotten* to circumcision (*beschneiden*).[35] Indeed, whenever the covenant—which is signified through circumcision—is broken, the children of Israel are threatened with extirpation (*ausgerottet*). The monument to nineteenth century German philology, *Grimms deutsches Wörterbuch*, ties this relationship between *ausrotten* and *beschneiden* to the tenet that "if one cannot uproot [*ausrotten*] a tree without harm, then one shall prune [*beschneiden*] . . . it."[36] *Ausrottung*, extirpation, is also the preferred term of Levin Varnhagen's contemporaries (such as Hundt-Radowsky) to describe their final solution to the Jewish question: they would exterminate German Jewry by supplementing circumcision with castration.[37]

Shame and despair scream from Levin Varnhagen's letter to her brother; it may have marked a turning point in her life. At least in the time since Napoleon marched on Berlin, Levin Varnhagen realized that when she and other Berlin Jews had exchanged the seamless garb of medieval corporate Jewry for the modern dress of *Bildung* and individuality, they had donned the Emperor's new clothes. The more original her intellect may have appeared, the more her empirical existence as the Jewess Rahel Levin was noted—to her discredit and humiliation. In the years that followed, she sought many ways to cover "the nakedness of jewishness"—through name changes, baptism, and intermarriage.[38] But on her deathbed, Levin Varnhagen is reported to have said: "What for most of my life was to me the greatest shame, the bitterest misery and misfortune—having been born a Jewess—I would not now have missed for any price."[39] Ironically, despite her own idealistic predilections, the irresolvable dilemma of Levin Varnhagen's social situation led this assimilating Jewess to assimilate German gentile culture's identification of Jewish character with the male—that is, circumcised—Jewish body. To describe how this birth had marked her as a Jewish woman she resorted repeatedly to the figure for male Jewish identity: circumcision.

Notes

1. See Katherine Goodman, ed., *In the Shadow of Olympus: German Women Writers Around 1800* (Albany: SUNY Press, 1992).

2. Drawing upon Milton Gordon's *Assimilation in American Life: The Role of Race, Religion and National Origins* (New York: Oxford University Press, 1964), historians of nineteenth-century European Jewry have adopted the distinction between acculturation and assimilation. See Marion Kaplan, *The Making of the Jewish Middle Class: Women, Family, and Identity in Imperial Germany* (New York: Oxford University Press, 1991); and Jonathan Frankel and Steven J. Zipperstein, eds., *Assimilation and Community: The Jews in Nineteenth-Century Europe* (Cambridge: Cambridge University Press, 1992). Against the traditional picture of thoroughly assimilated western and central European Jews, these historians recognize that synagogue attendance does not necessarily define a Jew; nor are the public practices and self-conceptions of male Jews necessarily normative for Jewish women. Accordingly, where assimilation with its mimetic appropriation of European identity implicitly disavows jewishness, acculturation recognizes that numerous forms of Jewish communal cohesion and practice existed, indeed thrived, despite the public adoption of many of the manners, appearances, and attitudes of the gentile majority.

3. Hannah Arendt, *Rahel Varnhagen. The Life of a Jewish Woman*, rev. ed. (1957; New York: Harcourt Brace Jovanovich, 1974); Arendt, *Rahel Varnhagen. Lebensgeschichte einer deutschen Jüdin aus der Romantik. Mit einer Auswahl von Rahel-Briefen und zeitgenössischen Abbildungen* (Munich: R. Piper & Co. Verlag, 1959); Liliane Weissberg, "Writing on the Wall: Letters of Rahel Varnhagen," *New German Critique* 36 (1985): 157–73; Weissberg, "True Confessions: Hannah Arendt, Rahel Varnhagen, and the Writing of (Auto)biography," lecture, Leo Baeck

Institute, New York, January 1990; Weissberg, "Stepping Out: The Writing of Difference in Rahel Varnhagen's Letters," in *Anti-Semitism in Times of Crisis*, ed. Sander L. Gilman and Steven T. Katz (New York: New York University Press, 1991); Weissberg, "Changing Weather: A Review Essay," *Germanic Review* 67, 2 (1992): 77–86; Weissberg, "Turns of Emancipation: On Rahel Varnhagen's Letters," *Cultural Critique* 21 (1992): 219–38; Dagmar Barnouw, "Society, Parvenu, and Pariah: The Life Story of a German Jewess," chap. 2 of *Visible Spaces: Hannah Arendt and the German Jewish Experience* (Baltimore: Johns Hopkins University Press, 1990); Heidi Thomann Tewarson, "German-Jewish Identity in the Correspondence between Rahel Levin Varnhagen and Her Brother, Ludwig Robert. Hopes and Realities of Emancipation, 1780–1830," *Leo Baeck Yearbook* 39 (1994): 3–29. Arendt's biography with its focus upon Levin Varnhagen's perceptions of her own pariahhood as a Jew and, although of secondary consideration for her biographer, as a woman, both revived interest in and greatly influenced modern perceptions of the salonnière.

4. Cf. *Rahel. Ein Buch des Andenkens für ihre Freunde*, ed. Karl Auguste Varnhagen von Ense, 3 vols. (Berlin: Duncker & Humblot, 1834), 1:43.

5. Robert M. Seltzer, *Jewish People/Jewish Thought: The Jewish People in History* (New York: Macmillan, 1980), 515.

6. This description of late eighteenth-century Berlin and the wealthy, privileged elite who made up a significant percentage of its Jewish community is drawn from Deborah Hertz, *Jewish High Society in Old Regime Berlin* (New Haven: Yale University Press, 1988); Steven M. Loewenstein, *The Berlin Jewish Community: Enlightenment, Family, and Crisis, 1770–1830* (New York: Oxford University Press, 1994); and Michael A. Meyer, *The Origins of the Modern Jew: Jewish Identity and European Culture in Germany, 1749–1824* (Detroit: Wayne State University Press, 1979).

7. The twenty-three-year-old Levin Varnhagen describes the frisson of riding on Shabbat in a letter to David Veit, *Briefwechsel zwischen Rahel und David Veit. Aus dem Nachlass Varnhagens von Ense*, 2 vols. (Leipzig: F. A. Brockhaus, 1861), 1: 76 (15 December 1793); cf. Lowenstein, *Berlin Jewish Community*, 99–100, 105, on the transgression and abandonment of ritual practices.

8. See Lowenstein, *Berlin Jewish Community*, 81–82 and nn.; Meyer, *Origins*, 60–70; Arendt, *Life*, 216–17, describes Levin Varnhagen's feelings of condescension, shame, and alienation regarding the poor Jews of Breslau during her 1794 visit there; also see Tewarson, "German-Jewish Identity," 12–13.

9. See Leo Spitzer, *Lives in Between: Assimilation and Marginality in Austria, Brazil, and West Africa, 1780–1945* (Cambridge: Cambridge University Press, 1989).

10. Letter to David Veit, in Varnhagen von Ense, *Briefwechsel*, 1:56 (18 November 1793).

11. *Wilhelm von Humboldts Briefe an Karl Gustav von Brinkmann*, ed. Albert Leitzman (Leipzig: Verlag Karl W. Hiersemann, 1939), 80 (3 November 1794), 87 (7 November 1796; cited in Meyer, *Origins*, 110); cf. 131 (29 May 1802): "Regarding the Levi one can now say that she is in fine form, let no one, who is not circumcised (*nicht beschnitten*), speak otherwise." In the 1796 letter to Brinkmann, Humboldt prides himself and Brinkmann on their

positive view of the Jews; he prefers the company of Jews to "noisy, trite Christians [who have] nothing sharp about them [*nichts Piquantes*; this phrase not only refers to tart, pungent conversation but also implicates the stereotypes of a strong Jewish stench, the *foetor judaicus*, and of Jewish fondness for garlic and onions], no black hair" (*Briefe*, 87). The identification of the Jew with *his* body is especially prevalent in the anti-Jewish pamphlets that circulated in Berlin at the beginning of the nineteenth century; see especially Karl Wilhelm Grattenauer, *Wider der Juden* (Berlin: Schmidt, 1803). Herz discusses Grattenauer's attacks on the Berlin salons in *Jewish High Society*, 259–64.

12. Letter to David Veit, in Varnhagen von Ense, *Briefwechsel*, 1:240 (16 October 1794).

13. The term, of course, is Arendt's. In *Life*, 201, Arendt cites Wilhelm von Humboldt, "I hear . . . that Varnhagen has now married the little Levy woman. So now at last she can become an Excellency and Ambassador's wife. There is nothing the Jews cannot achieve."

14. Letter to Rebekka Friedländer, in *Rahel Varnhagen im Umgang mit ihren Freunden (Briefe 1793–1833)*, ed. Friedhelm Kemp (Munich: Kösel Verlag, 1967), 273 (summer 1806); cf. the 19 September 1804 letter from Friedrich von Gentz to Karl Gustav von Brinkmann, in *Juden und Judentum in deutschen Briefen aus drei Jahrhunderten*, ed. Franz Kobler (Vienna: Saturn-Verlag, 1935), 149–50; cited in Barnouw, "Life Story," 56.

15. Letter to David Veit, in Varnhagen von Ense, *Briefwechsel*, 2:15 (16 November 1794).

16. Previous studies have emphasized different aspects of Levin Varnhagen's rhetoric about her jewishness. For Hannah Arendt, the salonnière and belletriste could recognize only a personal dilemma; she perceived her jewishness as a "fate" that one cannot fight but can only hope to escape, unless the long-awaited change in the social constellation takes place. More recently, Liliane Weissberg has focused upon Levin Varnhagen's ruminations about her Jewish birth as a fateful blemish; see Weissberg, "Stepping Out."

17. Letter to David Veit, in Varnhagen von Ense, *Briefwechsel*, 1:13 (2 April 1793); translated in Arendt, *Life*, 9. The translation of Goethe's original line and Levin Varnhagen's adaptation are mine.

18. That this citation testifies to her knowledge of the gospels is doubtful. Goethe's line recalls Matthew 3:9–10 (cf. Luke 3:8–9), in which the necessary relationship between truth and (ethnic) origin is negated. In that passage, John the Baptist is confronted by Sadducees and Pharisees whom he claims justify their authority and truth with the assertion "We have Abraham for our father." John tells them, "Even now the ax is lying at the root of the trees; every tree there that does not bear good fruit is cut down and thrown into the fire."

19. Johann Gottlieb Fichte, *Beitrag zur Berichtigung der Urteile des Publikums über die Französische Revolution. Erster Teil. Zur Beurteilung ihrer Rechtmässigkeit*, in *Schriften zur Französischen Revolution: mit zeitgenössischen Rezensionen*, ed. M. Buhr (1793; Köln: Röderberg, 1989), 144 n.

20. For example, an 1803 pamphlet that concedes that it would be unchristian to break the neck of a Jew at birth, and recommends instead that after the firstborn son all future male children be castrated: "We're only talking here about a couple more snips. But this couple more, what consequences would they have for the welfare of the state." In his 1819 *Juden-*

spiegel. Ein Schand- und Sittengemälde alter und neuer Zeit (orig. 1819; Reutlingen: Ensslin, 1821), Hartwig von Hundt-Radowsky would repeat the anonymous pamphleteer's recommendation, albeit more directly: "In order to prevent the Jews from further reproducing themselves, one could also in the future castrate (*verschneiden*) instead of circumcise (*beschneiden*) what of theirs p[i]d[dle]s on the wall"(144). These examples are drawn from Rainer Erb and Werner Bergmann, *Die Nachtseite der Judenemanzipation. Der Widerstand gegen die Integration der Juden in Deutschland, 1780–1860* (Berlin: Metropol, 1989), 175–78.

21. *Egmont*, in *Goethe's Plays*, trans. Charles E. Passage (New York: Frederick Ungar, 1980), 361.

22. Letter to David Veit, in Varnhagen von Ense, *Briefwechsel*, 2:79, 80, 80, 80 (22 March 1795).

23. Ibid., 2:80.

24. Although Weissberg ("Stepping Out," 148–50) notes in passing that there may be some connection between Levin Varnhagen's figuration of the lame (Jew) and the medieval representation of the diabolical, cloven-hoofed Jew, she does not attend to this conjunction of gender and jewishness in her otherwise extensive analysis of the parable.

25. Some twenty-three years later—eight years after she abandoned the patronym Levin, the manifest sign of her Jewish descent, four years after she had replaced her exclusively Jewish first name, Rahel—the woman now going by the name Antonie Friederike Varnhagen von Ense wrote to a recently baptized friend: "I hold this name changing to be of decisive importance. You will thereby to a certain extent become another person outwardly"; letter to an unknown addressee (16 May 1818), in Kobler, *Juden und Judentum in deutschen Briefen*, 184. More than baptism, the name change removed the stigma of Jewishness, for the name was the lingering outer mark that was coeval with the inner mark of Jewish identity. See Dietz Bering, *The Stigma of Names: Antisemitism in German Daily Life, 1812–1933*, trans. Neville Plaice (Ann Arbor: University of Michigan Press, 1992).

26. 20 December 1794 letter from Veit to Levin Varnhagen, 26 December 1794 letter from Levin Varnhagen to Veit, in Varnhagen von Ense, *Briefwechsel*, 2:40–47, 48–57.

27. Varnhagen von Ense, *Briefwechsel*, 2:41.

28. "One must but have a lot of courage (*viel Muth*) to parody Egmont"; ibid. The parody consists of his substituting "*Sie*" (you; i.e., Levin Varnhagen) for "*ich*" (I; i.e., Egmont).

29. Ibid., 2:45.

30. "I have the chutzpah (*gränzenlosen Mut*) to answer Egmont with Tasso," ibid., 2:41, 52. The passage is from *Torquato Tasso*, act 4, ll.1252–55; in *Goethe's Plays*; cited in ibid., 2:53.

31. Charles E. Passage, introduction to *Torquato Tasso*, in *Goethe's Plays*, 485.

32. Varnhagen von Ense, *Briefwechsel*, 2:53 (emphasis added).

33. Her two accounts of the costs of being a Jew are bridged with a reference to a similarly placed Veit non sequitur about his pen: "Also I have no pens (*Federn*); and soon—soon I can sharpen (*schneiden*) some." Here Levin Varnhagen writes: "You want me to carve the nibs?"

(*die Federn schneiden*). This exchange between Levin Varnhagen and Veit arose over the question of Levin Varnhagen's identity as constructed by her letters instead of through her actions. It is an identity and a life that exists only by an act of cutting. By cutting a little off the point of the quill she becomes the truth-telling letter writer, "the (male) Jew." See ibid., 2:55.

34. This excerpt from a previously unpublished letter to Ludwig Robert appears in Tewarson, "German-Jewish Identity," 16. As Tewarson states, the exact circumstances that motivated the plaint cannot be determined. Tewarson provides only her English translation; a shorter excerpt appears without source citation in Arendt, *Lebensgeschichte*, 117; cf. 205. Prior to her 1933 emigration from Germany, Arendt had access to all of Varnhagen's unpublished writings while preparing her biography.

35. Keith Spalding, *An Historical Dictionary of German Figurative Usage*, fasc.1–10 (Oxford: Basil Blackwell, 1959), 148 (s.v. "ausrotten"), credits Luther with having shifted the referent for *ausrotten* from the vegetable to the human world with his translation of this verse.

36. Jacob and Wilhelm Grimm, *Deutsches Wörterbuch*, vol. 1 (Leipzig: Verlag von S. Hirzel, 1859), 940 (s.v. "Ausrotter"), suggest another fruitful association between *ausrotten* and *beschneiden*: "When anguish (*der Ausrotter, kpdh* [Hebrew]/*eksilasmos* [Greek]) comes, they will seek peace" (Ezek. 7:25). Luther's translation of this hapaxlegomenon is then glossed by the *Wörterbuch* as a "device for pruning (*beschneiden*) nonfruitbearing branches from the tops of trees."

37. See note 20, above. The possibility of extirpating the Jews from Prussia reached into the state apparatus that same year (6 January 1806). A memo to privy councilor Sack reads: "Let us not extirpate [*Ausrotten*] them [i.e., that unfortunate race of men, the Jews], only restrict and better them, and this for the good of the Christians, and themselves, otherwise an unhappy destiny still stands before them, from which no government will be able to save them. We despise them only out of principle, the greater part of the nation however hates them out of instinct"; cited in Erb and Bergman, *Nachtseite*, 178.

38. Arendt, *Life*, 120.

39. As Levin Varnhagen's husband recounts in his foreword to *Rahel*, 1:43.

Jesus as Theological Transvestite

Susannah Heschel

Society doesn't exist, and the Jew is its symptom.
Slavoj Zizek, The Sublime Object of Ideology

An assumption common in Jewish feminist studies is that feminists study the history, activities, and images of women, or, at the very least, gender as a social construction. Feminists who turn to examine other issues, such as the case of Jewish-Christian relations discussed here, may find themselves accused of abandoning feminist scholarship.[1] But feminist theory can be applied to issues other than the explicitly gendered. In this essay I ask what happens when scholars engage in just such a move. Can there be a Jewish feminist scholarship that addresses a broad range of issues, themes, and topics?

Some years ago, at the same time that I was studying modern Jewish views of Jesus, I read Sandra Gilbert and Susan Gubar's now-classic study of nineteenth-century British women novelists, *The Madwoman in the Attic.* I noticed some striking parallels between the situation of women entering the English literary tradition and Jews entering the Christian theological tradition. I realized that feminist theorizing about women might fruitfully be applied to the experience of Jews. Gubar and Gilbert argued that in order to generate the language needed to produce their own literature, women were required to kill the "angel in the house," the aesthetic ideal of the female promoted in male literature.[2] Similarly, it seemed to me, the extensive project of modern Jewish theologians to clarify the origins of Christianity reflected a Jewish effort to destabilize Christian theology and create a space for Jewish theological self-definition.

Nina Auerbach has observed in connection with women writers in Victorian England who appropriate male-authored misogynous myths that the power of mythologies lies both in their ability to oppress and in their ability to endow strength.[3] To deny a myth or try to sidestep it will neither destroy its power nor subvert its meaning. The nineteenth century witnessed the rise of women's efforts to cope with the misogynist myths of literature by retelling the conventional narrative but subverting its plot. Similarly, modern Jewish thought was formed not simply by creating a Jewish historical narrative but by a rebirth of the Christian mythic potential under Jewish auspices. A crucial image for modern Jewish thought is the figure of Jesus as a pious, loyal Jew. Following Auerbach's lead, the surge of modern Jewish interest in Jesus can be interpreted as an effort to reclaim the power of the story of Christian origins for Jews. Like women characters in the English novel, the Jewish victim of Christian persecutions—slain, dismembered, powerless—is revived, made whole, and empowered through Jewish retellings of the Christian story. In this theological construction, Jews are all thereby enabled to become self-restoring heroes who try, in Auerbach's words, to merge "imperceptibly with the lives of those who believe in [the myth] and thereby into the history they make" (15). Seen in this light, the modern Jewish understanding of Christian origins is not merely a matter of Jews wishing to "set the records straight." Rather, it demonstrates a Jewish desire to enter into the Christian myth and thereby claim the power inherent in it. Reform Jews in particular may have concentrated so much attention on early Christianity in part to uncover a model for their own acts of revisioning Judaism, since they saw Christianity itself as beginning in a strong misreading of Judaism.

Liberal Protestant theologians in the nineteenth century had their own view of Jesus and his relation to Judaism. Although they advocated a historical approach to the New Testament, they set aside certain aspects of Jesus' nature from historical investigation. Regardless of his immersion in Jewish culture, they asserted, Jesus' religious consciousness was *sui generis*, immune to the surrounding culture and therefore not subject to historical causation. Such an intellectual move allowed Protestant theologians to delimit Jewish influence on Christian origins and separate Judaism from what was truly extraordinary about Jesus. They asserted that they sought the historical Jesus, but they elevated the ahistorical Christ elements within him.[4]

Increasingly, after the middle of the nineteenth century, Jewish theologians, beginning with Abraham Geiger, developed a counterstrategy, claiming Jesus in his entirety for Judaism. His extraordinary religious consciousness was not unique, Geiger argued, but simply a typical example of the religious genius of the Jewish people. Because Jesus was thoroughly immersed in the faith of Judaism, Geiger declared that Christianity, the religion constructed about him, bore little resemblance to Jesus' own faith. Geiger sought in this way to sever the connection between Christianity and Jesus, just as Christian theologians of his day were attempting to sever the link between Jesus and Judaism.

In their studies of the New Testament and of first-century Judaism, modern Jewish and Christian scholars have struggled over Jesus as a figure on the boundary of the two religions, the Jew who was the first and greatest Christian, a Christian who actually lived and taught Judaism. Yet both Christian and Jewish theologians were dissatisfied with the interpretations of Jesus they had constructed. After all, if Christian theologians were truly convinced by their own assertion of Jesus' ahistorical uniqueness, inherent in his superior religious consciousness, then why did they find it necessary to depict first-century Palestinian Judaism in such negative terms? Would not Jesus' superiority have been evident even if he had been surrounded by extraordinary people? Turning to Geiger, we might ask why, if Christianity was an unfortunate deviation from Judaism and Jesus, it was nonetheless invoked in the great reform project of "modernizing" the synagogue and its liturgy, which used the Lutheran church as its model.

Because the figure of Jesus stood at the boundary of Judaism and Christianity, the interpretation of his teachings called the self-understanding of both religions into question. Uriel Tal's study of Christian-Jewish theological debates in Imperial Germany has made it clear that the primary sources of theological anti-Judaism were not the conservative Protestants, with their exclusive and supersessionist definitions of Christianity, but the liberal Protestants.[5] Conservatives could find a theological niche for Judaism, but liberals could not. As Tal demonstrates, the struggle between liberal Protestants and liberal Jews concerned boundaries as liberal movements within both religions so reinterpreted their teachings that their similarities overtook their differences. Liberal Protestantism's rejection of the supernatural left little else than the historical figure of Jesus, whose greatness it derived not from his performance or miracles but from his teachings and force of personality. Liberal Jews' rejection of halakha similarly left only a nebulous ethical monotheism, whose message they defined in language nearly identical to the liberal Protestants' Jesus. The struggle that then emerged was not over points of difference in belief but over where to draw the line of distinction between the two faiths. If both religions promoted the same basic teachings, what was left to define their separate identities? In the end, liberal Protestantism and liberal Judaism, because each had shaped itself with such intimate reference to the other, ended up losing a sense of their own identities and resorting to polemics against each other, Tal concludes.

This destabilization of boundaries lies at the root of the progressively derogatory portrayal of early Judaism in modern New Testament scholarship. Earlier generations had sought parallels between New Testament passages and rabbinic literature as fodder for converting Jews to Christianity: if the Jews' own texts were in accord with Christian scriptures, Jews should take the logical step and become Christians. But in modernity the historical study of the relationship of the Jewish background to early Christianity became the site of an intense conflict motivated in large measure by territorialized claims to theological supremacy: Was Judaism the progenitor that had created Christianity? The mother of the daughter religion? Or was Christianity its own creator, having rejected Judaism in the face of its new, superseding, divine revelation? This debate came to be inscribed, for theologians and historians, on the figure of Jesus. Who was the real Jesus? *Whose* was the real Jesus?

In considering the inscription of Jesus at the boundaries, I suggest turning from a binary view of Judaism and Christianity to a more usefully complicated picture of religious development that recognizes the performative nature of religious activity. The interpretive language that makes this move possible comes from recent work in queer theory, which offers a corrective to some earlier feminist approaches. In particular, queer theory addresses the problem of binary thinking, in which male and female function as static terms of reference in dichotomous relation to one another. Instead this theory suggests that the binary construct of male and female is fictive, calling our attention to categories of overlap and confusion of sexual identify, in which male and female become so intricately intertwined that no effective separation of their components appears possible. The emergence of queer theory stems from theoretical innovations that see gender not as an identifiable essence, as in the modernist tradition, nor even a social construction, as in the postmodernist tradition, but as a performance without any fixed referential point.[6] Judith Butler writes that "there is no gender identity behind expressions of gender; that identity is performatively constituted by the very expressions that are said to be its results."[7]

Just as gender may be seen as performative, so too Jesus and even Christianity and Judaism can be seen as constructs of the modern period, which exist by the virtue of performative activity. The anxiety over the self-definition of the two religions, and over the boundaries between them, comes into relief through discussions of the jewishness of the historical figure of Jesus. Jesus, I argue, functions as a kind of theological transvestite, calling into question the constructions of Christianity and Judaism and destabilizing the boundaries between them.

The idea of the transvestite offers a useful figure on which to position an argument. Transvestism creates a sense of confusion and displacement that underlines the absence of a fixed referential to gender. The scandal of transvestism is its revelation of the truth about gender, namely, that gender exists only in representation or performance. The cross-dresser performs gender, rather than becoming or constructing it. The resulting indeterminacy of gender creates its power: the power to disrupt, question, and finally to undermine the binary categories of male and female. Indeed, transvestism disrupts not only the content of the categories "male" and "female" but even the very notion of "category." Marjorie Garber's classic study of transvestism, *Vested Interests: Cross-Dressing and Cultural Anxiety*, examines the phenomenon in terms of its wider cultural significance. She writes, "If transvestism offers a critique of binary sex and gender distinctions, it is not because it simply makes such distinctions reversible but because it denaturalizes, destabilizes, and defamiliarizes sex and gender signs."[8] Recent theatrical works, such as David Huang's play *M. Butterfly* and the film *The Crying Game*, present gender and sexuality as roles to be performed. Actors pass or trespass as male or female, heterosexual or homosexual, and the ultimate outcome is that neither category can be sharply distinguished from its putative opposition.[9] The confusion of categories leads to a breakdown of their function as oppositional points of reference. Ultimately, the concept of category as such breaks down as well.

Just as the transvestite breaks down the categories of an understood gender structure, so does Jesus, as theological transvestite, reveal the similarly fictive performances of Judaism and Christianity. Within modern theological efforts at Jewish and Christian self-definition, Jesus stands as an ambiguous figure. Jewish theologians dress him up as a rabbi; Christian scholars, even as they recognize his jewishness, dress him as a Christian. Gender, too, is a mixed category that furthers the possibilities for his transvestite performances. From the gospel accounts, modern scholars found that Jesus' teachings laud gentleness, the meek, and the cheek; he is himself pierced, wounded; he bleeds, suffers, and dies. At the same time, however, he is a man whose closest associates are men, not women; who proclaims himself one with the Father; whose death is overcome by the erection of resurrection.

This confusion over Jesus' religious identity, understood in terms of his boundary-crossing transvestism, accounts for the scholarly need to reestablish those boundaries. The highly denigrating portrayal of the Pharisees and first-century Palestinian rabbis is one example of this dramatic need for boundaries, and it is a portrayal that I would read as a kind of theological horror film. In this case, the horror was stimulated for Christians by Jewish claims that Jesus was a Pharisee. Geiger, for example, saw nothing original in the Jesus of the gospels. Far from being the founder of a new faith, Geiger asserted, Jesus espoused teachings and actions similar to those attributed to the Pharisees in Mishnaic and other rabbinic sources. Jesus, for Geiger, was no more than a pale imitation of his teacher, the first-century Palestinian rabbi, Hillel:

> Jesus was a Jew, a Pharisaic Jew with Galilean coloring, a man who joined in the hopes of his time and who believed that those hopes were fulfilled in him. He did not utter a thought, nor did he break down the barriers of [Jewish] nationality. . . . He did not abolish any part of Judaism; he was a Pharisee who walked in the way of Hillel.[10]

Christian scholars responded to Geiger's and other Jewish assertions with the view that any parallels between Jesus and the Pharisees were merely superficial because Pharisaic Judaism was degenerate at heart. From Emil Schurer to Julius Wellhausen, Ferdinand Weber, Wilhelm Bousset, and Rudolf Bultmann, among others, the parallels between Jesus and the rabbis were dismissed because, they said, the actual "life under the law" was sterile and devoid of religious meaning.[11]

At the turn of the century, Jewish writers, including Joseph Eschelbacher, Hermann Steinthal, and Martin Schreiner, polemicized against Christianity's allegedly impure monotheism and its reliance on miracles and dogma concerning Jesus' divinity.[12] Christian theologians responded by stating that early Judaism's monotheism had been rendered worthless by its sterile, degenerate legalism. While liberal Jewish theologians saw Jesus as a typical example of the Pharisees and rabbis, liberal

Protestants saw Jesus as having restored classical prophecy after it was smothered by Judaism's priestly and rabbinic traditions.

Thus, for both Christians and Jews in Germany, the jewishness of Jesus served as a central trope for defining the historical-theological consciousness of each group. The greater or lesser degree of Jesus' ties to Judaism measured the bond between the two religions and also the acceptability of Jews within modern German society. The more Jewish Jesus could be shown to have been, the more Christians would respect Judaism—or so the German Jews hoped. Christians had a different agenda. For them, the more Jewish Jesus was shown to be, the less original and unique he was. If Jesus had simply preached the ordinary Judaism of his day, the foundation of Christianity as a distinctive and unparalleled religion was shattered. The problem lay in the undeniability of Jesus' intimate relationship to Judaism. But the question was, what sort of relationship? As strongly as nineteenth-century Jews tried to show an identity between Jesus and Judaism, Christians tried to demonstrate a difference.

Ultimately, by the early twentieth century, Protestant theologians and scholars conceded that Jesus' moral message was derived historically from Judaism. Adolf von Harnack made just such a concession, but he then immediately insisted that it was precisely a sign of Jesus' extraordinary religious genius that he was able to extract moral teachings from the sterile legalism of his day. Harnack enshrined this idea in his classic statement of Protestantism, *Wesen des Christentums*, in which he wrote that although the religious message Jesus proclaimed had already been stated by the Pharisees, nonetheless the Pharisees "were in possession of much else besides. With them [religion] was weighted, darkened, distorted, rendered ineffective and deprived of its force by a thousand things which they also held to be religious and every whit as important as mercy and judgment. . . . [T]he spring of holiness . . . was choked with sand and dirt, and its water was polluted." With Jesus, "the spring burst forth afresh, and broke a new way for itself through the rubbish."[13] For Harnack, then, it does not matter that Jesus' teaching was not original, but instead, at least, that it was pristine.

Harnack's portrait of a legalistic Judaism was countered by the rabbi Leo Baeck, who distinguished between Jesus' criticism of Pharisaic Judaism and Paul's rejection of rabbinic law. Christianity, by following Paul, violated Jesus' own adherence to the law and created, in Baeck's words, a "romantic religion" of mysticism in which human beings remain trapped by their sinful nature, passively awaiting salvation through grace:

> In this ecstatic abandonment, which wants so much to be seized and embraced and would like to pass away in the roaring ocean of the world, the distinctive character of romantic religion stands revealed—the feminine trait that marks it. There is something passive about its piety; it feels so touchingly helpless and weary; it wants to be seized and inspired from above, embraced by a flood of grace which should descend

upon it to consecrate it and possess it—a will-less instrument of the wondrous ways of God.[14]

Feminine Christianity, Baeck argued, fails to foster moral responsibility, in contrast to the masculine "classical religion" Judaism, which places ethical commandments at the forefront and demands no belief in irrational dogma.

The debates over Jesus and Judaism were never resolved; they continue to this day. Ernst Käsemann's recent "Protest" in the journal *Evangelische Theologie*, that calling Jesus' teachings Jewish is insulting and renders Christianity meaningless, is a case in point. That one of the most highly respected and liberal figures in the field of German Protestant New Testament scholarship would continue to feel so threatened by Jesus' Jewishness indicates the depth and persistence of the theological dilemma.[15]

Käsemann and others react to this dilemma so heatedly because Christians have failed through so many centuries to make Jesus the signifier of Western civilization, the Christian *par excellence.* As Jacque Lacan uses the term, Jesus was to have been the ultimate cultural phallus, the center of power and meaning, for Christians and Jews alike. Just as the dissociation of penis and phallus strikes at the heart of patriarchy, so does the uncertainty of Jesus' identity as a Christian undercut the claims of the Christian message. "[I]f the penis was the phallus," writes Eugenie Lemoine-Luccioni, "men would have no need of feathers or ties or modals. . . . Display [parade], just like the masquerade, thus betrays a flaw: no one has the phallus."[16] Such compensatory mechanisms are found in theology as well. Had Jesus actually been the cultural phallus—that is, the first Christian—Christians may well have had no need for crucifixes or Jew-hatred.

The cross-dresser is at once both a signifier and that which signifies the undecidability of signification. It points toward itself—or, rather, toward the place where it is not. Jesus, too, destabilizes the self-definitions of both Judaism and Christianity, pointing out that the former could not retain its hegemony over monotheism and the Bible, while the latter has eternally reinvented untenable claims concerning its own origins. As a Jew and the first Christian, yet neither a Jew nor a Christian, Jesus is the ultimate theological transvestite.

Eve Sedgwick and others have argued that the transvestite becomes a third category, which reconfigures the relationship between male and female and places in question gender identities previously viewed as stable and known.[17] For Judaism and Christianity, Jesus is that third category, by which each religion inscribes the other, defining its relationship to him. Jews such as Geiger have claimed Jesus for the glory he brings to Judaism; he is the ultimate trump card whose Jewishness makes Christianity, for all its supersessionist claims, at best a deviant branch of Judaism. By standing on the boundary, Jesus links the two religions, but also makes their relationship ambivalent or even a reciprocal negation.

Christians, in contrast, have taken a fetishistic interest in first-century Judaism in the process of attempting to separate Jesus from his Jewish context (and modern liberal Protestantism from its liberal Jewish neighbor). Nineteenth-century Christian studies of the historical Jesus inevitably led to an examination of what is called "late Judaism" and which is described in a language designated to evoke horror in the reader. For example, Gustav Volkmar, one of the leading figure in the liberal Protestant Tübingen School of the nineteenth century, writes: "The Pharisees represent a wish to deceive oneself and, on top of it, God, [a wish] which turned out to be more than an ever-growing despair, the tighter and more hardened the shackles of the idolatrous power, which one hoped to evade through hypocrisy."[18] Indeed, throughout liberal Protestant writing, the descriptions of first-century Judaism, particularly of the Pharisees, are just about the only damnation left. Where Satan is in the world of liberal Protestantism, the Pharisees and rabbis are lurking close by.

What makes these negative depictions of Judaism so popular is the thrill of uncertainty, which is based on the ambiguity of Jesus. Because Jesus was Jew, Judaism cannot be fully denigrated, yet because Christians have broken with Judaism, it must be bad or inferior. There is connection, but also distance and a break. To strengthen the Christian side of Jesus, Judaism must be relocated to a space where its uncanny, demonic quality can be contained, and from which Jesus can be rescued, as in the gospel story of the Syro-Phoenician woman (Mark 7:24–30; Matt. 15:21–28). At first, Jesus refuses to heal the woman's daughter, but her persistence is rewarded and he eventually agrees. His refusal is generally attributed to the woman's being a foreigner, not part of the people of Israel. The story continues to be read by Christian commentators as teaching Jesus' breakthrough of the nationalistic fetters of Judaism, thanks to the help of a woman. In this reading, Jesus is transformed from being a Jew into being "no longer a Jew" but, rather, an opponent or even a destroyer of Judaism.[19] Jesus' cross-dressing is retained in the commentaries, in which Jesus is portrayed both as a female bonding with the woman who appeals for his help and as a man, successfully smashing through the chains of Judaism.

The sensibility of cross-dressing is retained in the rich detail and evocative imagery given to Christian descriptions of the first-century Judaism to which Jesus was born and from which he broke free. They use adjectives of bondage and even murder, suggesting imagery common to the modern horror film. Pharisaic religion is described, for example, as rigid, petrified, degraded, cankered, disfigured, wrathful, violent, and even as a cadaver; Pharisaism is a religion of materialism, deception, hypocrisy, abomination, and shackles; it murders the conscience, gentleness, and the true religious spirit, and, in the end, persecutes Jesus with enraged frenzy, to cite just a few of the adjectives used in modern Christian literature.[20]

How can Christian theological representations of the first-century Pharisaic-Jewish world out of which Jesus emerged be read as a kind of horror film? Feminist film theory has rested, until recently, on the premise first articulated by Laura Mulvey in the early 1970s, that the gaze of the film is the male eye whose pleasure is rooted in a voyeuristic sadism over the female object, the screen image.[21] Despite debate over aspects of Mulvey's analysis, her basic paradigm has remained fixed until recently, with most feminist analysts looking for the male viewer and the female object of the film's interest. In watching a film, Mulvey writes, the male "gazer salves his unpleasure at female lack by seeing the woman punished, and a fetishistic-scopophilic look [is generated], whereby the gazer salves his unpleasure by fetishizing the female body in whole or part." That gendered distinction between subject and object, male and female, might seem at first glance to be applicable to Christian studies of the Pharisees as well. Indeed, we might paraphrase Mulvey by suggesting that the Christian gazer salves his (*sic*) unpleasure at the realization that the historical Jesus was not a Christian but a Jew by fantasizing Judaism's presumed lack of the phallus, Jesus. For the Christian to gain mastery, the Jew must be punished by being made into a sadistic beast; Christian theology takes a scopophilic look at Judaism, fetishizing Judaism in whole or part through favorite tropes such as "the Pharisees," "the rabbis," and "the law." By so doing, they empty Jewish law of any authority, emasculating it even while describing its stereotypically masculine harshness, rigidity, and lack of mercy and sympathy. Like Jewish law, the Old Testament and its so-called God of wrath function within Christianity in similar terms, as both masculine and emasculated. It is neither the maleness of Judaism nor its feminine attributes but precisely its gender ambiguity that gives rise in Christian theology to the quality of horror.

Challenging the definition of Mulvey, Carol Clover has defied the neat distinction between gazer and object, sadist and victim, male and female.[22] Instead, she locates the success—the pleasure—of the horror film in its sexual vacillation between male and female performance. The thrill of the horror film is created, she argues, precisely by confounding the representation of gender. For example, the female victim assumes masculinity in the horror film when she sets out to seek revenge on her attacker. The uncertainty of male and female gender is promoted further by the mutations found in slasher films, in which women begin to look like men, or in possession films, in which men are pressured to become like women, and in other films, in which some people are genitally so ambiguous that even a doctor does not know what sex to assign.[23] It is a confusion of gender that Clover also finds even in some of Freud's own readings, such as his assertion that the clitoris is a "little penis," or his fantasy of anal procreation.[24] As much as the sexuality of the male killer or slasher of the horror film is ambiguous, it is his feminine component that is abnormal and hence responsible for his monstrous atrocities.

The Jews' lack is an analogous problem, based on the proposition that the male is not always what he appears to be. Like the horror film, the appeal of Christian anti-Judaism is rooted in the masochistic fears and desires of its Christian audience. The horror here is figured as "Jewish." It draws its power from the suggestion that Judaism belongs not to a separate realm but within Christianity itself. That is, it is grudgingly acknowledged by liberal Protestant theologians such as Harnack that Jesus was indeed a Jew, a rabbi, whose teachings were no different from those of the Pharisees. To compensate, Jesus is read as a feminine victim whose valiant escape from the horror of Judaism makes him a man. That transformation, of course, is never a fully successful operation. In its lack of success, the threat of ambiguity, of losing the boundaries that constitute self-definition, becomes present to the Christian as well. If Jesus can so easily lose his Christian identity and slide into the morass of Jewishness, how much more so is the Christian vulnerable to a comparable danger.

There is a metaphoric architecture to the female body that constructs both genders, and there is a metaphoric architecture to Judaism in Christian theological writings that constructs both religions; both the female and the Jewish become the sites for production of the uncanny. The question to be asked, however, is if the horror film is presented with an implied male viewer, and Christian theology is written for Christian readers, what is the pleasure of the man or the Christian in the sadistic, voyeuristic side of horror? What is the Christian pleasure in the horror of the Pharisees? If the Pharisees, in fact, are solely representing Judaism, there would be no thrill to the horror; only because of the indeterminacy that results from identifying Jesus, the Christian, as a Pharisee can the thrill be generated. As much as Jesus lies within the camp of the Pharisees, the Pharisees must be an element within Christianity. The indeterminacy of boundary is overcome only with the unfulfillable hope that those who save themselves are male, and those who are saved by others are female. The ultimate hero who saved himself is, of course, Jesus. Eluding the dybbuk of Judaism that invades from the inside out, he resisted the Judaization and fled the orbit of the Jews by becoming the first Christian. The reader, by identifying with Jesus, hopes to resist the danger of Judaization and flee to the presumably safe space of the Christian.

Perhaps the rage Jewish interpretation evoked among Christian theologians demonstrates just how powerful a Jewish gaze can be. Slavoj Zizek suggests that antisemitism functions by fantasizing the "Jew" as the barrier to ultimate satisfaction.[25] Theologically, for Christians, the "Jew" functions similarly, as the supposed barrier to an ultimate apotheosis. As Amy Newman has argued, Christians continually fantasize about the "death of Judaism" because it would overcome so many of the inconsistencies in their religious claims—or at least draw the gaze away from them.[26] The Jew who writes on Jesus is like the woman who writes on men; by reversing the position of the observer, from Christians writing about Judaism to a Jew writing about Christianity, the power relations of the viewer and the viewed are reversed, transforming Christianity into a semiotic representation within the economy of Judaism. Feminist scholarship has similarly destabilized not only the canon but the very gaze of the scholarly eye. The Jew, in narrating the Jesus story, becomes the hero, claiming the power that inheres in the story and attempting the same destabilization of Christianity that Christians have attempted of Judaism. The theological gaze may indeed be reversed, but its ferocity is not thereby diminished. As much as Jews dressed Jesus as a rabbi, Christians intensified the negative depiction of Judaism, particularly of the Pharisees, and insisted upon the opposition between Jesus and Judaism. By contrast, Jesus as theological transvestite unsettles and "queers" our understanding of the "boundaries" between Judaism and Christianity.

Notes

1. A recent collection of essays, *Feminist Perspectives on Jewish Studies*, ed. Lynn Davidman and Shelly Tenenbaum (New Haven: Yale University Press, 1994), illustrates the point: the parameters of the subject at hand are limited to the study of women, or at most, what men have written about femaleness.

2. Sandra M. Gilbert and Susan Gubar, *The Madwoman in the Attic* (New Haven: Yale University Press, 1979).

3. Nina Auerbach, *Women and the Demon: The Life of a Victorian Myth* (Cambridge: Harvard University Press, 1982), 12.

4. For example, see Daniel Schenkel, *Das charakterbild Jesu* (Wiesbaden: C. W. Kreidel 1864); and Theodor Keim, *Geschichte Jesu von Nazara in ihrer Verkettung mit dem Gesammtleben seines Volkes* (Zürich: Orell, Fussli, 1867–1872).

5. Uriel Tal, *Christians and Jews in Germany*, trans. Noah Jacobs (Ithaca, NY: Cornell University Press, 1975).

6. Judith Butler, *Gender Trouble: Feminism and the Subversion of Identity* (New York: Routledge, 1990). See Donald Morton, "Birth of the Cyberqueer," *PMLA* 110.3 (May 1995): 373.

7. Butler, *Gender Trouble*, 25.

8. Marjorie Garber, *Vested Interests: Cross-Dressing and Cultural Anxiety* (New York: Harper Collins, 1992), 147.

9. On *The Crying Game*, see Marilyn Reizbaum, "Not a Crying Game. The Feminist Appeal: Nationalism, Feminism, and the Contemporary Literatures of Scotland and Ireland," *Scotlands* 2 (1994): 24–32.

10. Abraham Geiger, *Das Judentum und seine Geschichte* (Breslau, 1875), 117–118. Unless otherwise indicated, all translations from the German are my own.

11. Ferdinand Weber, *Jüdische Theologie auf Grund des Talmud und verwandter Schriften* (Leipzig, 1897); Rudolf Bultmann, *Das Urchristentum im Rahmen der antiken Religionen* (Zürich, 1949); Wilhelm Bousset, *Die Religion des Judentums im neutestamentlichen Zeitalter* (Berlin: Reuther & Reichard, 1906); Emil Schürer, *Geschichte des jüdischen Volkes im Zeitalter Jesu Christi* (Leipzig: J. C. Hinrichs, 1898); and Julius Wellhausen, *Pharisäer und Sadducäer: Eine Untersuchung zur inneren jüdischen Geschichte* (Greifswald: L. Bamberg, 1874).

12. Joseph Eschelbacher, *Das Judentum im Urteile der modernen protestantischen Theologie* (Leipzig, 1907); Martin Schreiner, *Die jungesten Urteile über das Judentum, kristisch untersucht*

(Berlin: Cronbach, 1902); and Hermann Steinthal, *Über Juden und Judentum: Vorträge und Aufsätze*, ed. Gustav Karpeles (Berlin: 1906).

13. Adolf von Harnack, *Des Wesen des Christentums* (Berlin, 1900), 30–31.

14. Leo Baeck, "Romantic Religion," in *Judaism and Christianity: Essays by Leo Baeck*, trans. and ed. Walter Kaufmann (Philadelphia: Jewish Publication Society, 1958), 192, 189–292; originally Leo Baeck, "Romantische Religion," *Festschrift zum 50 jährigen Bestehen der Hochschule für die Wissenschaft des Judentums* (Berlin, 1922), 1–48.

15. Ernst Käsemann, "Protest!" *Evangelische Theologie* 51.5(1991): 458–467.

16. Eugenie Lemoine-Luccioni, *La Robe* (Paris: Seuil, 1983), 124; cited in Garber, *Vested Interests*, 356.

17. Eve Kosofsky Sedgwick, *Epistemology of the Closet* (Berkeley: University of California Press, 1990).

18. Gustav Volkmar, *Die Religion Jesu* (Leipzig: F. A. Brockhaus, 1857), 60.

19. Ernest Renan, *Vie de Jesus* (Paris, 1863), trans. as *The Life of Jesus* (New York, 1927), 224–25; for a more recent feminist analysis, see Sharon Ringe, "A Gentile Woman's Story," in *Feminist Interpretation of the Bible*, ed. Letty Russell (Philadelphia: Westminster Press 1985), 68.

20. Michael Wirth, *Die Pharisäer, Ein Beitrag zum leichtern Verstehen der Evangelien und sur Selbstprüfung* (Ulm: Stetten, 1824), iii; Joseph Langen, *Das Judentum in Palaestina zur Zeit Christi* (Freiburg im Breisgau: Herder Verlag, 1866), 189; Anon., "Pharisäer," in Georg Benedict Winer, *Biblische Realwöterbuch zum Handgebrauch für Studirende*, Candidaten, Gymnasialleher und Prediger, 2 vols. (Leipzig: Carl Heinrich Reclam; vol. 1, 1847, vol. 2, 1848), volume 2, 244–48; and Christoph van Ammon, *Du Geschichtie des Lebens Jesu*, 3 vols. (Leipzig: Vogel, 1842–1847), 3:225; Renan, *Life of Jesus*, 299.

21. Laura Mulvey, "Visual Pleasure and Narrative Cinema," in *Visual and Other Pleasures*, ed. Laura Mulvey (Bloomington: Indiana University Press, 1981).

22. Carol Clover, *Men, Women and Chain Saws: Gender in the Modern Horror Film* (Princeton: Princeton University Press, 1992).

23. For example, Clover points to the film *God Told Me To*, or the rapist in the film *The Incubus*, whose ejaculations consist of equal parts of semen and menstrual blood. Ibid., 15.

24. Ibid.

25. Slavoj Zizek, *The Sublime Object of Ideology* (New York: Verso, 1989), 125.

26. Amy Newman, "The Death of Judaism in German Protestant Thought from Luther to Hegel," *Journal of the American Academy of Religion* 61.3 (Fall 1993): 455–484.

Mengele, the Gynecologist, and Other Stories of Women's Survival

Sara R. Horowitz

During the earliest phase of my project on gender, genocide, and Jewish memory, I spoke to a group from an Orthodox Jewish women's organization about the portrayal of women's experiences of pregnancy and childbirth during the Shoah. Scattered among the American-born midwestern women between the ages of thirty and fifty were a few older women, some of whom spoke in accented cadences that told of another place, another time.

In the middle of the ensuing question-and-answer period, one of the older women stood up, stared intently at me, then announced to the group, "Mengele was my first gynecologist."

After a moment of stunned silence, the woman continued. She explained that as a young adolescent, she had been one of a group of teenagers selected for "reproductive experimentation" at Auschwitz. She had never before been subject to a pelvic exam, never before been touched by a man. After the war, she went on, "I was afraid. I was afraid he had done something to me, I was afraid I couldn't have children. I didn't know what he did when he examined me, I couldn't remember anything. I was afraid I couldn't have children." The girls in her group survived the war. Although they dispersed to different parts of the world, they remained in loose contact with one another. "When the first one from our group had a baby, we all heard about it, and we were so happy. It meant maybe we weren't sterile, maybe I could have a child, too." Each time another in the group gave birth, the remaining women would take heart. The woman who related this story explained that she was by this time already a grandmother. She had spoken to her children about the Shoah, about being a survivor. But about Mengele, she found it difficult to speak.[1]

I begin with this story about a particular survivor I have met, for several reasons. First, to make clear that in my work on women survivors, my point of departure and return is always the voices of survivors. Only my careful attentiveness to their voices authorizes my own voice in this area. Second, because the story makes clear that the atrocity and trauma of the Nazi genocide did not end with liberation of the camps. Third, because this story illustrates to us that Jewish women survivors experienced the war and also reflect back upon it both as Jews and as women. A careful consideration of this one woman's Holocaust remembrance indicates what the perspective of gender brings to our attempt to comprehend the events of the Shoah. Embedded in her account of forced participation in Mengele's notorious medical experimentation is a narrativizing of the extremity and lasting effect of the trauma suffered and atrocity endured, and an intimation of the importance of gender analysis of Shoah literature.

"Mengele was my first gynecologist." Her choice of terminology and fear of infertility indicate that in her eyes, she suffered a particularly female wounding. Some men, too, suffered forced sterilization and castration in medical "experimentations." But as this Mengele survivor recounted it, the invisibility of her wounding marks it as female. The woman recollects not knowing precisely what Mengele was doing in his "examinations," neither at the time nor in retrospect: "I didn't know what he did when he examined me, I couldn't remember anything." Nor could the lasting effects of Mengele's unknown or unremembered actions be revealed until her future life unfolded—"I was afraid I couldn't have children." Her fear and subsequent relief connects her to the other women who also endured this specifically female atrocity and feared its consequence, and whose escape from consequence was the only source of reassurance to the other women. "When the first one from our group had a baby, we all heard about it. . . . It meant . . . maybe I could have a child, too." The woman's language underscores the specifically female nature of the atrocity and the trauma. Given her age at Auschwitz and her religious background, her reference to Mengele as "my first gynecologist"—rather than a "doctor," a "monster," a "torturer"—suggests a sexual violation and also a gender wounding, a shattering of something innate and important to her sense of her own womanhood. This idea of gender wounding emerges in women's testimony—in stories women tell publicly and privately, in memoirs, in literary texts, and differently, in works by men.[2]

As my encounter with this Mengele survivor indicates, stories prompt other stories, and empathetic listeners facilitate the telling. Listening to the memories of atrocity and survival I was recounting secondhand, and feeling the intense compassion and sorrow that pulled together the women in the room that evening, made this woman choose to tell this most intimate and scathing chapter of her life story publicly for the first time. In developing my current project, "Gender, Genocide and Jewish Memory," I write the lives (and deaths) of women victims of Nazi atrocity. Although initially conceived as "literary"—that is, treating written narratives—this project quickly evolved into a multidisciplinary study exploring also videotaped testimony, oral history, and personal interviews with survivors. In several instances, a series of taped interviews with a survivor led to her publishing a memoir. In other cases, I conducted ongoing interviews with known authors of published fiction. These interviews considerably reshaped my view of the published works, the writers, and the experience of survival.

Just as my conversations with survivors shaped me, I became aware that my questions—indeed, my presence as listener—could shape their testimony. As a real audience/reader, I stood in for the ideal, imagined, or implicit reader whose concerns, interests, and sensibilities were to be addressed. The "interviews" quickly turned into wide-ranging conversations. On several occasions, I chose not to bring out a tape recorder, preferring the promise of a nascent friendship to the possibility of a published interview.

As I built precious friendships with the remarkable women whose lives constituted the basis for my academic work, it became clear that I was not simply a scholar. In their eyes and in my own, I too had become a witness. To borrow a phrase from the poet Paul Célan, I was a witness for the witness. I became increasingly self-conscious of my own participation as another sort of witness, one who witnesses the witness. But as I move from listening and reading to writing, I find myself uncommonly stuck. I delete paragraph after paragraph, page after page, from articles whose deadlines overtake me. I find it impossible to write the lives of women survivors of the Nazi genocide, impossible to write even the little I have come to know about their unimaginable experiences of victimization, survival, trauma, and triumph. I am not referring here to the muteness that informs all writing about the Shoah,[3] the blankness of page that comes about because, as Charlotte Delbo explains, "*Tous leurs mots sont lègers*" (All their words are light),[4] or, as Primo Levi complains, "Our language lacks words to express the offense, the demolition of a man,"[5] or, as Maurice Blanchot observes, "The disaster de-scribes."[6] Nor am I speaking of the muteness of the witness, the words and images left unuttered because the self shattered by atrocity cannot fully articulate its own unmaking.[7] Although all of these are implicated in my own attempts to write, I struggle also with other problems specific to my current project. As I move beyond published texts and archival testimony to personal encounters, interviews, and friendships, as I move from Holocaust atrocity generally to the gender-wounding of women in the Shoah, I confront the unwritability of women's lives and deaths during the Holocaust. Their experiences are unwritable on several levels: the confidentiality or delicacy of certain revelations, the desire not to commodify the individual rememberer as "a survivor," the reluctance to open up this material to a prurient voyeurism. Several concrete examples illustrate my difficulties.

I was introduced to a woman I'll call "Judith," a concentration camp survivor who wanted my assistance in producing her memoirs. Initially, I thought she was asking advice on getting published, or perhaps on writing. When we first met, she had already begun writing her life. Although she asked, I had qualms about providing editorial suggestions. I did not want my voice to intrude on the "authentic" voice of the survivor, to reshape her memories. As a close reader of texts, I believe that truth is embedded in the details of language and narration. My "improvements" would carry the resonances of my memory, my psyche, not hers. I wanted to bear witness for the witness, not to displace her.

But what transpired between Judith and me became more problematic. I soon became the listening ear, the receptive listener whose presence enabled the flow of testimony. For Judith, writing, like speaking, required not merely an implied audience but a physical presence at the moment of writing or speaking. Sometimes we would meet, and she would read aloud passages of memory she had composed. This reading would trigger other fresh, new memories. She eventually asked to tape-record our conversations because she found herself recollecting events long buried in "the ruins of memory," to borrow a phrase from Ida Fink. When we could not meet, she would continue her memory work with me by phone. Sometimes she would break off the conversation in search of a pencil to jot down something she had just remembered. Occasionally she wept.

Judith did not require my active participation in the conversation; once we had finished chatting about our present lives, she would say, "I remembered something recently. May I tell you?" That would begin a plunge into the past that might last for several hours.

An opportunity arose to publish some of Judith's memory writing in an anthology of women's writing. To shape the essay, we began by transcribing the taped conversations and meshing sections of it with some her written memories. The taped narratives consisted of three related components: vividly recollected testimony, incidents in her life before, during, and after the Nazi upheaval; historical narrative, drawn not so much from her personal recollections as from her exhaustive reading; and historical analysis. Given an austere page limit, I pushed to include as much of the personal narrative as the editors would allow, at the expense of the historical and analytical sections. This meant culling chunks of writing from different sessions and manuscripts. I resisted any attempt by the editors to "normalize" or refine her writing. I thought her an eloquent witness, whose occasionally nonidiomatic or Yiddish expressions testified to the events that had so radically displaced her. Eventually, she produced a long narrative that served as the first draft of the published essay.

Each subsequent draft began with a long passage consisting of the names of her murdered relatives in Europe, with her family network laid out in elaborate detail, and reaching back several generations. These were the people who had constituted her intimate world as a child. Her beloved maternal grandmother, her maternal uncle, her mother's sister—all named, the relationships carefully traced. The editors felt that the passage impeded the flow of narrative and, moreover, took up valuable space that could be used to narrate further episodes of her life. The names and family network would not be meaningful to the readers of the volume. But Judith would not yield. I eventually realized why. The people named in it had all vanished. With the exception of her grandmother, all had been murdered and had neither burial nor gravemarker. They exist only in her memory, only at the moment she recollects them—and now, in her narrative. I suggested she substitute for the passage a family tree—as detailed and extensive as she desired—so that her lost loved ones would be given some permanence on the page, and her narrative could flow.

As I reread the transcripts of our conversations, I began to notice that Judith repeated herself. I don't mean this trivially. Sometimes, when Judith would call me to tell me an anecdote, her language corresponded almost word for word with what she had said on the tapes or in her handwritten memoir. She would recite the stories almost verbatim, and with the same affect, as though telling each one for the first time. Yet, repetition notwithstanding, her anecdotes were not frozen snapshots that had lost emotional resonance by virtue of having been told before.

As I came to know Judith, I was reminded of Coleridge's ancient mariner, compelled to recite his harrowing tale of death and survival over and over, without the relief of what today we would call "working through." Judith was unaware of the exactness of her repetitions. Yet it was clear to me that she had to tell her story just so. The ritualized telling, it seemed to me, was both a form of remembering and a form of forgetting. Her recollections were contained by language—in two senses. First, that language held memory, as a bucket holds liquid that would otherwise flow into the ground and be lost. And second, that language held it in check, as concrete walls hold in or contain an explosion. Judith's recollections tell the truth—that is, they actually happened—and they still carry an emotional charge. Because of the massively traumatic nature of her experiences, she has memories that may never be "worked through," no matter how often recited. At the same time, the memories she tells me are ordered, selected memories, not chaotic ones. Her involuntary memories are quickly given shape and meaning. Telling her stories in this way and no other, I believe, she protects herself from ways of remembering that are too painful to bear.

The novelist Ilona Karmel, another survivor of Nazi concentration camps and author of *An Estate of Memory*, once distinguished between two types of Holocaust memory. One type she describes as her "coat": dates and details she can tell and retell without great anguish, because the words and events she selects protect her deep self. In contrast, "real memories" are private and searing, difficult to think, speak, and write. I sensed that in Judith's tellings, the repetitive narrations serve as such a "coat," insuring that other, more searing memories be protected. Thus, Judith's repetitiveness tells me something about the atrocities she witnessed and endured, about the lasting effects of massive trauma. I would like to speak to her about this, and to write about it in greater detail. But I cannot. If I tell her that she repeats herself verbatim, I risk hurting her feelings. Far worse, should I choose to push her beyond this self-protective device, I may upset the crucial balance she has struggled to maintain between memory and forgetting. I feel compelled to respect the boundaries she has set for herself. But at the same time, I cannot help but wonder what memories locked inside her are lost to the world.

Like Judith, other women survivors have entrusted me with personal and intimate memories, on the condition that I not reveal them. Sometimes particular recollections involve other people, or would evoke unwanted pity or unwanted admiration. Some memories are simply too private or too painful to open to public display. What I learn from the women whose confidences and friendships I value deepens my understanding of their experience and their writing; it surely deepens our friendships. I know I may not divulge things told to me in confidence, nor information gleaned from being welcomed into a woman's home and observing her family interactions. But at the same time, I regret this silencing of testimony—mine and theirs.

What I have heard and observed speaks powerfully about memory, survival, trauma, victimization, loss, resilience, and ethics.

For example, I am frequently shown or handed copies of the intimate artifacts of family life—homemade birthday and Mother's Day cards; children's drawings, poems, and school projects; photographs and letters—that reveal the resonances of Holocaust trauma in the lives of second and third generations. One woman showed me the Mother's Day poem her child had written to her many years earlier, which she had carefully preserved. The verse begins by invoking Hitler, the murdered six million, and a world of hate and prejudice; it concludes with praise to the child's mother, "the greatest mom," who strives to build a world filled with peace and love. The mother, a concentration camp survivor, consented to my writing about this card as a means of illustrating the deep knowing that comes out of examining household items, with the provision that I disguise her identity. For this reason, I do not quote at length from the poem, but instead approach it more descriptively.

The Mother's Day poem reveals its author, a child born into post–World War II America and a legacy of genocide. The poem combines elements of American culture and European Jewish memory by coalescing the evocation of the Holocaust with the occasion, Mother's Day, an invention of American commercialism. Opening with the specificity of Jewish history, the poem closes with a Hallmark-esque praise of the child's mother. As such, it unintendedly mimics the mother's own life trajectory from Auschwitz to a working-class section of a northeastern American city. To arrive from its point of origin to its destination, the poem expands or universalizes the Holocaust, so that the imperative to remember the Jews of Europe encompasses also a universalized mandate—to quest for "world peace," for example. Coalescing the child's Jewish and American identities on the fixed point of the Holocaust, the poem suggests that the child's dual cultural memories can serve as a basis for life-affirming values. Finally, the poem ends by rhyming "mom" with "bomb," suggesting a darker undercurrent to the poem's upbeat surface, one made explicit in a note written at a different time: "I wish you could forget about the Holocaust, so you will stop crying already."

The Holocaust is situated at the zero degree point for the dual axes of the child's American and Jewish identities. Equally important, the Nazi genocide is an integral component of the intimate connections between mother and child. In the child's perceptions, the destruction of the Jews of Europe constitutes part of the mother's self, part of the relationship between them, and because of this, part of the child's self.

The mother is aware of the ambivalences of these connections, of some of the complicated ways in which her experiences mark her relationship with her children and shape her children's sense of their place in the world. She reflects, "To others, the Holocaust is just a word, but to me, it is my life, it is my history, and part of my experience. Part of what my children and grandchildren are deprived of now. . . . Their roots begin with us. We've brought them a legacy of pain. That is all we have to bring them. We have nothing left to show them."

At the same time, she weaves remembrances of atrocity into her articulation of values, with which she consciously informs the moral education of her children. "That I could come out of a hell like that . . . and still had the courage to go on, to continue . . . I know now that I love life. . . . And do you know what? . . . If your life is important, and mine is important too, it's only as important as everyone else's." She reaches deeply back into her past before the Holocaust, to her own childhood, to reconstruct a Polish-Jewish family whose interactions can instruct her present Jewish-American family. She tells her family anecdotes about their ancestors, focusing on their sense of ethics, humaneness, and compassion.

As the child's poem indicates, the mother serves up a plate that is both empty and full. The memories that she retells her children make their ancestors both intimately present in, and horribly absent from, their lives. By sharing those memories, she becomes both close to and distant from her children and their more fortunate existence. Like her child's poem, the mother attempts to bridge the absence and the presence, the Polish then and the American now, by universalizing her experience, by inscribing its history into American history. She visits schools, synagogues and churches, state penitentiaries, hospitals.

My position in this memory work is not without disquieting complications. Sometimes a survivor wants to talk at length when I would prefer not to; other times, I want to know something specific and ask survivors probing questions shaped by my desires and not theirs. At moments, I have fancied myself a character in a yet-to-be-written Cynthia Ozick story, the Holocaust scholar who can't get off the phone with a garrulous survivor. Indeed, Ozick's novella, "Rosa," points to the dangers of academic work focusing on living survivors—dangers of commodification, appropriation, and dehumanization. Through the consciousness of Rosa, a Holocaust survivor who witnessed the death of her only child in a concentration camp, Ozick holds up to scrutiny the growing academic concern with the Holocaust in America, where the enthusiasm for the details of research may inadvertently lead scholars to dehumanize the victim once again. Rosa receives "university letters" whose professorial writers seek to use her memory as "data."[8] In the scientific language, devoid of empathy, Rosa discerns an "excitement over other people's suffering" (36). In reading the letters, she herself feels diminished:

> Consider also the special word they used: *survivor.* Something new. As long as they didn't have to say *human being.* It used to be *refugee,* but by now there was no such creature, no more refugees, only survivors. A name like a number. . . . Blue digits on the arm, what difference. They don't call you a woman anyhow. *Survivor.* . . . Who made up these words, parasites on the throat of suffering! (36–37)

Positioned as the subject of academic research by scholars and scientists who do not know her, Rosa finds her situation powerfully reminiscent of her initial experience as a subject of genocidal practice. This suggests a critique of academic memory work, which, Ozick indicates, may miss the mark entirely even as it compiles more and more data.

To mitigate against such commodification of the survivor, the academic writer purposefully "writes-himself" into the story of the Jewish catastrophe, to use Berel Lang's term, writing against "the abstraction of theory or explanation" that "proposes to *think* rather than to feel or imagine" the events of the Nazi genocide.[9] As such, the stories of the women survivors—while remaining intimately their own—become, in some way, mine, as well. The line between "telling oneself" in these stories and appropriating them is a fine one, demanding constant negotiation and attentiveness.

Perhaps the most difficult subject to negotiate is that of the sexual violation of women during the Holocaust. On the one hand, some feminist scholars believe that stories of sexual violation have been deliberately omitted from constructions of the master narrative of the Holocaust. On the other hand, I find myself disturbed by the frequency of questions about rape and prostitution during the Holocaust whenever I speak to a general audience about women's experiences. Some of these inquiries seem motivated by deep concern for women victims as well as historical curiosity. But sometimes I sense other motives behind the questions. It is perhaps too harsh to see in the queries a certain voyeurism that sees the concentrationary universe as erotic exotica. But the woman victim as erotic object has become a trope of Holocaust representations, a prevailing image in narrative, film, and popular culture. Woman as erotic object figures as treacherous seductress (as in Peter Wyden's *Stella*) or as one drawn amorally to men in power (as in Marcie Hershman's *Tales of the Master Race*), or as one, more frequently, as alluring in her helplessness (Helen Hirsh in Spielberg's *Schindler's List*) or sexually violated (as in Sheri Szeman's *The Kommandant's Mistress*).[10]

When particular patterns of imagery recur, we are compelled to ask why. I confess to some hesitation in embarking on this topic, whether in literature, testimony, or the popular imagination, which is too easily given to sensationalism. Yet precisely because I cannot easily understand it, cannot easily speak of it, I find myself attempting to write about it. Three questions drive my writing: How do we account for the prevalence of erotic imagery, on the one hand, and the paucity of women's testimony on sexual violation, on the other? What are the limits of representation for this subject? What are the ethics of representing sexual violation?[11]

Steven Spielberg's film *Schindler's List* represents the alluring dark Jewish beauty of European literature and folk stereotypes. In Nazi anti-Semitic propaganda, the Jewish woman's physical beauty veils her racial repulsiveness. This visual comeliness permits the Jewess to tempt Aryan men into *Rassenschande*, the crime of miscegenation whose monstrous offspring serve to reveal the Jewess's real inner ugliness. Imagining a Jewess who entices men into dangerous liaisons, the trope of the alluring Jewess positions Jewish women as agents of their own sexual violation, projecting male desires onto them. Through the relationship between Amon Goeth and Helen Hirsch, *Schindler's List* exposes this mixture of attraction, fear, and revulsion; as Schindler's cellmate comments, "Jewish girls . . . cast a spell on you."

In Jewish American women's writings about the Holocaust, the trope of the eroticized female protagonist is sometimes unraveled, sometimes reproduced, sometimes used to discuss sexual violation more generally, outside the context of the Holocaust. Sheri Szeman takes a daring tactic in *The Kommandant's Mistress*[12] that juxtaposes the perceptions of perpetrator against those of victim by revealing both the erotic memories of a concentration camp kommandant and the recollections of the Jewish woman camp inmate forced to perform sexual service for survival.

The Kommandant's Mistress reproduces and then disrupts the eroticization of the Jewish woman victim. In the novel, other characters frequently refer to the Kommandant's prisoner/mistress as a "whore": Jewish prisoners envious of what they perceive as her privileged position ("Oh, no, Kommandant," Sharon said breathlessly, her hips pounding. "Please don't torture me this way" [154]); the Kommandant's wife, jealous of her husband's obsessive philandering and repulsed by the prisoner's Jewishness ("Max, even you couldn't love a Jew," she tells him); the Kommandant's adjutant, simultaneously appalled by the *Rassenschande* and lusting after the Kommandant's mistress; the Kommandant's best friend who begs to "have" her "just once." The sexually charged Kommandant's narrative titillates the reader, just as the camera work in *Schindler's List* invites the viewer to participate in Goeth's lascivious gaze at Helen Hirsch.

Against the Kommandant's erotic recollections and the repeated epithets "whore," are the woman's own reflections. Referred to only as the Kommandant's mistress in his narrative, the woman names herself in her own. Rachel's memory interrupts the erotic pleasure of the Kommandant's text by concentrating on her physical sensations at the Kommandant's exhilarating moments. The Kommandant focuses on his own sensations of desire and pleasure, and on his possession of the woman's body. Their encounters take place in small, contained spaces, such as the guardhouse or the Kommandant's office. The isolation of the closed rooms emblemizes the compartmentalization of the Kommandant's relationship with his "mistress" from the reality of the Nazi genocide—his work life and social context—in order to maintain the fantasy of a lovingly reciprocal relationship. The Kommandant's erotic memories focus on his physical pleasure and emotional happiness:

> I rubbed my cheek against her face and throat as I stretched my body along hers. I wrapped my arms around her and hugged her to me, my knee sliding between her legs. She closed her eyes. She always closed her eyes. I covered her face and throat with kisses. I held her breasts in my hands and I kissed them. . . . I pressed her onto her back, and her thighs were soft on either side of mine. . . . I brushed the back of her thighs and lifted her hips. . . . I wanted her to sigh my name against my chest and throat. . . . I was happy." (91–92)

By contrast, Rachel's memories expose not only her physical pain but also the context in which these encounters occur—the Nazi death camps.

> As he undid his pants, he leaned against me, his mouth open and wet and stinking of alcohol. He pressed me hard against the desk. . . . He pushed against me until I was flat on the desk. When he got on top of me, I turned my head away, toward the window.
>
> Outside, in the camp's yard, rows of men, women, and children stood, naked, waiting to go into showers. The chimneys belched out the black smoke that had been their comrades, and the smoke hung in palls over the shivering Jews. They clung to each other for warmth, or used their hands to hide their nakedness from the soldiers who walked slowly back and forth, their rifles ready. The Kommandant's fingers dug into me as he thrust, and he rubbed his face against my cheek. He hadn't shaved. His shoulder jammed my chin. . . . If I said his name, he would cry out and be done. (176–77)

The Kommandant's narrative focuses on erotic pleasures and the fantasy that his desire also represents hers. Rachel's narrative incorporates physically unpleasant sensations—the Kommandant's breath and the roughness of his unshaved face, the hard surface of the desktop—with death-camp sights and sounds. Although some Jewish prisoners envy what they take to be her "living a good life, there in his office" (154), Rachel's narrative indicates that the inside of the Kommandant's office is, in fact, a continuation of the outside, the death camp. In her nakedness, the narrative identifies her with the "rows of men, women and children . . . waiting to go into the showers," and places her torment as a piece of theirs.

By means of its narrative structure, *The Kommandant's Mistress* traps the voyeuristic reader. The dual narratives first titillate then expose the reader's acquiescence to the combination of eros, victimization, and violence. Szeman's novel thus intensifies our understanding of the ethics of representing sexual violence. The sequential memory narratives alert the reader to the dangers of such representations: that the retelling of stories of rape and sexual violation may serve to eroticize victims, thereby reenacting, to some measure, the initial atrocity.

Explaining instances of sexual violation of women during the Holocaust expands our knowledge of Nazi atrocity and ensuing trauma. It particularizes the experiences of Jewish women and allows a silenced testimony to speak belatedly. On the other hand, a focus on the sexual violation of women, more generally, outside the context of Nazi atrocity runs the danger of viewing women purely in sexual terms, and in eroticizing their image. In addition, sexual violation universalizes the experience of Nazi atrocity, making it more accessible to American readers and writers. Interestingly, some of the issues that emerge in survivor writing—the struggle against silence, belated witnessing, mistrust of memory, the duration of trauma—parallel issues that emerge in remembering sexual violation. Melanie Kaye/Kantrowitz, for example, opens *The Issue is Power: Essays on Women, Jews, Violence and Resistance*,[13] with the following parallelism:

> First I learned about rape. I mean, I always knew, cannot remember learning. First I learned about the Holocaust. I mean, I always knew, cannot remember learning. (i)

Pushed to its extreme, the idea of seeing the Holocaust solely in terms of eros and sexual violation (as in Emily Praeger's novel, *Eve's Tattoo*) domesticates the Holocaust, diminishing its horror to something more ordinary and sparing the reader a more disturbing confrontation.

At the same time, certain aspects of the Holocaust for women—for example, nakedness in front of strangers, exposure and shaving of genital hair—connect even atrocity of a nonsexual nature with a sense of sexual violation. What are the limits of representing sexual violation? The rabbinic protest against the photograph at Yad VaShem depicting Jewish women forced to disrobe moments before their murder, and the delicacy with which the U.S. Holocaust Memorial Museum shields unwilling and unwary viewers from film footage of similar scenes, underscores the complexity of this issue. Like all Holocaust testimony, evidence and remembrance of sexual violation should not be suppressed. But how should it be represented without re-creating the original offense, without again exposing these women to the gaze of strangers?

In narratives by men, the focus on eroticized female victims compartmentalizes the horror according to gender: men read (or write) their own desire, thus reaffirming agency; women represent helplessness and victimization. Scholars have observed a similar pattern in the narratives of African American slaves, where the scenes of the most visceral, corporal torture are frequently depicted as inflicted on a female victim, who is often unclothed. There, the gendered compartmentalization shores up the slave unmanned by atrocity; in Toni Morrison's novel about slavery and the traumas of memory, *Beloved*, Paul D., a former slave, repeatedly wonders whether one can be both a man and a slave. In addition, to the extent that the two central female tropes—mother and erotic object—coalesce, they reveal the fear of many women survivors that something essential to their womanhood has been damaged. Many women survivors have spoken to me of their fears of sterility after the war because of medical expermentations or the cessation of their menses. Others complain that without a mother to initiate them into womanhood, they did not learn how to function adequately as adult women, as mothers, as wives.

As I investigate the memories of women survivors, I become aware of parallels between their act of witnessing and my own. Just as they mediated history through personal memory, so I mediate their stories through writing and teaching. The women whose lives I write search continually for ways to make the world cohere. The radical negativity of the Holocaust decenters all fixed points: the values and political philosophies of the West; Jewish identity, faith, and politics; assumptions about community, friendship, family, gender. My interactions with these women and their memories unhinge my own fixed points. Actively listening to their testimony means becoming a witness not only to their lives but also to my own. It means importing into my life and work their desire to act ethically in conditions that made this nearly impossible; the sense that one's choices count, even (especially) under conditions that constrict choice. As these women, catastrophically displaced from Europe to the United States, reflect on their brutal treatment in their native lands, they ask that their witnesses reflect on how America treats our own outsiders.

Notes

1. October 27, 1994, Etz Nashim, Jewish Community Center, Cleveland, OH.

2. The gendering of Holocaust tropes, testimony, and trauma, of course, informs memory work by and about men as well as women. See, for example, my discussion of the trope of the wounded tongue in the works of H. Lervick, Elias Canetti, and Elie Wiesel in *Gender, Genocide and Jewish Memory*, forthcoming.

3. For further discussion of the function of muteness in Holocaust narratives, see Sara Horowitz, *Voicing the Void: Muteness and Memory in Holocaust Fiction* (New York: SUNY Press, 1996).

4. Charlotte Delbo, *Aucun de nous ne reviendra* (Paris: Editions de Minuit, 1970), 61.

5. Primo Levi, *Survival in Auschwitz: The Nazi Assault on Humanity*, trans. Stuart Woolf (New York: Collier, 1969), 22.

6. Maurice Blanchot, *The Writing of the Disaster*, trans. Ann Smock [L'Ecriture du désastre] (Lincoln: University of Nebraska Press, 1986).

7. For further elaboration of the function of the mute witness, see Sara Horowitz, "Rethinking Holocaust Testimony: The Making and Unmaking of the Witness," *Cardozo Studies in Law and Literature* 4.1 (Spring/Summer 1992): 45–68.

8. Cynthia Ozick, *The Shawl* (New York: Knopf, 1989), 37.

9. Berel Lang, *Act and Idea in Nazi Genocide* (Chicago: University of Chicago Press, 1990), xii.

10. Peter Wyden, *Stella* (New York: Simon & Schuster, 1992); Marcie Hershman, *Tales of the Master Race* (New York: HarperPerennial, 1991); Steven Spielberg (director), *Schindler's List* (1993); Sheri Szeman, *The Kommandant's Mistress* (New York: HarperPerennial, 1993).

11. The question of establishing an ethics of representing sexual violation is part of the larger issue that I address in this essay: the ethics of representing trauma and testimony more broadly speaking, without participating in a kind of voyeurism, exploitation, or appropriation. As interpreters of texts and as listeners to and transmitters of testimony, we are accountable for developing reading and writing practices that respect the witness and the testimony.

12. Szeman, *Kommandant's Mistress.*

13. Melanie Kaye/Kantrowitz, *The Issue is Power: Essays on Women, Jews, Violence and Resistance* (San Francisco: aunt lute books, 1992).

(The Problem with) Embraces

Laura Levitt

These reflections begin with a problem: what does it mean to do Jewish feminist scholarship at the end of the twentieth century in the United States? How do feminist scholars of Judaism work with texts? How do we read, write and speak about a whole range of issues? From where do we speak? With which texts do we engage?

I begin this exploration by resisting what is familiar to me in Jewish Studies, the (however varied) roles of "reader" demanded by certain kinds of Jewish reading practices, those often labeled as "traditional," "religious," or "Wissenschaft." *Since I cannot read from the position of these normative masculine readers, I have had to find other stances, other ways of reading, writing, and speaking. In part this is what this essay is about. It is my attempt to claim how I work with texts as a Jewish feminist critical practice.*

This essay is but one approach to these problems. It comes out of my extended engagement with feminist literary theory. Although I initially came to this theory in order to explore issues of identity in their complexity, this move to theory has also had other ramifications. More specifically, it has helped me think about how issues of identity inform my critical practice. In other words, I speak from somewhere about lots of things not only about my self. At times this has led me to write autobiographically, but, in this case, I want to argue that the autobiographical can also be understood as a part of broader critical practice.

With these issues in mind, I explain in what follows how I understand reading and writing as a kind of embrace. I then offer a reading of Nancy K. Miller's "Dreaming, Dancing and the Changing Locations of Feminist Literary Criticism, 1988" in order to demonstrate how I work with Jewish texts. By writing about my interaction with this text in particular, I hope to make explicit the ambivalent desires that inform my critical practice.

Part One: The Embrace

Perhaps *embrace* is an odd word to use to explain a methodological turn in one's work, but it captures well the way I work with Jewish texts. According to the *American Heritage Dictionary, to embrace* means

> to clasp or hold with arms, usually as an expression of affection. . . . To surround; enclose. . . . To twine around. . . . To include as part of something broader. . . . To take up willingly or eagerly. . . . An act of holding close with the arms, usually as an expression of affection; a hug. . . . An enclosure or encirclement. . . . Eager acceptance.[1]

Implicit in this definition is a desire, an attraction that calls for a response. An embrace is such a response. But equally implicit is a basic tension. An embrace can be a loving gesture, a tender act of affection, or protection, but it can also suggest control over others, even and perhaps especially the other who is the object of one's affection.

In the *American Heritage Dictionary*, to embrace is to surround or enclose. I worry about the danger of holding on too tight, of not allowing the other enough space to breathe and grow on its own. When I think about being entwined, I am reminded of vines like kudzu. They take over all the trees and bushes that come into their grasp; they kill whatever they embrace.

Reading is about desire, and about different kinds of embraces. When you read a text, something brings you in, captures your imagination, hooks you. To embrace a text is to give yourself over to your desire for it. This is a joy, but it comes with dangers. One danger is holding on too tightly, so that the text loses its distinct character and becomes a reflection of the reader. As the reader takes the text into herself, it becomes an extension of her. Another danger, an inversion of the first, is that the reader loses herself in the text. In the first danger, the text gets swallowed; in the second, the reader's difference dissolves. She is reduced to another instance of the text's argument. Becoming the text, she loses her own voice and takes on that of the text. Both of these forms of reading blur boundaries. Distinctions between reader and text are lost.

When reading is a part of the writing process, this blurring of distinctions can get especially tricky. Academic scholarship, like many other forms of writing, depends on the citation of other writers' texts. And often we make use of citation because, in the process of finding and staking out our own positions, we encounter other texts whose commitments are similar to ours. Staking out new positions is risky, and the similarities we find in other texts can offer us an (em)brace. Our citations hold us up as we attempt to take a stand, especially for the first time. These citations of other people's writing can brace our own argument, providing weight, authority, and precedent. But sometimes in this process, a writer gets lost. As readers who write about other people's writing, we can lose our own voices, holding on too tightly to the authority of other people's writing. And so in writing this essay, I find myself a bit unsteady. I have texts to bring into this discussion, passages to cite as proof for what I am saying. But, for the moment, I will resist the temptation. I will let my words stand alone.

Reading and engaging with the texts of others has helped me find my own voice as a writer. The text that speaks to me right now—pushing through the seams of my essay with such force that I can barely keep myself from quoting it at length—is Susan Rubin Suleiman's *Risking Who One Is: Encounters with Contemporary Art and Literature.*[2] In her introduction Suleiman writes about how she reads and writes about contemporary art and literature. As she explains, in writing the book she had become aware of the fact that she was "constructing one version of the shape of my own life." She continues:

> Since these are all critical essays dealing with the work of others . . . , they are not what I would call "straight autobiography." Rather, they are a form of mediated autobiography where the exploration of the writer's self (which I take to be a defining characteristic of autobiography) takes place not directly but through the mediation of writing about another. (3)

What I love about this passage is the recognition it inspires. I identify with Suleiman's narrative voice. I recognize myself in her writing, and yet there is something in this identification that feels uncomfortable. I remember discussing this issue with Miriam, early in my writing process. I explained that I was thinking about the notion of embracing texts, that I was pulling out the tension in critical practices of reading, writing, and citation, looking closely at the relations between me and the text. I couldn't resist reading her this passage, so that she would understand what I was doing by hearing it in Suleiman's voice. I assumed that my point would be obvious, but it was not. Instead, I discovered that although Suleiman's text spoke to me, what I heard was not self-evident. Reading the passage to Miriam, she did not hear what I heard in the text. Despite my desire for clarity through citation, my point was lost when I gave voice to my argument through a reading from Suleiman's text.

Miriam understood my argument without reference to the text. She was not the one who needed the citation, and in fact, she did not see me reflected in Suleiman's text as clearly as I saw myself. This led me to wonder about the differences between my project and Suleiman's. What had drawn me into her description, and at what point did I see myself most clearly? The attraction, I found, lay in her discussion of the ambivalence of mediated autobiographical writing. As she explains in the passage just quoted, her essays are "a form of mediated autobiography where the exploration of the writer's self . . . takes place not directly but through the mediation of writing about another." In this particular sentence, I found both the desire—and the difference. Embracing text is not identical to "autobiographical" writing. An attraction to the autobiographical is already present in my explanation of what it might mean to "embrace" a text, but I am not solely concerned with "the exploration of the writer's self." The point is not merely to read and write "my self" but to recognize the self who always reads and writes from somewhere, who is already positioned (in various and contradictory ways) in relation to particular texts. To read and write, in other words *as* my self with delicacy about many different things.

I encounter this tension as I read and write about a broad range of Jewish texts, and it is a tension I wish to explore carefully. With all this in mind, in what follows I demonstrate some of the difficulties and possibilities involved in trying to embrace texts as a feminist and a Jew. I do this by writing about Nancy K. Miller's essay "Dreaming, Dancing, and the Changing Location of Feminist Criticism, 1988,"[3] a feminist critical essay in which the author tries to speak as a Jew and a feminist critic. Out of this reading I suggest how different kinds of critical embraces offer ways to configure Jewish study as a feminist practice.

Part Two: Reading and Writing for Others as One's Self

I believe that it is possible to write as one's self about others. Consequently, I am troubled to find a text that passionately confronts precisely these issues but that ostensibly makes the opposite claim: that reading and writing as one's self about others is impossible. This claim is at the heart of Miller's "Dreaming, Dancing." In her essay, Miller first makes use of the strategy of citation as a means of speaking for others. She presents a series of texts on dreaming and dancing through many citations of other people's writings, without any apparent intervention of her own. Having demonstrated the limitations of this approach, she then offers an alternative. She writes about fewer texts and positions herself within the essay as a Jew doing feminist criticism. Because Miller is one of very few feminist critics to write as a Jew, I was especially interested in her assessment. At the end of her essay, reflecting back on her efforts, Miller writes:

> To some extent the difficulty of these two occasions was an effect of context; it was also, and more importantly, a symptom of the project of identity writing itself: impossible to elude: the co-implication, which always seems to find its borders in violence, of the "speaking as a"s and "speaking for"s. . . . It is for this reason that I have not tried, even in the space of written revision, to master the crisis by a conclusion that would put things back together again. This could only be done by a discourse of containment that depends finally on making an abstraction of that violence. (97)

In this passage Miller connects writing and speaking. The two activities are intertwined and not unconnected to what I have referred to thus far as the relationship between reading and writing. Despite the connections between these activities, my efforts to read and write for others as my self are not the same as what Miller calls "the project of identity writing." For Miller, "identity writing" is a singular activity. It is either a writing "for others" or a writing "as something," in this case, a Jewish woman. She wants to find a way to negotiate both of these moves without causing discursive violence to herself or to those others for whom she speaks.

I begin with Miller's quotation as a way of saying yes, in Miller's essay I see a partial reflection of my desire to embrace texts and others, to speak as my self. I identify with her, at least, in part. And, yet, I also see a rather dramatic difference. Miller is sure that these efforts, "the speaking for's" and "the speaking as a's," are impossible; I am not so certain. I want to know more about the dangers involved. What harm do these kinds of writing inflict? In what ways are they violent? Miller suggests that this violence is about a loss of meaning or intention, but she clearly links this injury to other kinds of harm. According to the *American Heritage Dictionary*, among other things, "violence" can be an "abuse or injury to meaning, content, or intent." What I want to focus on here are the dangers posed by a loss of meaning.

In the first section of Miller's essay, the "Whose Dream?" portion, she attempts to offer a kind of "meta-critical fiction whose author would spin off into the interstice between acts" (97). But, here Miller loses control of the meaning of her text, and in the confusion of so many different passages, her editorial voice is lost. The reader loses sight of Miller's specific engagement with these other texts. It is not clear who is speaking for or to whom. Although her "use of quotation in 'Whose Dream?' was meant to both foreground the social plural of dreaming . . . and to destabilize [her] own position in relation to that project" (76), this is not how I read the text. Because she did not give her readers enough clues about how she wanted the text to be read, readers can find whatever they want in her essay. Echoing her title back to her, my question is, whose dreams are these?

The question points to the problem. As Miller explains,

> allowing my reading of the quotations to speak for me without my signing them (evaluating them and historicizing them, . . . against each other) turned out to mean letting readers read for me—which meant their placing, identifying, and *worst of all, perhaps, misreading me: in my own text, in my place.* [my emphasis] (97)

Having experienced this kind of loss of meaning as a loss of self, Miller attempts to correct the situation in "Personal Histories, Autobiographical Locations," the second section of her essay. She attempts to enact this correction by writing as a Jew. In the end, however, she dismisses this effort as "an even greater failure" (97). I disagree. I want to risk misreading Miller in order to argue that there is much more to be said about these efforts at speaking and writing about others as one's self. Instead of sticking with her final judgment that these gestures are impossible, I will demonstrate that it is possible to read, write, and speak as one's self for others not—as Miller argues—as an act of identity writing but as a kind of embrace.

Letting go of the opposition between "speaking as" and "speaking for," "Dreaming, Dancing" demonstrates both the dangers as well as the possibilities opened up by this sort of reading, writing, and speaking. I propose that Miller is able to read, write, and speak as a Jew about at least a single text precisely because, as she puts it, "The fact . . . of being both Jewish and a feminist is a crucial, even constitutive piece of my self-consciousness as a writer; and in that sense of course it is also at work—on occasion—in the style and figure of my autobiographical project" (97). It is for this reason that at least, "on occasion" Miller is able to write as both a Jew and a feminist.

In reconsidering what it might mean to "speak for" others, I offer a reading of the final section of "Whose Dream?" I do so because it points to the possibilities and illustrates the limitations of a certain kind of citational practice. Miller begins this section with a passage from Adrienne Rich's 1971 essay "When We Dead Awaken."[4] She offers this passage as a feminist answer to Jacques Derrida's dream of "incalculable choreographies." Instead of a dream like Derrida's that moves "beyond all local contingencies of history and place," Miller uses Rich's piece to argue for the necessity of a feminist dream that "never escapes the social." The Rich passage that appears in Miller's essay reads as follows:

> In closing I want to tell you about a dream I had last summer. I dreamed I was asked to read my poetry at a mass women's meeting, but when I began to read, what came out were lyrics of a blues song. I share this dream with you because it seemed to me to say something about the problems and the future of the woman writer, and probably of women in general. The awakening of consciousness is not like the crossing of a frontier—one step and you are in another country. (89)

In this story, and in general, the interrelationship between reading (or listening, as here) and writing, is complicated. Our own voices are always already formed and informed by what we know of the works of others. In 1971 Rich already seemed to know, in some sense, that her poetry was built on the work of others, specifically on the songs of African American women. Rich's dream also points to a larger sense of borrowing and/or appropriation, the relationship between white feminist and African American liberation struggles.[5] Although I am not so sure that Rich appreciated the potential violence in these kinds of appropriations, she does seem to understand here that the dream poses a problem for her feminist politics and writing.

Miller follows her citation of Rich's "dream" with this sentence:

> In a footnote to this passage added in 1978, Rich asks herself: "When I dreamed that dream, was I wholly ignorant of the tradition of Bessie Smith and other women's blues lyrics which transcend victimization to sing of resistance and independence?" (89)

In placing this footnote after her citation from Rich, Miller uses a strategic quotation to reinterpret the text significantly. Whereas Miller presents the two texts (citation and footnote) in direct succession, in Rich's original essay, they are separated by another sentence. The footnote on resistance does not actually refer to the dream but relates more directly to the interim sentence that Miller has omitted: "Much of women's poetry has been of the nature of the blues song: a cry of pain, of victimization, or a lyric of seduction."[6] In its original context, the footnote meant something different. Its significance is that by 1978 Rich had realized that the blues were not only about pain and victimization, or even seduction, but also about resistance and liberation.

In contrast, Miller's reading of the text changes the location of the note and makes its significance much less specific, less engaged with women's oppression and resistances to oppressions. Given Miller's desire for a feminist dream that will "never escape the social," it is ironic that in her text Rich's dream is taken out of its broader social context. After all, Rich's dream is a dream about the complicated interrelationship between African American and feminist struggles for liberation, set within a gathering of women. Miller's dream offers no concrete location for her own or other women's struggles. Instead, she uses the final image of Rich's dream, "another country," to move even further away from any social context. With the image of "another country" Miller sets up a series of increasingly abstract analogies to the process of feminist consciousness raising.

> Like the philosopher who wonders where the " 'dream' of the innumerable would come from, if it is indeed a dream" . . . , and the poet who has already discovered that "poems are like dreams: in them you put what you don't know you know" . . . , the dream of feminist critics, I think, already includes some linguistic knowledge of the culture of another country, even if we haven't traveled there. (89)

I wish to question this "the dream of feminist critics," which, according to Miller, "already includes some linguistic knowledge of the culture of another country, even if we haven't traveled there." Dreams may contain truths that we do not always know we know, but Miller's formulation is a problem. It loses track of the legacy of the blues as an embodiment of a country that is and is not other. Rich does not say that feminist critics have some linguistic knowledge of another place. Rather, she argues the opposite: "The awakening of consciousness is *not* like the crossing of a frontier—one step and you are in another country" (my emphasis) (89). Thus, in her citation of Rich, Miller reverses the meaning of Rich's statement. In so doing, what drops out of Miller's reading is the social, the interrelationship between those who inhabit other and the same places, the African American blues singers of Rich's dream, white feminist poets and activists such as Rich, and white feminist literary critics. In Miller's reading, the boundaries between these different positions are effaced. The white feminist critic can continue to enter whatever territory she likes without social implications. Those others whose words and songs have been reclaimed in the name of this kind of consciousness raising drop out of the picture while the (white) feminist critic remains unmarked. Never acknowledging her own social location, the white writer takes no responsibility for her appropriation of "the culture of another country," since she never stands anywhere in particular.

It is precisely this stance that changes when Miller attempts to write as a Jew in "Personal Histories," the second section of her essay. In one of the strongest moments in "Personal Histories," Miller offers an embrace of sorts. She does this by reading and writing as a Jew about Minnie Bruce Pratt's powerful autobiographical essay "Identity: Skin Blood Heart,"[7] Pratt's contribution to *Yours in Struggle: Three Feminist Perspectives on Anti-Semitism and Racism.* In this essay Pratt writes about herself in relation to the ongoing legacies of anti-Semitism and racism in the United States. In her reading of Pratt's essay, Miller writes about how it feels to read about herself—her Jewish self—in someone else's autobiographical project. "As a Jew," Miller is keenly aware of the distorted characterization of Jews, even within Pratt's careful narrative. What Miller finds there is something that approximates, but is not quite, her self. In the prose of "Personal Histories," Miller presents her reactions to teaching Pratt's essay in a seminar at the Graduate Center of the City College of New York. During the class she and her students discussed this passage from Pratt's essay:

> I had no place for Jews in the map of my thoughts . . . except that they had lived before Christ in an almost mythical Israel, and afterwards in Germany until they were killed, and that those in this country were foreign, even if they were here: they were always foreign, their place was always somewhere else.[8]

Seeing, but, then again, not seeing herself reflected in this characterization of Jews, Miller responds by describing how, in the process of teaching this piece, she suddenly realized that she was the only Jew in the room. She describes feeling intensely uncomfortable reading the phrase "my Jewish lover" embodied and fixed within Pratt's narrative. As she explains: "I didn't like reading the (negative) signifiers—Jews/foreign/somewhere else—and then feeling interpellated as 'the Jewish woman' in the record of this white woman's awakening (working her anti-semitism through 'on' me)" (95).

In sharp contrast to her reading of Rich's dream, in this case, Miller no longer speaks from the position of the unmarked (white) feminist critic. Instead she finds herself in the uncomfortable position of the other woman who is being spoken for. She inhabits someone else's "other country," she is the foreigner. In responding to this discomfort, she sees the lack of fit between Pratt's description of Jews and her own sense of jewishness. For Miller, jewishness is figured in terms of isolation and fear even in her own classroom. "I didn't say much, if anything, about it at the time—being the teacher—and I think now that this was an error of pedagogy" (95). Although she questions her inability to speak up as a Jew in that classroom and even regrets it, her inaction is itself an important statement. As she explains, calling attention to the fact that she was the only Jew in the room might have offered her a useful way of complicating the terms of that classroom discussion. Such an intervention might have allowed Miller to speak more directly to a central contradiction within Pratt's essay, the way in which she is and is not able to celebrate others in her narrative. According to Miller, the problem is "a failure in the writing: the shifting line between the poignancy of self-representation and the didactics of representivity" (95). In other words, Pratt's essay is another example, according to Miller, of the impossibility of writing as oneself about others, in this instance, Jewish others.

In this way, Miller writes about her jewishness in relation to a text that also explicitly struggles with issues of identity and representation. By questioning what happens to Jews in Pratt's autobiographical project, Miller begins to articulate the feeling of being spoken for. She makes explicit the disjuncture between Pratt's good intentions and her own experience of being interpellated. In this sense Miller reverses her "Whose Dream?" reading of Rich. She begins to address what it might have felt like for a black woman to read about a legacy of the blues in Rich's text. She articulates the combination of familiarity and distance that comes with finding a semblance of yourself within the text of another. She articulates her ambivalence about the terms of inclusion.

As a result of this "different kind of reading," Miller expresses a feeling of isolation. She is lonely. She is the only Jew in a room full of people reading a text that includes a depiction of Jews that she cannot fully identify with. There is little room for her to maneuver. Miller sees this as "a failure in the writing." Despite its "solemn celebration of the other," Pratt's narrative is unable to capture the complexity of Miller's jewishness. In part, I agree with Miller's assessment. There is something missing in Pratt's text. But there is something else going on in Miller's. Her reading constitutes more than just an assessment of Pratt's narrative. By finally situating herself within a particular context, the graduate classroom, Miller offers another possibility. Instead of "escaping the social," she demonstrates that it is possible to engage a text within a social context. What she offers is an embodied reading. In both identifying with Pratt's project and rejecting it in that classroom, Miller offers an embrace of sorts. She begins to stake out a Jewish position.[9]

Part Three: Embrace as a Jewish Feminist Critical Practice

As I see it, "speaking for" others and "speaking as" one's self are always already intertwined. They operate in tension: doing one does not preclude the possibility of doing the other. When we write about or "for" others, we already do so from somewhere "as" lots of contradictory things. The danger is in losing sight of this interrelationship, of trying to do one without taking the other seriously. In part, this is what happened in "Whose Dream?" Because there was no marked "I" (or better still, "we"), the distinctions between self and other, between Rich and Miller, between the unmarked feminist critic and Bessie Smith, were all lost. In contrast to these potentially dangerous depictions of self and other, I see the possibility of a writing in relation. In part, this is what Miller enacts in her reading of Pratt. She reads Pratt from a particular Jewish location and, in so doing, is able to maintain distinctions between her self and the text.

Although this Jewish reading differs markedly from my own, what draws me to Miller's essay is her Jewish presence in the text. In watching Miller move between the stance of an feminist critic whose whiteness and jewishness are present but unmarked to her attempts to position herself as a Jew, I have come to learn something about my own critical practice.

The textual embrace I desire acknowledges the tensions and ambivalences in reading and writing about texts, it lets doubled voices converse together in both their similarities and in their differences. Writing about Jewish texts, I do not wish to collapse these distinctions into the autobiographical; "they" are not merely about "me." Such a collapse brings with it a loss of all that is not "me" in these texts, the difference, for example, between Suleiman's "mediated autobiography" and my "textual embrace" or between my position and Miller's. Unlike Miller, I do not experience being Jewish in terms of isolation. When I read "as a Jewish feminist" I am surrounded by many Jewish voices and texts: those of colleagues, friends, and students, those of the various Jewish texts I read, write and teach about.[10]

Standing in relation to most Jewish texts, mine is an ambivalent embrace. As in my readings of both Miller and Suleiman, I wish to maintain my voice even as I write about the interplay between familiarity, intimacy, and distance between me and these texts. Acknowledging these tensions as I read and write is part of what it has meant for me to engender Jewish knowledges.

Notes

I want to thank Miriam Peskowitz for her ongoing critical engagement with this essay, and David Watt and Maxine Grossman for their careful reading of earlier versions. I also want to thank Susan Shapiro, Chava Weissler, Elliot Wolfson, Hannan Hever, and Larry Silberstein for rereading Miller with me during the 1995 Judaism and Postmodernism Conference at Lehigh University.

1. *The American Heritage Dictionary of the English Language*, 3d ed. (Boston: Houghton, Mifflin, 1992).

2. Susan Rubin Suleiman, *Risking Who One Is: Encounters with Contemporary Art and Literature* (Cambridge: Harvard University Press, 1994).

3. Nancy K. Miller, "Dreaming, Dancing, and the Changing Location of Feminist Criticism, 1988," *Getting Personal, Feminist Occasions and Other Autobiographical Acts* (New York: Routledge, 1991), 72–100. For a different reading of this discursive violence and its larger material implications, see my extended reading of Miller's essay in Laura Levitt, *Ambivalent Embraces: Jews, Feminists and Home* (New York: Routledge, forthcoming).

4. Adrienne Rich, *On Lies, Secrets, and Silence: Selected Prose, 1966–1978* (New York: Norton, 1979), 31–49.

5. Many of those involved in early second-wave U.S. feminist organizing were women of color, white, and Jewish women who had worked in civil rights and more radical black liberation struggles. For a tracing of some of this history, see Elly Bulkin, Minnie Bruce Pratt, and Barbara Smith, *Yours in Struggle: Three Feminist Perspecitves on Anti-Semitism and Racism* (Brooklyn: Long Haul Press, 1984). Moreover, Rich presumably also knew that many first-wave nineteenth-century U.S. feminists were also abolitionists actively engaged in efforts to end slavery. On this history, see Alice S. Rossi, ed., *The Feminist Papers: From Adams to de Beauvoir* (New York: Columbia University Press, 1973).

6. Rich, *On Lies, Secrets, and Silence,* 48.

7. Minnie Bruce Pratt, "Identity: Skin Blood Heart," in *Yours in Struggle,* 9–64. Pratt's essay has become a classic in feminist studies, where it is widely read. Miller contrasts her reading of Pratt's essay to Chandra Mohanty and Biddy Martin's reading of the essay. See Chandra Mohanty and Biddy Martin, "Feminist Politics: What's Home Got to Do with It?" in Teresa de Lauretis, ed., *Feminist Studies/Critical Studies* (Bloomington: Indiana University Press, 1986). For Miller's reading of Mohanty and Martin's essay, see Miller, "Dreaming, Dancing," 90–94. For a radically different Jewish reading of these essays see my introduction to Levitt, *Ambivalent Embraces.*

8. Miller, "Dreaming, Dancing," 95; and Pratt, "Identity," 31.

9. For a somewhat different assessment of Miller's attempts to speak as a Jew, see Laura Levitt, "Rethinking Jewish Feminist Identity/ies: What Difference Can Feminist Theory Make?" in Steven Kepnes, ed., *Interpreting Judaism in a Postmodern Age* (New York: New York University Press, 1996), 361–377.

10. These texts include a standard rabbinic ketubbah, Napoleon's questions to the Jewish notables, a series of poems by Irena Klepfisz, and Miller's own text, among many others. For some of these readings, see Levitt, *Ambivalent Embraces,* and "Reconfiguring Home: Jewish Feminist Identity/ies," in T. M. Rudavsky, ed., *Gender and Judaism: The Transformation of Tradition* (New York: New York University Press, 1995), 39–49.

Notes on Contributors

AMMIEL ALCALAY teaches at Queens College and the CUNY Graduate Center. Most recently he edited *Portraits of Sarajevo* by Zlatko Dizdorević. His books include *After Jews and Arabs: Remaking Levantine Culture* (University of Minnesota Press), *The Cairo Notebooks* (Singing Horse Press), and *Keys to the Garden: Israeli Writing in the Middle East* (City Lights Books).

REBECCA ALPERT, Assistant Professor of Women's Studies at Temple University, has written extensively on contemporary Jewish themes. Her publications include *Exploring Judaism: A Reconstructionist Approach* and a forthcoming study of lesbian issues in Judaism.

JOËLLE BAHLOUL is Associate Professor of Anthropology and Jewish Studies at Indiana University (Bloomington). She has done extensive research in the ethnography of Jewish cultures in France. She is the author of a forthcoming book, *The Architecture of Memory* (Cambridge University Press, 1996).

ROBERT J. BAIRD is an independent scholar writing in the areas of religion and culture. His book *Inventing Religion in the Western Imaginary* (forthcoming from Princeton University Press) analyzes the cultural forces behind the construction of the modern category of "religion." His current research is on nineteenth-century discourses of "religion" and "ethics" and their role in the construction of colonial and postcolonial societies. He is currently a Chief Academic Officer and Senior Vice President at The National Faculty.

JUDITH R. BASKIN is Professor and Chair of Judaic Studies at the University of Albany, State University of New York. She is the editor of *Jewish Women in Historical Perspective*; *Women of the Word: Jewish Women and Jewish Writing;* and, with Shelly Tenenbaum, *Gender and Jewish Studies: A Curriculum Guide*, as well as numerous articles on women in rabbinic and medieval Judaisms.

KALMAN P. BLAND is Associate Professor of Jewish Studies and Director of the Center for Jewish Studies at Duke University. He is currently at work on a monograph titled *The Idea of Jewish Art: Medieval and Modern.*

DANIEL BOYARIN is Taubman Professor of Talmudic Culture in the Department of Near Eastern Studies at the University of California at Berkeley. His two most recent books are *Carnal Israel: Reading Sex in Talmudic Culture* (1993), and *A Radical Jew: Paul and the Politics of Identity* (1994), both published by the University of California Press. He forthcoming book is *Unheroic Conduct: The Rise of Heterosexuality and the Invention of the Jewish Man.*

JONATHAN BOYARIN is an independent scholar trained in anthropology. His work centers on the relation between Jewishness and Western discipline. He is currently attending Yale Law School.

PAULA CHAIKEN is Assistant Curator of Education at the Spertus Museum of Judaica, Chicago. She also teaches a course on gender and Judaism to high school students.

TAMAR EL-OR is Lecturer of Sociology and Anthropology at the Hebrew University, Jerusalem. Her book *Educated and Ignorant: Ultraorthodox Jewish Women and Their World* (1994) focuses on a matrix of literacy, gender, and religion. She currently studies the constitution of gender, nation, and Jewish identity among religious zionist young women.

JAY GELLER teaches Judaic studies at Vanderbilt University. In addition to publishing articles on Benjamin, Freud, Hegel, Hitler, Schreber, and representations of the male Jewish body, he has coedited *Reading Freud's Reading* (New York University Press) and is completing *The Nose Job: Freud and the Feminized Jew*, forthcoming from SUNY Press.

KARLA GOLDMAN received her Ph.D. from Harvard University in 1993 and is Assistant Professor of American Jewish History, and the first woman faculty member, at Hebrew Union College-Jewish Institute of Religion in Cincinnati. She is at work on a study of the place of women in the development of American Judaism.

SUSANNAH HESCHEL holds the Abba Hillel Silver Chair in Jewish Studies at Case Western Reserve University, where she also directs the Samuel Rosenthal Center for Jewish Studies. She has written extensively on feminist issues, as well as on Jewish-Christian relations.

SARA R. HOROWITZ is Director of the Jewish Studies Program, and Associate Professor of English literature in the Honors Program at the University of Delaware. She is the author of *Voicing the Void: Muteness and Memory in Holocaust Fiction* (Albany: SUNY Press, 1996), and is currently completing a book called "Gender, Genocide, and Jewish Memory." In addition to teaching courses on film and literature, she has published articles on Holocaust literature, women survivors, Jewish American fiction, and pedagogy. She is founding coeditor of *KEREM: A Journal of Creative Explorations in Judaism*, and served as fiction advisory editor for *Jewish American Women Writers: A Bio-Bibliographical and Critical Sourcebook*, ed. A. Shapiro, S. Horowitz, E. Schiff, and M. Glazer (Westport: Greenwood Press, 1994).

IRENA KLEPFISZ is a poet/activist in the lesbian and Jewish communities, former executive director of New Jewish Agenda, and teacher. She is author of *A Few Words in the Mother Tongue* (poems) and *Dreams of an Insomniac* (essays), both published by Eighth Mountain Press. Most recently she published "Feminism, Yidishkayt, and the Politics of Memory," in *Bridges* (1994), and "Queens of Contradiction: A Feminist Introduction to Yiddish Women Writers," in *Found Treasures: Stories by Yiddish Women Writers*, ed. Frieda Forman et al. (Toronto: Second Story Press, 1994).

AMY-JILL LEVINE, Professor of New Testament Interpretation at Vanderbilt Divinity School, has numerous publications on the Gospel of Matthew, Jesus, formative Judaism, and feminist approaches to biblical texts. She is working on *Threatened Bodies: Women, Culture, Apocrypha* for Harvard University Press.

LAURA LEVITT is Assistant Professor of Religion at Temple University, and also teaches in the Women's Studies Program. Her writing attends to feminist theory and contemporary Jewish culture. She is the author of the forthcoming book *Ambivalent Embraces: Jews, Feminists and Home* (New York: Routledge).

ANN PELLEGRINI teaches in the Department of Women's Studies at Barnard College. She is the author of *Performance Anxieties: Staging Psychoanalysis and "Race"* (New York: Routledge, 1996).

MIRIAM PESKOWITZ is Assistant Professor of Religion and Jewish studies at the University of Florida. Trained as a historian of Judaism in the Roman period, her recent articles appear in venues such as *Religious Studies Review* and the *Journal of Feminist*

Studies in Religion. Her forthcoming book is titled *Spinning Fantasies: Rabbis, Gender and History* (Berkeley: University of California Press).

RIV-ELLEN PRELL, an anthropologist, is Associate Professor of American Studies at the University of Minnesota. She is the author of *Prayer and Community: the Havurah in American Judaism* (Detroit: Wayne State University Press), and *Fighting to Become Americans: Jewish Women and Men in Conflict in the Twentieth Century* (New York: Basic Books, forthcoming).

NAOMI SEIDMAN is Assistant Professor of Jewish Culture at the Center for Jewish Studies of the Graduate Theological Union in Berkeley. Her first book, *A Marriage Made in Heaven: The Sexual Politics of Hebrew and Yiddish*, is forthcoming from the University of California Press. She is also working on a book titled *From Senderl the Woman to Yentl the Yiddish Boy: A Queer History of Yiddish Literature.*

SUSAN E. SHAPIRO teaches Jewish philosophy and philosophy of religion in the Department of Religion at Columbia University. Her research and writings span a variety of subjects. Some of her more recent publications include "Rhetoric as Ideology Critique: The Gadamer-Habermas Debate Reinvented," *Journal of the American Academy of Religion* 62 (1994): 123–150; "*Écriture judäique*: Where are the Jews in Western Discourse?" in *Displacements: Cultural Identities in Question*, ed. Angelika Bammer (Bloomington: Indiana University Press, 1994); "Elie Weisel and the Ethics of Fiction," in *Rhetoric and Pluralism: Legacies of Wayne Booth*, ed. Frederick Antczak (Columbus: Ohio State University Press, 1995); and a forthcoming book, *Recovering the Sacred: Ethics, Hermeneutics and Theology after the Holocaust.*

LAURENCE J. SILBERSTEIN is Philip and Muriel Berman Professor of Jewish Studies in the Department of Religious Studies at Lehigh University, and Director of the Berman Center of Jewish Studies. He is author of *Martin Buber's Social and Religious Thought*, editor of *New Perspectives on Israeli History* and *Jewish Fundamentalism in Comparative Perspective*, and coeditor of *The Other in Jewish Thought and History.* He is currently engaged in a study of the emergence of postzionist discourse.

ELLEN M. UMANSKY is the Carl and Dorothy Bennett Professor of Judaic Studies at Fairfield University in Fairfield, Connecticut. Author of numerous works on women, Judaism, contemporary Jewish theology, and modern Jewish history and thought, her publications include many articles, a monograph study of Lily Montague, and the coedited *Four Centuries of Jewish Women's Spirituality: A Sourcebook* (Boston: Beacon Press, 1992).

Beth S. Wenger received her Ph.D. from Yale University and now teaches modern and American Jewish history at the University of Pennsylvania. During the 1995–96 academic year, she was a visiting fellow at Princeton University's Center for the Study of American Religion. Her articles have appeared in *American Jewish History* and the *Journal of Women's History*. A forthcoming book about New York Jews and the Great Depression will be published by Yale University Press.